Revealing Architectural Design

- How do you use methods to create unique outcomes in the architectural design process?
- How do you set up methods that have a high degree of success based on your intentions?
- How do you develop and apply conceptual tools to assist in the design process?
- How do you use methods to satisfy the cultural needs of innovation and usability?
- How do you make an architectural design inherently defensible?

All of these questions and more are answered by examining the architectural design process from the point of view of knowledge domains, domain syntax, coherence, framing, thinking styles, decision-making and testing. Using straight-forward language, the book connects general design thinking to underlying frameworks that are used in the architectural design process.

The book provides historical grounding as well as clear examples of real design outcomes. It includes diagrams and explanations to make that content accessible. The frameworks and their methods are described by what they can accomplish, what biases they introduce and the use of their final outcomes.

Revealing Architectural Design is an advanced primer, useful to anyone interested in increasing the quality of their architectural design proposals through under-standing the conceptual tools used to achieve that process. While it is intended for undergraduate and graduate students of architectural design, it will also be useful for experienced architectural practitioners. For the non-architect, this book opens a window into the priorities of a discipline seldom presented with such transparency.

Philip D. Plowright is Associate Professor of Architectural Design, History and Theory at Lawrence Technological University. He is a founder of the systems-based think-tank synchRG, a registered architect, and Managing Editor of *Enquiry/The ARCC Journal of Architectural Research*. He has published and lectured widely on issues of meaning, interpretation and process in architectural design.

Revealing Architectural Design

Methods, Frameworks and Tools

Philip D. Plowright

Routledge
Taylor & Francis Group

LONDON AND NEW YORK

First edition published 2014
by Routledge
2 Park Square, Milton Park, Abingdon, Oxon OX14 4RN

and by Routledge
711 Third Avenue, New York, NY 10017

Routledge is an imprint of the Taylor & Francis Group, an informa
business

British Library Cataloguing in Publication Data
A catalogue record for this book is available from the British Library

Library of Congress Cataloging in Publication Data
Plowright, Philip D.
Revealing architectural design : methods, frameworks & tools /
Philip D. Plowright.
pages cm
Includes bibliographical references and index.
1. Architectural design--Methodology. 2. Design--Methodology.
I. Title.
NA2750.P59 2014
729--dc23
2013025918

ISBN: 978-0-415-63901-9 (hbk)
ISBN: 978-0-415-63902-6 (pbk)
ISBN: 978-1-315-85245-4 (ebk)

Typeset in Bembo Std 11/14pt
by Fakenham Prepress Solutions, Fakenham, Norfolk NR21 8NN

Printed and bound in Great Britain by
TJ International Ltd, Padstow, Cornwall

For Suzanne, Madeleine and Sophia.

Contents

Contents

Contents

Preface

There are so many great works of architecture, the majority of which never grace the glossy pages of design magazines or websites – nor photograph well as they need to be *experienced* rather than *viewed*. The projects chosen to illustrate the method examples in this book are from architectural designers with whom I have discussed their work, been intimately involved in the design process or studied extensively through documentation, lectures and seminars. Through these actions, I understand the final architectural proposal to be authentic in terms of the methods described, although reduced in complexity. It is easy to post-rationalize design projects and any misunderstanding or misrepresentation of the projects is my responsibility alone. The trend in the past decades explicitly to discuss the process of design for individual projects, led by Rem Koolhaas and OMA, has made the act of understanding methods easier.

While the general origins of this work can be traced to my persistent interest in meaning as a core concern of art and design spread over the past twenty years, the current project is the result of a series of investigations that originated with a comment by Thomas Daniell. At a conference several years ago, he asked me for a concrete, built example of the process theory I was discussing. This single comment, which he perhaps thought was casual and has subsequently claimed to have forgotten, started a five-year investigation explicitly to connect architectural theory to application. It led me on a journey that started with postmodern architectural theory, and followed a line of enquiry through intellectual history of design theory, process and pragmatist philosophy, design studies, cognitive science and studies in creativity. I finally arrived back where I started but with a new set of tools to structure an understanding of current and historical practices of architectural design. Was it an innocent question to ask to be shown evidence of a persistent theoretical structure as part of built work? No, I don't think so. Thanks, Tom.

Acknowledgements

It is necessary to thank all those individuals and architectural practices that have had a hand in shaping this book ... and there are many. Anirban Adhya, Leonard Bachman, Mollie Claypool, Ralph Nelson, and Stephen Winter need to be acknowledged for their invaluable comments, disagreements, and suggestions. Anirban helped broaden my understanding of typology and was invaluable in the overall flow of the book. Leonard was wonderful in his ability to extend any point with a dozen new connections that needed to be examined. Mollie would make a single three-word comment that resulted in half a chapter rewritten, two new paragraphs and six new footnotes. Along with his critical commentary, Ralph, of LOOM Studio, was instrumental in challenging many of my hypotheses as well as being a great aid in the argument against considering architectural design as a problem-solving mentality. Stephen has now become a voice in my head with his sharpness of intellect, precision of thought, and writing skills. While they all gave freely of their time, I am pretty sure they enjoyed pointing out my moments of overt casualness, extreme obscurity, and inability to make subject–verb agreements. Nick Cressman, Rosie Curtis, Erin Smith, Suzanne Sonneborn, and Jim Stevens provided advice on various drafts while Doris Grose assisted in some of the foundational research. In addition, I would like to thank Alexander D'Hooghe of MIT and ORG for many conversations around theory, philosophy, type, and typology. Dale Clifford of Carnegie Mellon provided clear examples of biological to architecture domain transfer and first principles reduction. Amale and Dan of WORKac extended my understanding of hyper-rationalism and $1 + 1 = 3$ mentality which is behind force-based and synthesis-focused design work. My interest in hyper-rationalism as an example of a force-based framework originated with the work of Lewis.Tsurumaki.Lewis and conversations with Mark Tsurumaki of that practice. Kathryn Moore was wonderfully generous with her time and intellect, especially when engaging in discussions of the use of pragmatist philosophy and aesthetics in design processes.

I also need to thank all those designers and photographers not mentioned above who graciously allowed me to use their work in order to illustrate these ideas. In no particular order, OMA, Studio Gang, Steven Holl Architects, Snøhetta, Mitchell Joachim, Atelier Tekuto, Juliet Symes, Ying Xiao, Shengchen Yang, Malwina Dzienniak, Christopher Hess, Shuang Wu, Joseph Adams, Katherine Piasecki, Glenn Gualdoni, Lauren Hetzel, Rachel Kowalczyk, Zachary Verhulst, Justine Pritchard, Erin Smith, Brendan Cagney, Joy Sportel, Jason Campigotto, Jonathon Krumpe, Chris Telfer, Steve Cooper, Blake Chamberlain, Lily Diego, Rushiraj Brahmbhatt, Kathryn Grube, Amanda Joseph, Jia Liu, Ryan Mccourt, Rana Salah, Erica Sanchez, Raman Shamoo, Eric Henry, Tomos Karatzias, Quang Lam, Jason Rostar, Brian Eady, Mike Gee, Kathleen Lilienthal, Ellen Rotter, Jennifer Breault, Priya Iyer, Pierre Robertson, Paul Warchol Photography, Pragnesh Parikh Photography, and Hedrich Blessing Photography were generous in allowing their illustrations, renderings, diagrams and photographs to be used.

Francesca Ford at Routledge has my eternal gratitude for her endless enthusiasm, trust, and faith in the development of this project. Finally, many years ago, Margaret Priest set me on this course and instilled a critical framework of enquiry. Thank you.

Introduction

Recipes of course are just information we can access, select, refine, tailor and interpret freely, but the better the recipe, the better the dinner and a really good recipe can apply innovative ideas to readily available and inexpensive ingredient materials so as to create valuable results. That added value is the basis of postindustrial production and the intelligence coded into the recipe is the strategic design component of how that value is conceptualized, produced, and realized.

Leonard R. Bachman[1]

This book presents conceptual tools and embodied processes foundational to architectural design. It also examines patterns of thinking and decision-making that are shared between various architectural design proposals. Like learning to cook at Le Cordon Bleu in Paris, the intention is to illustrate a set of tools, techniques, and base recipes persistent in the practice of architectural design. As in cooking, the purpose isn't to give a rigid set of instructions to follow absolutely, but rather to offer a foundation of understanding to develop or refine design skills. As such, while particular outcomes of personalized compositions are presented, they are used as a way of illustrating the underlying conceptual structure of the ingredients.

A method is present in architectural design every time a student, academic or professional designer takes on a project. *Every* time. And those methods are not random but belong to larger frameworks that support the priorities of an architectural designer. While method and methodology are the more technical terms, in architectural culture *design process* is used to mean a sequence of steps taken to arrive at a conclusion. This term can be heard often in design studios, with instructors and design practitioners mapping out a set of assignments or sequences in order to guide a student through *how to do design*. Knowing the design process is important. Strangely, though the design process is embedded in every project and is at the heart of the education and business practices of architects, the exact nature of that process is often obscure. It is under-documented, often invisible, and explained to students in anecdotes and one-off conversations.

Why is this? There are reasons – some historical, some cultural, and some traditional. In general, the reasons relate to the type of knowledge in architectural design, as in all the design fields, which is tacit. Tacit knowledge is knowledge which is difficult to document and transfer. It might be knowledge that is taken for granted so never examined; it might take too many resources to record as it contains many variances and complex information; or the knowledge might be so subtle that it resists documentation. Tacit knowledge is often transferred through the master–apprentice format of education. This is the format we find in architecture, where knowledge is transferred through personal experience, narrative, and hands-on practice.

In addition to the nature of ill-defined knowledge that is used in architectural design, there is also the personal angle. Generally, there are two camps of architectural designers working from different opinions of what is important and what should be prioritized. These camps have formed as a result of Western intellectual development creating a framing semantic. The framing, as a point of view, affects how events in the world are interpreted. Generally, the camps map well onto two alternative Western cultural positions of those who see the world in terms of 'art' and those who see it in terms of 'science'. Because of the different ways of interpreting the world, the members of these two camps have different opinions about the use and application of methodology.

One camp consists of those who resist any documentation of how to design based on a belief that that documentation will undermine the sense of artistry, exploration, and innovation with which design is tasked (*designer-artist*). At the heart of this way of framing architectural design is the opinion that architecture is an artistic pursuit. As methodology implies the codification and standardization of what is considered a personal, unique process, it is resisted.[2] Decisions are measured against the background frame of architectural design as personal expression in this first camp. As such, most of the approaches are experiential, focusing on the individual designer.

The second camp is looking for a single, strict, and repeatable structured method that can be applied to all applications of design in any situation and at any time (*designer-scientist*). In this case, the term *method* becomes interchangeable with *scientific method*. The approach is inclined to explain design in general terms which have little specificity that can be used by a designer as a robust applied process. It also tends to see design as a discipline unto itself, one that can separate particular design processes from their application in applied disciplines such as architecture. Other methods come out of this way of thinking, such as building performance simulation tools and fitness evaluations. However, these are not *design* methods. A design method requires the ability to generate something, to propose, refine, organize, and arrange relationships in a context with a shared purpose or intention. Design methods are generative. However, most of the approaches from this second camp are analytical. The approach is good at identifying what we have done but not what we will do or should do, or *why* we should do it in social or cultural terms.

The position adopted in this book attempts to change the dialogue slightly. Rather than approaching architectural design from either one of these framing semantics that are based on large ideological positions – how people believe the world should work – the book attempts to clear away some of the clutter and mystique. This is done in order to see, as clearly as possible, how architectural design methods can be both flexible enough to allow unknown outcomes yet codified enough to produce repeatable patterns of success. Approaching architectural design in this way groups methods into larger sets or methodologies. These methodologies can then be defined based on an exploration of conceptual frameworks – a basic structure which underlies a more complex system. A framework is a meta-organizational structure that works as a guide to more specific methods. It helps apply particular content to outcome desires, locates when to do certain kinds of thinking, what disciplinary devices to use, when to set up and apply judgement, and how to scale thinking.

The parts that operate in the framework are examined as tools, including understanding the syntax owned by architecture, using philosophy and theory to set bias and judgement, how thinking styles generate content, the location of decision-making, how disciplinary structure affects access to knowledge, and how to move knowledge between disciplines. When tracing the organization of these tools in historical and contemporary processes of architectural design, there are three major methodological frameworks. These frameworks are based on patterns, forces, and concepts. As overarching structures, they are not listed in any particular order or implied hierarchy – one is not better than another. The frameworks are just used for different design purposes as they produce different priorities of outcomes.

The three foundational frameworks and the context of architectural design are explored as conceptual processes. The first section of the book addresses the nature of architecture as a discipline with a particular syntax. This is followed by a section on conceptual tools and thinking patterns that are used in these architectural design frameworks. The final section examines each of the three framework structures in detail, explores their historical development, and presents examples of variations of the basic framework. The purpose is to explain how persistent frameworks are applied as design methods in the contemporary practice of architecture, allowing both persistent structure and originality to be present.

The frameworks and methods presented in this book are meant for the early development of designers – those learning how to think in terms of systems, formal proposals, social content, and cultural effect. Experienced designers use methods implicitly rather than explicitly. Although, like all practitioners who wish to excel in their discipline, bringing awareness to an implicit practice is a way to reflect, adapt, and improve that practice. Most people might instinctively learn how to swim after a couple of lessons, but Olympic swimmers need a great deal of training and understanding of the factors involved in swimming. These would include strength, conditioning, and nutrition along with the minute examination of technique to make them swim faster. In the same way, to become a better architectural designer, deep knowledge and clear visibility of the process of design are required.

The method examples presented here are in a simplified form to make the concepts clearer. In practice, there will be a dominant framework, but within that framework aspects of the design investigation might combine several nested design processes focused on particular outcomes. These would be integrated back into the major framework as a decision. Moreover, the tools within frameworks can be adjusted once both the framework structure and conceptual tools are understood. The frameworks are then recipes that can be tweaked and adapted for personal use which will produce a unique or personalized method. Design frameworks are simply containers of thinking that scale content, pre-select tools, and identify points of decision-making. They are not – nor should they be considered – rigid sequences of detailed steps with predetermined outcomes in which the decisions are made by the process and not by the designer. Various starting points and content can be introduced by the designer which will affect outcomes, while the underlying structures of the design process remain fixed.

Decision-making, theory, and the visibility of method

What became interesting to me, as a design practitioner, was the absence of a clear communication, or even documentation, of the structure of the design process in architecture. Design methods were obviously present – as noted, each time a suggestion of how to proceed on a project is offered, that is a method. Every studio and practice has developed an approach to design which includes an overall framing position that biases what is important to that office as well as a set of steps on how to develop the design. How did this occur in the absence of any clear documentation? Mostly, it seemed to be constructed over years by the transfer of tacit knowledge from a master to an apprentice – be it the studio critic or office principal. Many times, the results are considered intuitive and part of the genius of the individual designer, an opinion which negates the learning environments in which many of these designers have been nurtured. In those learning environments, designers have been exposed to various aspects of knowledge as part of the design process. These include site analysis, case studies and precedents, theoretical writing, philosophical texts, historical dialogues, environmental studies, and cultural readings. Knowledge areas are joined by the technical skills of drawing, engineering systems, and structural systems. However, more often than not, these elements are not integrated into larger patterns of cognitive activity which can relate their use to specific predictive outcomes. As a case in point, one can question why architectural programmes isolate history, research methods, and theory classes from design studios, making these knowledge areas independent from each other.

Given the current disconnection between aspects of architectural knowledge, why do we need visible and accessible methodology in architectural design? Simply stated, to produce viable architectural design it is necessary to have strong decision-making. A more complicated response to the question goes like this: architectural design is pursued through proposals of meaning, which operate through intentionality; in turn, these are developed through exploration, analysis, and decision-making at contextual and disciplinary levels. In either case, it is important to know how, why, and which decisions need to be made. It is also important to know when a decision should happen in the process and on what scale the decision-making occurs. Without this knowledge, designers are working blind as it is impossible to develop or critique work towards a particular situation. There is hope of a strong degree of relevance between the intentions of the position and the final outcomes. In order to know if this relevance has occurred, there has to be some way to determine success. How can we know if a proposal is successful in the context it is applied? The answer is by understanding the structure of the process so that the elements selected by decisions in the proposal align with priorities which have been identified as being important. It is the role of the designer, and not of methodology, to create intentions by identifying priorities and making decisions accordingly. Our intentions need to be connected to outcomes which are testable; otherwise we are falling into the fallacy of being 'romantically speculative about the power of vague ideas'.[3]

Another way of defining architecture is as a moment of enrichment in the fabric of our environment. Architecture is an act of enrichment which brings additional content and experience to physical space so that the summation of the parts of that space equals more than merely the parts themselves. This definition of architecture considers architecture as a system based on syntax, process, elements (physical, social, and peripheral), and proposal, not as an object. Ideas of meaning, intention, and decision-making are the core of the conceptual process which arranges the relationship between elements in space in order to create architecture. Again, success is judged on the basis of how that conceptual process is considered through development, testing, refinement, and finalization. The visibility of method is important in order to engage questions of quality and relevance as well to ensure a richness of response.

Another concern, when considering methods in architectural design, is the role of theory. Traditionally, a set of seminal writings has been used to develop critical thinking abilities in architecture. Theoretical writing in architecture develops greater sensitivity towards spatial, experiential, socio-cultural, and environmental issues. Often, writings are pulled from other disciplines, such as biology, sociology, political science, cultural theory, economics, linguistics, and literature. Some of these are found in their original format, but many are reframed by architectural scholars and thinkers to be adapted to the disciplinary content of architecture. As such, architectural theory, as a body of work, should be considered to hold the core intellectual content of the discipline.

My own educational experience reinforced the importance of theory. It located this territory as the source of priorities in art and design as well as the path to interpretation of that work but it *failed completely to connect it to design processes*. Theory, as a body of knowledge, became marginalized through the retreat of architecture into academia during the 1970s and 1980s, where it was used to create class distinction within the architectural profession. I still believe in the importance of theory, from my first taste of semiotics in the late 1980s to current publications. But questions of the relevance of theory are constantly raised when dealing with the practice of architectural design, including issues of use, application, adaptability, and effect. The basis of these questions can be roughly restated in this format: this theory is interesting, it is provocative, it makes me consider things that I hadn't thought of before,[4] but how do I use it in design? In professional practice, the role of theory can be problematic and obscured, many times removed from visibility in normative design practice.

Thinking and frameworks

The purpose of this book isn't to document or research the design process by applying sociological or other non-architectural research methods. Instead, the book evolved through precedent and case study analysis, connecting the writings of architects, the decisions they made through the process, stated priorities, and philosophical framing to completed proposals of architecture, whether built or on paper. This information was combined with research into documented methods using design tools such as first principles and engaging in many discussions with active designers. What became clear was the ability of a designer to know how to structure a process to make it work for their desires, connecting intentionality to judgement criteria. This is a different way of thinking about design methods when compared to the approach of a researcher, scholar, or scientist. As such, many issues will be suppressed or ignored in terms of design methods research, architectural theory, design theory, cognitive science, psychology, and philosophy. Many analytical and theoretical concerns, while very important, are not the focus of this book and are not addressed. Instead, the attempt here is to produce repetitive, transferable knowledge about the frameworks and tools we use to do architectural design. There is a conscious attempt to avoid introducing an ideological position that creates a hierarchy of importance between these frameworks.

In the following chapters, the term *framework* is used to mean the schematic conceptual structures which underlie all processes in design; *methodology* is used to mean a set of working methods which share a framework; and *method* is used to mean the particular way the framework is applied in practice as a variation of the methodology. A framework can be adapted and applied to many different situations. However, they will not determine a *starting state* – that place of beginning. Nor will the frameworks identify significance or relevance, or help identify bias. These roles are still the mandate of the designer. No methodology will ever magically 'solve' an architectural design proposal.

One of my colleagues, who is heavily embedded in digital fabrication and algorithmic processes, refers to this fallacy of believing in an automated design process as the *magic red button approach*. Designers, and this seems especially true in current parametric and algorithmic design, seem to think that somewhere there is a magic formula or process that will automatically make the best design ever: complex, novel, cool-looking, bendy shapes, flashing lights, and so on. However, there is no replacement for personal interest, exploration, iteration, and considering why we should care or why something matters. Methods should not be seen as magic buttons. What they can do is help a designer understand where and when decisions need to be made, how to arrange scales of thinking, and how to set up criteria to judge proposal success at the scale of the parts-to-whole and the parts-to-parts relationships.

In the end, this book illustrates persistent frameworks at the base of all architectural design proposals, as well as the variation possible in those conceptual structures. The flexibility occurs as the same framework, operating below content, can structure many methods which can then be populated by priorities in different contexts to produce different outcomes.

Notes

1 Bachman, Leonard R., *Two Spheres: Physical and Strategic Design in Architecture.* Abingdon and New York: Routledge, 2012: 6.
2 The origin of this attitude can be traced philosophically to Immanuel Kant's introduction of genius when he developed aesthetics as the foundation of metaphysics. In this he separated the creator and user of art into different facilities. More recently, Donald Schön's book, *The Reflective Practitioner*, introduced concepts originally found in pragmatist philosophy by thinkers such as John Dewey and William James. In the book, Schön stressed that theory and practice are integrated by improvisation on the part of a professional knowledgeable of his syntax and discipline. He treated design methods as a series of intuitive

steps based on prior experience rather than structured frameworks. See Schön, Donald A., *The Reflective Practitioner: How Professionals Think in Action*. New York: Basic Books, 1983.

3 Winston, Patrick H., 'Learning and Reasoning by Analogy.' *Communications of the ACM* 23, no. 12 (1980): 689–703, at 690.

4 Andrew Ballantyne made this point well in his short, but excellent, book written for architects on the process philosophy of Deleuze and Guattari. See Ballantyne, Andrew, *Deleuze and Guattari for Architects*. London and New York: Routledge, 2007.

SECTION I

CONCEPTUAL FOUNDATIONS

Chapter One

Disciplines and syntax

> Architecture remained conceived by man, representing man and his condition. It assumed physical structure and shelter to be absolute conditions of architecture, and when it considered signification it was in terms of a meaning which was extrinsic to architecture itself; that is, to ideas which related architecture to man, rather than to intrinsic ideas which explained architecture itself.
>
> Peter Eisenman[1]

In the Introduction, two general definitions were suggested as a way to think about architectural design. The first spoke of meaning, intentionality, and decision-making which could be acted upon by someone working on ideas that are architectural. The second defined architecture as a moment of enrichment in the fabric of our environment using syntax, process, and proposal rather than the creation of an object. What is implied by both of these definitions is that architecture has a particular set of responsibilities and knowledge which makes it identifiable *as* architecture and not as something else. It is, in fact, what is called a *discipline*, and a discipline has a *domain of knowledge*.

A *domain of knowledge*, or simply a *domain*, refers to an area of information tied directly to specialized activity or a discipline. Each discipline makes up a territory of knowledge, something that is considered owned by that discipline and contains its priorities and expertise. Michel Foucault, the influential French philosopher and historian, considered a discipline as 'defined by a domain of objects, a set of methods, a corpus of propositions considered to be true, a play of rules and definitions, of techniques and instruments: all this constitutes a sort of anonymous system at the disposal of anyone who wants to or is able to use it'.[2] A discipline exists by defining boundaries and setting rules so they can be accessed by its members with consistency. This is what makes a discipline a discipline. In order to define a boundary, a sense of separation is required. Separation is achieved in several ways, from titles and professional membership to education and degrees, but also by the creation of terminology *owned* by a discipline (*archispeak* is an example of this, not as an expression of arrogance, as has been claimed, but as a deep disciplinary-specific vocabulary). We can understand the separation mainly as a way a discipline has set up its priorities and to claim a territory of knowledge. For example, baking and pastry arts is a discipline that is related to the discipline of microbiology. Both disciplines are interested in, for example, yeast. Someone who is baking bread might be concerned about the health of yeast and the fermentation process from the point of view of rise, flavour, and proportion of materials – since the priority is the quality of the product of bread. However, the baker will not generally be concerned with knowledge about cell cycles, spore genetics, or binary fission, although these are all parts of the process of baking that uses yeast to put gas bubbles into dough. In return, the microbiologist doesn't have discussions of crumb, crust, rise, proofing, or spring as part of their disciplinary domain. While both disciplines are concerned with yeast, the two have different ways of thinking and looking at the same basic material. Each has its own focus and priorities for outcomes, and different ways to judge success. All of this is reflected in the words the disciplines use (terminology) as well as in the tools they have developed to pursue their disciplinary study (the proofing bowl versus the microscope). In the end, the yeast is left unchanged (well, maybe not physically, but at least conceptually) by their attention. It is still yeast.

Architecture, as a discipline, is no different. It has its own concerns, focus, priorities, terminology, and content, while sharing many objects of its attention with other disciplines. Recognizing architecture as a discipline allows us to understand that the boundary between types of knowledge is very real. Some things are *inside* architecture while others are *outside* architecture.

Inside and outside architecture

So what is 'inside' the domain of architecture and to what content can architecture lay claim? What do these terms 'inside and outside' and 'interior and exterior'[3] even mean? Some clarity can be brought to these concepts by examining the nature of disciplines through syntax, tool use, and domain-particular priorities.

If we return to the definition by Foucault, a discipline is a system defined by a set of focused interactions between objects, methods, beliefs, rules, definitions, and tools. Each of these items, from objects to tools, is constrained by a boundary. It is the boundary that makes the idea of inside and outside possible. The boundary is present so rules can be set for access by everyone involved, creating a consistency of approach. Disciplines are regulatory in nature, and it is the boundary, being clearly identified and defended, which makes the discipline – as a body of knowledge and a practice – possible. The boundary can primarily be defined by what has been produced as final outcomes of the processes found within the discipline – what product/proposal is identified as being owned by the discipline and what types of knowledge go into its production. The boundary of a discipline such as architecture, which evolved naturally over centuries, is also extremely stable as it is part of a historical structure.[4]

However, while a boundary is stable in terms of priorities (inside), it is also open in terms of influence (outside). The boundary defines and codifies knowledge of a disciplinary domain – it fixes it in place. It is the role of discourse to explore the content of that knowledge. A discourse also attempts to extend outwards to probe the possible annexing of new territories. The definition of a discourse is: a lengthy discussion about a subject or an ongoing and persistent dialogue. Like a boundary, a discourse in a discipline is about protection and control; but unlike a boundary, it is not static. Discourses are exploratory and attempt to define, as well as extend, the territory found in the discipline.[5] This is an active exploration to map the boundaries of the territory which it controls.

The relationship between a boundary and a discourse is what makes it possible to define normative and avant-garde styles of practice. Normative practice explores the well-defined territory within the disciplinary boundary, while avant-garde practice is focused on pursuing a discourse in order to extend the boundary. Both can be critical though they have different disciplinary roles. When Vitruvius wrote on building construction, machine fabrication, material science, urban design, surveying, astronomy, and clock making, he was participating in a discourse in order to define a boundary clearly. He was writing to regulate the discipline. Leon Battista Alberti, in the first major theoretical work after Vitruvius, mapped an architectural territory which had narrowed by the Renaissance to material science, construction, building, and urban design. Jean–Nicolas–Louis Durand

and Eugène-Emmanuel Viollet-le-Duc operated with a discourse and body of knowledge which included Vitruvius' contribution. They, as part of the changing culture of the Enlightenment, did not simply regulate but rather extended the scope of the territory using new intellectual tools of rationalism.

The discourse continues today, building on past discussions either in agreement or in contradiction. Current architectural theorists such as Stan Allen, Peter Eisenman, Jeffrey Kipnis, Rem Koolhaas, Sanford Kwinter, Winy Maas, Thom Mayne, Patrik Schumacher, and Bernard Tschumi, to name just a few, all continue to probe and extend the location of the architectural disciplinary boundary. At the same time, the boundaries of architecture will resist redefinition from exploratory discourse as naturally occurring disciplines have ultra-stable boundaries.[6]

This brings us back to the idea of *inside* and *outside*. Now that we have a good idea of how a boundary is defined, how do we identify it? The easiest way to identify *inside* versus *outside* knowledge in architecture is to look at both final outcomes and the tools used to achieve those outcomes. In these we will find the particular thing that the discipline of architecture defines itself as being. This is because while someone working within a discipline may be influenced by content not generally found in the beliefs or definitions of the discipline, the final outcomes will always be based on tools, language, and objects that are clearly identified as parts of the discipline. If they were not, then that outcome would not be considered architectural.

When we look at the final proposal of something considered architecture, rather than writings about architecture, we find continuity from the earliest documents to the latest exploration. Architectural outcomes are always physically based on the arrangement of form and of a particular scale, regardless of the starting position. The formal composition involves a complex relationship to the human body, social content, technical position, and cultural representation. The language used, the *syntax*, is based on negotiating these relationships with formal arrangements in space. All the tools that have developed to access architectural ideas are based on this premise. These include very traditional tools of plan, section, elevation, axonometric, isometric, and model, but also newer tools such as digital visualization, algorithms, and environment simulations. Production tools involved in project delivery, such as specification and schedules, are also focused on formal arrangement and physical manifestation. They are used to create coherence between intention and results. Even the diagram, as it is used in architecture, is a representation of forces which, ultimately, become physically located and defined in space. The tools have a tendency to be based in the visual field or to be visually biased, prioritizing sight over the other senses. However, olfactory (smell) and auditory (sound) knowledge can also be considered as critical components in the discipline of architecture, especially contributing to the interpretation of a place. While our tools tend not to engage this information directly, it can be notated by them graphically and is part of the interpretation of the quality of a space. Taste, as a sense, is outside of the domain of architecture. Tools used in considering architectural solutions can access information based on its syntax directly. For example, we can use plan-based drawing to address circulation, sequence, rhythm, hierarchy, and field; or elevation to represent texture, surface, rhythm, massing, and materiality.

If we look at architecture as a domain of knowledge and a discipline, it is not necessary to define architecture simply as the design of a building. Instead, architecture can be defined through the content of its boundary and its discourse. Both of these are engaged through syntax. The syntax is considered to be anything that can be directly engaged or manipulated by the tools of architecture. This is *inside* the discipline. Anything that needs a form of translation in order to engage architectural syntax is *outside*.

Architectural syntax

Disciplinary syntax does not have quite the same definition as *syntax* in linguistics. In the latter case, *syntax* is used to denote the rules that exist between words which allow a language to be structured and understood. As Adrian Forty notes, 'it is one thing to say that architecture has certain things in common with language, for example that it can mediate things apart from what is contained within its own materiality, but it is quite another thing to say that architecture fully conforms to the various syntactical or grammatical rules that are found in spoken languages'.[7] In a discipline, a syntax is used to define a territory, not to set up explicit rules. The syntax contains the objects, forces, priorities, thinking structures, and habits which have been defined by the discipline. We may consider syntax as the representation of the culture of a discipline. All conclusions of an architectural design process will, necessarily, be manifested in architectural syntax.

As noted above, architectural syntax is biased towards form-making, but also involves the engagement of the human body and environmental conditions considered at a particular scale. In this way, rather than being a discipline of design that is focused on the production of a discrete artefact, architecture is focused on the *development of an experience through constructing physical environments.*[8] The manipulation of form is, then, a primary aspect of architecture, and one of the main ways in which the discipline is engaged. It is not the goal, however, but a means to an end.[9] Form-making includes the introduction of primary elements, such as cube, sphere, or pyramid. Through disciplinary syntax, these elements are reinterpreted as architectural objects such as wall, column, vault, dome, arch, and so on.[10] While the pieces are particular, the heart of formal design is systems-based and is about an *arrangement* of content − form, body, space, and event. It is the arrangement of the pieces, not the pieces themselves, that is important.[11]

Our understanding of architectural syntax can be built from foundational operations of manipulating form. The basic operations of formal manipulation are shared among many aspects of human existence and mental processing. It is the act of mentally associating form with virtual actions and relationships such as movement, pressure, and directionality which makes architecture possible. These activities can be found in the standard reference books used to teach architecture.[12] The basis of formal design includes considering form in the following ways:

- Located in space: *position, direction, orientation, centre, surface*;
- A sense of visual inertia: *stable, unstable, balanced, neutral*;
- Defining a container: *border, enclosure, bounding of void (perceptual or physical), frame*;
- Associated with other elements: *number, geometry, proportion, hierarchy, repetition, rhythm, front to side, entry, centre, edge*;
- Pressures and forces between elements: *interlacing, stretch, fragmentation, decomposition, fold, graft, rotation, shift*;
- A sense of identity: *superimposition, superposition.*

It is important to understand that the types of formal manipulations at the core of architectural design are conceptual actions, not physical.[13] When considering the visual inertia of a form, for example, the architect does not literally make it unstable. It is visually and conceptually unstable in its context, not physically unstable. In addition to the formal manipulation, a series of factors relate directly to surface and build upon the basic formal foundation. Decisions focused on surface representation including texture, pattern, plane, colour, massing, and materiality. For architecture to occur, the properties of formal composition need to be strongly influenced by the social context of space. The presence of the human body brings event, circulation, sequence, procession, presence, and occupation into architectural syntax.

Finally, environmental factors associate formal and social content with physical context by addressing adjacency, light, air and surface temperature, humidity, air movement, extension, biofilia, and field (as datum and context). All of these aspects have been historically associated with the architectural discipline and can be directly engaged by the tools of the discipline. The extents of each of these factors combine to present the boundary of architecture as well as providing the syntax by which discourse occurs within architecture (Figure 1.1). As the discipline's boundaries, these factors determine what is considered inside and outside. Many architectural projects may start with external influence or inspiration. However, when methods are considered in terms of disciplinary boundaries, it is clear that syntax factors will need to be engaged directly as the core of the process or risk a proposal that is irrelevant, misinterpreted, or non-architectural.

It is with the idea of syntax that we can return to bias. The syntax shapes what is probable as an outcome, and what can or cannot be addressed. In the domain of architecture, syntax is biased towards form-making that contains the human body, rather than considering form-making from the point of view of the human body holding the form. It is also biased towards considering the movement of the body through the form as critical to the experience, refinement in terms of comfort and health, and a scale that fully engages the human body's visual field. While architecture is fundamentally experiential, bias through syntax prioritizes the visual field and formal composition. As such, architecture has a tendency towards visual

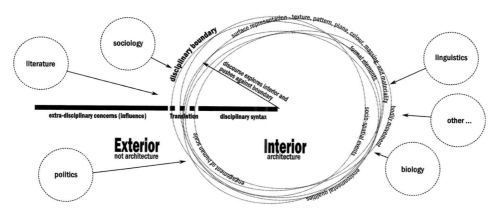

Figure 1.1: Architecture as a disciplinary structure with boundary, syntax, and influences

symbolism as cultural interpretation, and undervalues other sensory interpretations based on disciplinary syntax.

Bias as introduced by disciplinary syntax is important as it makes a generic design process operational in practice. Disciplinary syntax contains values. These values affect how context is applied, how information is gathered, scales of effect, judgement criteria, and phase definitions. The range of possible conclusions to a design process, along with the choice of framework, is predetermined by the values which define the content at the starting point of the design process. While it might be possible for design disciplines to share frameworks, it seems less probable that they can share specific methods. Methods require content which is held by the disciplinary syntax in order to operate. This makes a generic design process difficult to achieve.

Notes

1 Eisenman, Peter, 'Aspects of Modernity: Maison Dom-Ino and the Self-Referential Sign.' In *Oppositions Reader: Selected Readings from a Journal for Ideas and Criticism in Architecture, 1973–1984*, edited by Hays, K. Michael. New York: Princeton Architectural Press, 1998: 189–198, at 191.

2 Foucault, Michel, 'The Order of Discourse (Inaugural Lecture at the Collège de France, Given 2 December 1970).' In *Untying the Text*, edited by Young, Robert. Boston, MA: Routledge & Kegan Paul, 1971/1981: 52–64, at 59.

3 In architectural terminology, issues that are inside architecture might be called *interiority* while anything considered outside the discipline would be *exteriority*.

4 Although Patrik Schumacher and Zaha Hadid Architects, the practice where he is a partner, consider themselves as avant-garde, exploratory, and arts based, they still recognize the existence of a disciplinary boundary that divides architectural content from non-architectural content. See Schumacher, Patrik, *The Autopoiesis of Architecture*. Chichester: John Wiley & Sons, 2011.

5 Iser, Wolfgang, *How to Do Theory*. Malden, MA: Blackwell, 2006: 172.

6 A naturally occurring discipline is one that has developed over time and has developed a boundary based on historical occurrences of outcomes. The discipline is then defined by what it has done and what it has been, resisting any redefinition due to the weight of historical content. Andrew Benjamin addresses aspects of this in his essay 'Eisenman and the Housing of Tradition'. In *Rethinking Architecture: A Reader in Cultural Theory*, edited by Leach, Neil. New York: Routledge, 1997: 286–301.

7 Forty, Adrian, *Words and Buildings: A Vocabulary of Modern Architecture*. London: Thames & Hudson, 2000: 64.

8 This is in contrast to how industrial and product designers approach their work. See Krippendorff, Klaus, *The Semantic Turn: A New Foundation for Design*. Boca Raton, FL: CRC/Taylor & Francis, 2006: 210.

9 Leonard Bachman, in personal communications, reformulated these ideas as: 1) experience as the goal, 2) form as the tactic, 3) design as the strategy, and 4) representation as the objective.

10 Alexander, Christopher, Sara Ishikawa, and Murray Silverstein, *A Pattern Language: Towns, Buildings, Construction*. New York: Oxford University Press, 1977; Ching, Francis D. K., *Architecture: Form, Space, and Order*. Hoboken, NJ: John Wiley & Sons, 2007; Prina, Francesca, *Architecture: Elements, Materials, Form*. Princeton, NJ: Princeton University Press, 2008.

11 Hanlon, Don, *Compositions in Architecture*. Hoboken, NJ: John Wiley & Sons, 2009; Aureli, Pier Vittorio, *The Possibility of an Absolute Architecture*. Cambridge, MA: The MIT Press, 2011.

12 Standard introductions to architectural composition through formal studies include: Hanlon, Don, *Compositions in Architecture*. Hoboken, NJ: John Wiley & Sons, 2009; LaVine, Lance, *Constructing Ideas: Understanding Architecture*. Dubuque, IA: Kendall/Hunt Publishing Company, 2008; Ching, Francis D. K., *Architecture: Form, Space, and Order*. Hoboken, NJ: John Wiley & Sons, 2007; Conway, Hazel and Rowan Roenisch, *Understanding Architecture: An Introduction to Architecture and Architectural Theory*. New York: Routledge, 2005; von Meiss, Pierre, *Elements of Architecture: From Form to Place*. New York: E. & F. N. Spon/Routledge, 1998.

13 For a more technical understanding of the conceptual basis of formal manipulation, see Plowright, Philip, 'Agency and Personification: Core Analogical Operators in the Architectural Design Process'. In *Proceedings of the 2013 ARCC Architectural Research Conference*, University of North Carolina at Charlotte, 27–30 March 2013: 156–164.

Chapter Two

Architecture as a type of design discipline

> A discipline is defined by a domain of objects, a set of methods, a corpus of propositions considered to be true, a play of rules and definitions, of techniques and instruments: all this constitutes a sort of anonymous system at the disposal of anyone who wants to or is able to use it.
>
> Michel Foucault[1]

Design, rather than being an isolated activity or even a discrete discipline, can be seen as a way of thinking found throughout all of human activity and shared among many disciplines. We find the activity of design not only in the clearly labelled 'design' disciplines (architecture, interior design, industrial design, graphic design, etc.). As a conceptual process, it is present in any discipline which concerns itself with accomplishing a goal or achieving an objective. This includes the hard sciences such as physics, chemistry, and biology but also fields such as business and law. It has been said that there 'is no area of contemporary life where design – the plan, project, or working hypothesis which constitutes the "intention" in intentional operations – is not a significant factor in shaping human experience'.[2] Design is an important human activity – we could speculate that it might even be the thing that makes us human – the ability to conceive, evaluate, innovate, and propose.

For architectural design there is a question raised in terms of methods if design is considered as a broad activity. A discipline has an implied ownership over a set of methods that is part of its definition. Yet, if design is considered as a broadly defined practice based on specifying outcomes, there should be a commonality to all methods. The question becomes: is there a general method common for design as an activity or is architecture unique in the way it approaches design? The answer to both positions is 'yes', implying an apparent contraction. A rationalist position would seek to achieve a clear choice between the two options. However, architectural design involves shared types of thinking common to any design process and not just those in traditional design disciplines. Yet, as a discrete discipline, architecture focuses those thinking structures on particular expectations based on syntax and relevant outcomes. The discipline itself has a strong influence on shaping particular methods.

Design methods

The study of methods in design as a general enquiry began rigorously in the 1960s and 1970s. A large body of knowledge was developed by design researchers as part of what has become known as the Design Methods Movement. This group, still in existence today as the Design Research Society (DRS), is concerned with producing design methodology and addressing design research for a culture viewed as becoming ever more complex. Out of this research came not only some excellent studies on the generic nature of design,[3] but also the attempt to make design into a discrete discipline independent of application or discipline concerns.[4] Since the basis of the Design Methods Movement was to bring a structured rational thinking bias into design, it is not surprising that many proposed methods that movement developed were based on *technical rationality*. This is a form of rationalism that believes our social reality is objective, measurable, and explainable. Technical rationality in design methods focuses on problem-solving through scientific procedures and theories. Accordingly, methods based on rationalist beliefs attempt to provide a detailed, comprehensive, linear, and universal approach to design, seeing the results as 'solutions' to problems.

The most influential design methods found in the technical rationality model are called normative theories[5] or rational problem-solving.[6] There have been two generations of development in these theories in the Design Methods Movement. Rational or normative methods also exist in other disciplines independent of this movement, such as urban planning and studies of creativity. The first-generation researchers in the Design Methods Movement, who included Christopher Alexander and J. Christopher Jones, approached the design process as a way to produce 'rational criteria of decision making, and trying to optimize the decisions'.[7] In application, the methods, when applied by others, tended to be simplified and distorted from the original intention. This made them less than useful and consequently highly criticized for a lack of relevance in practice (Figure 2.1). The second generation of researchers, led by Horst Rittel, focused on identifying the *problem* so as to assure a correlation between the designer's *solution* and the user's expectation and needs. These methods borrowed from sociology and anthropology to involve the users as part of the design process.[8]

The planning industry as a design practice has probably been the most robust at proposing and applying normative methods. The dominant Synoptic or Rational Comprehensive Model was proposed by Edward Banfield in 1955, but as in the Design Methods Movement, the approach was challenged by issues of real-world use. Multiple second-generation processes are currently used in planning, such as Transactive, Advocacy, and Radical planning methods.[9] These engage the community and stakeholders as a way to set priorities. While participatory models have had some influence on architectural design, that influence has been very limited. Or perhaps it is more correct to say that these rationally based, explicit methods have not become part of the culture of architecture, which has its own implicit, but unexamined, methods of design.

A counter-proposal to the rational problem-solving models of design methods is found in Donald Schön's *reflection-in-action* approach. The reflection-in-action[10] model positions the designer as a designer-artist, an individual who adapts and shifts his or her approach based on experience and need but without any explicit understanding of methods. Schön's approach seems to address the disconnection identified in the rational methods between how design methods are described and the actual activity of a practising designer. However, reflection-in-action didn't

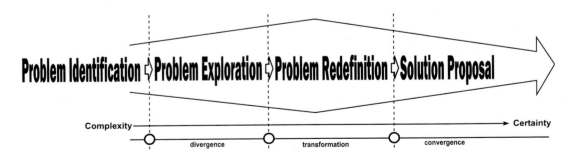

Figure 2.1: A first-generation design method based on J. Christopher Jones

introduce any methods explicitly usable by a designer. Experienced designers do reflect upon their practice, but how do they become experienced? In addition, reflection-in-action still positions design as a series of responses to problems. Problem identification remains a primary tool of the process; however, the model has more feedback implied. The reliance on disciplinary mastery in order to identify a response to a 'problem', along with the rejection of any identified method framework, ultimately relies on intuition and the genius-model of architectural designer.

The approaches of rational problem-solving and reflection-in-action can be seen as representative of the science/art division discussed in the Introduction. Yet both poles reinforce the same dominant attitude. Design disciplines, including architecture, are engaged in a problem-solving activity.

Problem-solving

Why has problem-solving become so dominant as an attitude in architecture and design? To paraphrase Viollet-le-Duc, before beginning to design, architectural designers must know what they wish to do, and once they know what they wish to do, they need to consider how to do it.[11] The idea of 'problem-solving' addresses the *what to do* portion of that statement. A problem-solving approach allows the act of design to respond to a particular dilemma and (hopefully) makes the world a better place. What *a better place* means, who it addresses, or how it is represented is certainly up for debate. Our Western society deals with a strong legacy of the representation of progress as purpose, a view with origins in the Enlightenment with the rise of relativism and pleasure as a replacement for beauty. Western attitudes are further shaped by nineteenth-century Realism's portrayal of art's social responsibility to guide society.[12] These attitudes continue today and create tension for a designer obliged to satisfy their demands. Responding to these pressures, one of the easiest ways to structure a design process is to isolate an issue or respond to a crisis. It is an easy target.

Problem-solving, as a focus for architectural design, didn't just develop in the 1960s and 1970s. It came into the discipline as part of Enlightenment Rationalism during the eighteenth century and was reinforced by the codification of architecture into a profession. The focus of all professions has been claimed to be problem-solving.[13] When Jean-Nicolas-Louis Durand first documented a rational architectural design method around 1802, he clearly stated that his focus in this method was to solve a problem which was a building.[14] His problem-solving would be considered simplistic today as it was based only on the composition of the plan and was shaped by ideas of efficiency. Efficiency, for Durand, was a consideration of cost.[15] Earlier than Durand, we find architects involved in what would be defined as social problems. Sebastiano Serlio, practising architecture in the early sixteenth century, worked on designs for a series of houses for the poor. These designs were made in response to social and political pressures occurring in Venice at that time.[16]

While it is useful to focus design activity, there are issues with the thinking of architecture as a rational problem-solving process. The problem/solution model may work well in disciplines which deal with discrete and containable project definitions. However, architecture rarely has a discrete and containable project or context. Architectural design constantly engages the synthesis of incomplete, obscure, and ill-defined social, cultural, and technological content into formal responses which are then reinterpreted through the experience of a diverse public. The term coined by Horst Rittel, and adopted by the design research community, to refer to this type of situation is *wicked problem*.[17] A wicked problem is one that cannot be easily defined, has incomplete or complex information associated with it, and is resistant to resolution. It might be questioned whether it is really a problem at all.

The entire problem-solving approach presupposes that viewing design as the solution of a problem is a useful strategy. It also assumes that the problem used for driving the architectural design is real. But often it is not. Instead, problems are fabricated in order to 'do design' since design is *supposed* to respond to problems. In architecture, there really aren't any problems; rather, there is a complex layering of pressures, forces, perceptions, desires, priorities, and values. These are not problems. Defining the goal of architectural design as a problem, then, in practice, is less than constructive. This attitude becomes reductive, approaching the richness of the architectural fabric as a limited and discrete set of issues rather than orchestrating a multi-level, system-based proposal. One example is the much-discussed failure of modern architecture. Modern architecture and planning of the 1920s was seen as the solution to problems emerging from Western industrialization. Urban poverty, crime, slum creation, and social alienation were rampant. Since many of the issues of an industrial society were based on issues of density, overcrowding, and urban life, there seemed to be an architectural 'problem'. Modernist avant-garde designers armed with a utopian belief system set out to make a better world through changing our physical environment. They did this, however, by reducing the issues to space planning and aesthetics, ignoring the complex relationship that included a sensitivity to context, the social dynamics between family and community, and the relationship to politics, policy, and social welfare. The result was a public failure and the declared 'death' of modern architecture.[18] The problem of social housing and the quality of urban life was not really a problem of architecture. While the spatial and formal arrangement of the housing complex aggravated the situation, the architectural proposal was not the cause of the failure; nor could it alone be its solution. The issue was far larger and more complex than anything the formal resolution could solve or even influence significantly.

Architecture is a design profession which refines a complex network of social, cultural, and technological factors to provide *quality* as part of the human ecosystem and addresses the potential of a social effect or occupation. Because of this, approaching design through architectural priorities will transcend a 'problem statement to solution' definition. Since architecture is socio-cultural in nature, even if conceptualized as problem-solving, those 'problems' addressed are not actually solvable but only negotiable as 'in the social realm, problems are never solved (and thereafter forgotten); they more likely involve conflicts that may be *re*solved by consensus – only to resurface later as other kinds of conflicts, calling for further resolutions, and so on'.[19] Architectural design, as a design discipline, has multiple stakeholders and non-discrete layers of content, and it is context-dependent rather than product-focused. This doesn't mean that a type of problem-solving cannot be attempted, only that it tends to be detrimental to the outcome. The idea of what a problem is should be considered broadly or isolated to a fragment of the overall process, such as when programmatic conflicts must be 'solved'. Holistically, architecture responds to a situation or a context. It does not solve discrete problems.

Why do we need to address attitudes to problem-solving? Simply because the starting bias – the filtering process that limits which information used in the initial set-up of an architectural design process – has so much influence on the final proposal. Many times, the starting bias will presuppose the potential of the final outcome. If architectural design is defined as needing to identify a comprehensible and isolated problem, the content of the process is affected in a significant way. It doesn't actually affect the framework or the method, but it does affect the content, types of information, testing criteria, and types of decisions which are variables in the method. The framework of the method only structures these aspects, allowing focus and predetermining tools. Jumping ahead to design frameworks, methods based on a pattern-based framework do not need to identify problems to solve in order to have a successful outcome; the attitude isn't even part of the process. Force-based methods, focused on the negotiation of assets, constraints, and opportunities, is probably the closest to what most design researchers would consider a standard problem-solving approach. However, identifying a problem isn't necessary as the methods of this framework can ignore a clearly identified problem to use a rigorous analysis of context instead. Concept-based methods also *could* approach design as problem-solving through identifying a question. These methods would then use the question as an organizational device for the process and would generate varied formal responses in a coherent structure. They do not *need* to do this; it is only an option as there are other ways of developing a central focus that also work.

To reiterate the main point of this book, methods only structure content, tools, types of information, thinking styles, location of judgement, and points of decision-making. They do not make decisions, but act as types of filter to address complex situations. Philosophical approach, starting bias, and selection of elements in the design are the role of the designer, *not of the method*. None of these aspects can be automated as they are non-linear and complex. None of them can be reduced to discrete, isolated problems.

Cognitive styles

There are shared, generic aspects to design activities. However, generic aspects are useful only when put into context. That context includes intentions, specific syntax, embedded histories, disciplinary culture, bias, and priorities. Identifying and studying the generic basis of design without the context makes it difficult to extract useful information. This is because the context, intentions, and chosen framework all apply detail to the generic structure.

So what are the generic aspects of design? Emerging from studies of design, creativity, innovation, and human behaviour, a fundamental aspect of a design process is the importance of using different *cognitive styles* or *thinking styles*. Thinking style is combined with the nature of human decision-making, which is based on heuristics rather than logic. Heuristic decision-making uses shortcuts in mental processing power – these are usually called rules-of-thumb, trial-and-error, educated guesses, or common sense. The process results in a decision which might not be perfect but will be *good enough*. Design, at a basic level, is then a conceptual process that uses two different types of thinking with a decision-making event (selection) related to them. Regardless of the discipline being studied, be it architecture, engineering design, or studies of innovation in business, a mapping of process reveals an exploratory, divergent, or expansive type of thinking (creative) combined with a reductive, convergent, evaluative (analytical) type of thinking (Figure 2.2). J. Christopher Jones called this 'divergence, transformation and convergence'[20] in his early studies.

Divergent (exploratory) and convergent (evaluative) thinking styles are not exclusive to design but they are basic human processes. If the ability to design is considered as an expression of being human, this means the ability to explore, evaluate, and innovate. Taken alone, thinking styles are not a method but only very basic elements found in all methods.[21] They are, however, a serious tool that all designers, architectural and otherwise, need to hone. Design is made possible by combining these thinking styles with disciplinary syntax to form a framework which holds the potential of a relevant and significant outcome for the discipline. The thinking styles are located within phases of the method. The phases then scale and focus the type of information explored and analysed by the thinking techniques to arrive at decisions (and there will be hundreds of these in a design method). Each decision is the result of a divergent–convergent sequence. The heart of architectural design, and all design, is an intellectual structure – the active thinking of the designer. The foundation of the intellectual structure is the types of thinking that are involved.

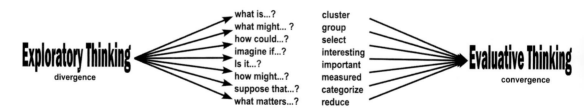

Figure 2.2: Exploratory (divergent) thinking and evaluative (convergent) thinking

Notes

1 Foucault, Michel, 'The Order of Discourse (Inaugural Lecture at the Collège de France, Given 2 December 1970).' In *Untying the Text*, edited by Young, Robert. Boston, MA: Routledge & Kegan Paul, 1971/1981: 52–64, at 59.

2 Buchanan, Richard, 'Wicked Problems in Design Thinking.' *Design Issues* 8, no. 2 (1992): 5–21, at 8.

3 The core writings of this period are those by Christopher Alexander, J. Christopher Jones and Horst Rittel. Alexander was awarded the first Gold Medal for Research in 1972 by the American Institute of Architects (AIA) for his book *Notes on the Synthesis of Form*. See Alexander, Christopher, *Notes on the Synthesis of Form*. Cambridge, MA: Harvard University Press, 1964; Jones, J. Christopher, *Design Methods: Seeds of Human Futures*. London: Wiley-Interscience, 1973; Rittel, Horst and Melvin Webber, 'Dilemmas in a General Theory of Planning'. In *Developments in Design Methodology*, edited by Cross, Nigel. Chichester: J. Wiley & Sons, 1984: 135–144.

4 The statement regarding design as a discipline was made by the Editorial Board introducing two articles by Bruce Archer in the first issue of *Design Studies*, the journal of the Design Research Society. The Board clearly stated that the new journal was possible because design was an independent discipline and could 'be identified as a subject in its own right, independent of the various areas in which it is applied to practical effect'. See *Design Studies* 1, no. 1 (1979): 17.

5 Stempfle, Joachim and Petra Badke-Schaub, 'Thinking in Design Teams: An Analysis of Team Communication'. *Design Studies* 23, no. 5 (2002): 473–496.

6 Simon, Herbert A., *The Sciences of the Artificial*. Karl Taylor Compton Lectures. Cambridge, MA: The MIT Press, 1969.

7 Bayazit, Nigan, 'Investigating Design: A Review of Forty Years of Design Research'. *Design Issues* 20, no. 1 (2004): 19.

8 Ibid.: 21.

9 John Friedmann's Transactive planning placed citizens and civic leaders at the centre of planning processes. Paul Davidoff's Advocacy planning addressed social and economic issues and grounded the act of design to the location where it was to manifest. Stephen Grabow and Allan Heskin attempted to redefine planning processes to address the poor through decentralization, ecological attentiveness, spontaneity, and experimentation. See Davidoff, Paul, 'Advocacy and Pluralism in Planning'. *Journal of the American Institute of Planners* 31, no. 4 (1965): 331–338; Friedmann, John, *Retracking America: A Theory of Transactive Planning*. Garden City, NY: Anchor Press, 1973; and Grabow, Stephen and Allan Heskin, 'Foundations for a Radical Concept of Planning'. *Journal of the American Institute of Planners* 39, no. 2 (March 1973): 106–114.

10 Schön, Donald A., *The Reflective Practitioner: How Professionals Think in Action*. New York: Basic Books, 1983.

11 Viollet-le-Duc, Eugène-Emmanuel, *How to Build a House: An Architectural Novelette*. Translated by Bucknall, Benjamin. 2nd edn. London: Sampson, Low, Marston, Searle, and Rivington, 1876.

12 Morris, Pam, *Realism*. London and New York: Routledge, 2003.

13 Schön, Donald A., *The Reflective Practitioner: How Professionals Think in Action*. New York: Basic Books, 1983: 23–24.

14 J-N-L Durand was critical in shifting architectural concerns away from decoration of surfaces to the arrangment of spatial distribution for particular purposes. In his introductory chapter of the *Précis*, through rational argument, he reduces architecture down to 'the solution of two problems: (1) in the case of private buildings, how to make the building as fit for its purpose as possible for a given sum; (2) in the case of public buildings, where fitness must be assumed, how to build at the least possible expense.' See Durand, Jean-Nicolas-Louis, 'Introduction'. In *Précis of the Lectures on Architecture; with Graphic Portion of the Lectures on Architecture*. Translated by Britt, David. Los Angeles, CA: Getty Research Institute, 2000: 77–88, at 86.

15 Ibid.

16 Serlio, Sebastiano and Myra Nan Rosenfeld, *Serlio on Domestic Architecture*. New York: Courier/Dover Publications, 1997: 43, 48.

17 Rittel, Horst and Melvin Webber, 'Dilemmas in a General Theory of Planning'. *Policy Sciences* 4 (1973): 155–169. [Reprinted in *Developments in Design Methodology*. Edited by Cross, Nigel. Chichester: J. Wiley & Sons, 1984: 135–144.]

18 The 'death' of modern architecture was declared by Charles Jencks when the Pruit Igoe housing development was demolished on 15 July 1972 (St Louis, Missouri). The massive housing development was based on modern planning theory, and the architect, Minoru Yamasaki, developed the project with a high Modernist aesthetic. However, living conditions in the housing centre declined almost as soon as the project was completed, and the entire complex was destroyed as a failure of public policy. While the failure of Pruit Igoe was complex, the event became a symbol for Postmodernist architects of the failure of Modernism. See Jencks, Charles, *The Language of Post-Modern Architecture*. New York: Rizzoli, 1977.

19 Krippendorff, Klaus, *The Semantic Turn: A New Foundation for Design*. Boca Raton, FL: CRC/Taylor & Francis, 2006: 27.

20 Jones, J. Christopher, *Design Methods: Seeds of Human Futures*. London: Wiley-Interscience, 1973.

21 Many first-generation design research methods, such as those developed by C. Alexander and J. C. Jones, had issues of connecting a reduced structure to relevance in practice as they reduced methods to core thinking structures of divergence, convergence, and decision. However, those structures are generic to any creative act based on formulating a plan. They cannot be used successfully *as a method* within a particular context and discipline without being applied in a framework which contains the connective elements to a practice.

Chapter Three

Revealing methods in architectural design

'BEFORE resuming your pencil,' said the cousin, 'you must know what you wish to do.'

Eugène-Emmanuel Viollet-le-Duc[1]

Design methods are repeatable patterns of activity occurring systematically and recognized to produce certain results in the process of architectural design. That is, they have the *potential* to produce results and they *should* be able to be taught, learnt, and applied. More often than not, this potential is not realized. Many, if not most, intern architectural designers and students learn through practice and trial-and-error, overseen by an experienced architectural designer. When method is introduced as part of learning architectural design, it isn't often done in a systematic way in order to show its relationship to larger design concerns. Much information, coming from either theory or outside the discipline, is used as early 'inspiration' rather than deeply connected to the decision-making process as part of designing. To make deep connections, theoretical positions need to be connected to structured techniques of mapping, transfer, and application as an integral part of the design process.

The misunderstanding, or lack of visibility, of how external information is used to generate architectural design encourages intuitive responses in the process of architectural design. Intuitive responses are capable of developing rich projects if the designer is well experienced. However, more often than not, the result is a proposal that is difficult to defend and less rich than it could have been. The designer might sense that something is interesting or has significance in a context but have little clue how to develop that work in order to reinforce those qualities. Many times the result simply becomes a shallow, symbolic representation of the initial idea, focused on an object of cultural but not architectural meaning. While form is the final manifestation of architecture, that form needs to be accessible by conceptual layers of architectural syntax and domain knowledge. Considering that the basic activity of architectural design has to do with the translation of intellectual intentions into tangible form, the lack of clear processes to connect thinking to formal realization seems problematic.

There are reasons why these barriers exist between architectural designers and access to core knowledge of their design processes. For example, there is a very strong belief that architectural design operates by intuition and genius, a concept borrowed from architecture's association with the fine arts.[2] The concept of genius as a cultural and social construction can be traced back to the influence of Immanuel Kant on the development of aesthetics. Kant wrote that for 'judging of beautiful objects as such[,] *taste* is requisite; but for beautiful art, i.e. for the *production* of such objects, *genius* is requisite'.[3] Following the direction of Vitruvius, before the onset of modernity in the 1700s, architecture was classified as a craft. However, from the eighteenth century onwards, art was shifting in its responsibility to society and architecture was repositioned as a fine art.[4] This meant that the rules for making art were applied to making architecture. The rules were important as, without them, there was no ability to have meaning and understanding. Yet, as art shifted from imitative work based on nature to concerns expressed through the imagination, it became more difficult to identify the rules to follow.[5] For Kant, the solution was to consider genius as a type of pre-conceptual intuition by which the rules could be accessed yet were not apparent. If genius was used, the rules did not need to be known for the artist to respond to them. Any decision related to those rules occurred prior to conscious, rational thought. This allowed an artist to work with originality by applying rules that had not yet been defined.[6] Yet genius cannot be taught, studied, or transferred – a person must simply be born with the facility. Genius as a source for art and architecture became institution-alized through the legacy of nineteenth-century Romanticism and integrated as an unexamined attitude in architectural Modernism and Postmodernism.

Genius replaces the need for method as knowledge of the structure to produce architecture is not required. The architectural designer will just know what to do because of the intuition fuelled by his or her genius. Decision-making then becomes personal, arbitrary, and intellectually inaccessible. The result of this attitude is an opposition to 'being told what to do' as this infringes on the idea of free will and personal expression. There is also great resistance to introduce any framework of thinking which appears 'deterministic and authoritarian',[7] as evidenced from the accusations thrown at Christopher Alexander's robust contemporary method for use in architecture. Although Alexander examined design processes as tools in which to access complex environments, those tools were often interpreted as rigid directives. In addition, most people look to methods and expect, or require, the process to create a fixed series of steps which produces exactly the same results each and every time. This is a fallacy of rationalism. Genius and rigid directives represent the poles of artist and scientist. Both positions misunderstand how methods work in design *as structures of thinking which produce cohesive relationships among elements* resulting in a design proposal. In the sense that architecture is constructed by relationships between bodies and forms in space, architectural design is an activity applied to systems rather than objects. Those systems include human and environmental factors. Due to this, the best we can hope for in applying structure to our thinking in terms of design methods are *potential* effects and *probable* interpretations. This doesn't mean that intuition is not found *within* method, only that it should not *replace* method.

The contemporary suppression of explicit methods in architecture design doesn't mean there haven't been, aren't still, and can't be some classic methods available to the architect – it is just a question of revealing access to these processes through examining historical approaches to architectural design. In general, approaches fall into two large organizing categories. These categories parallel an attitude in Western culture which divides access to knowledge, justification, and truth into two sources: do we primarily gain our understanding from our *senses* or is our *mind* alone responsible? We find these two poles of accepting either our senses or our mind as the dominant mode of understanding echoed throughout many disciplines and called by different terms. It is the subject–object conflict, rationalism versus empiricism, intuition versus logic, experience versus reason, nature versus nurture, and, in very broad terms, art versus science. Amazingly, the two sources of knowledge are set up as a conflict, with one being dominant over the other. If knowledge comes from the mind, then knowledge from the senses is subordinate to it, and vice versa.

The history of architectural design is not free of this division between the mind and the senses but the division is fairly problematic if someone actually wants to *practise* design rather than just talk about or study it. There are other problems created for an architectural designer which are more subtle in nature. Accepting a natural and preordained division between poles such as art and science, or intuition and logic, separates one type of content from another without ever really examining the relationship between the two.[8] In architecture, 'science' is often left to the technical side – building systems, environmental controls, and structure – while 'art' is claimed for design – usually focused on aesthetics and the visual appearance of buildings. However, current research in cognitive science and evolutionary psychology is showing that division to be completely artificial and culturally constructed.[9] Historically, architectural design methods have developed through a rational approach (mind) yet discussions around qualities of space are experiential and phenomenological. Considering the Western division between these two types of information, there are issues rigorously connecting intellectual reasoning to sensory-based experience. Yet, design methods are based on a rational structure that contains intuition through exploratory thinking and a heuristic decision-making process.

Underlying foundations

Marcus Vitruvius Pollio wrote the first known treatise on architecture, *de Architectura* or *The Ten Books of Architecture*, in the first century BCE. This single book was used as the benchmark for the foundation of architectural judgement and quality from the resurgence of interest in Classical antiquity during the fifteenth century to the final defence of Classically inspired work in the nineteenth century.[10] Vitruvius gave the requirements of architecture as consisting 'of Order, which in Greek is called *taxis*, and of Arrangement, which the Greeks name *diathesis*, and of Proportion and Symmetry and Decor and Distribution, which in the Greek is called *oeconomia*'.[11] It was assumed that an architect would integrate each of these factors when considering an architectural design. And much of the theoretical discussion between the fifteenth and nineteenth centuries was exactly that – a dialogue on the merits and interpretation of Vitruvius' categories of judgement. Even after the philosophy of Classicism was abandoned as a valid source for architectural design, the mantra of firmness, commodity, and delight (translated elsewhere as 'durability, convenience, and beauty'[12] or 'strength, utility and grace'[13]) is still heard today as the cornerstone definition of architecture. It doesn't tend to be used in architectural design or educational circles, unless the school still holds to classical beliefs, but the terminology has entered general societal knowledge. These three words were the first and oldest presentation of an architectural theory. They were never, however, a design method. While Vitruvius presented a system for determining priorities for architectural intentions, the first explicit documentation of a design method didn't occur until the early nineteenth century. Its arrival was inevitable considering the shifting concerns towards knowledge in Western culture through the Enlightenment and the growing belief in rational, scientific thinking.[14]

Rational thinking and critical discourse were at the heart of a series of changes in Western society that moved us from being medieval to being modern in the way we defined ourselves, our cultural values, and our beliefs.[15] When a change is this large and far reaching into all aspects of society, it is known as a *paradigm shift*. The major catalyst of this shift was a change in the way knowledge was pursued, and our ability to access what was perceived as universal truths. What made the paradigm shift possible was a fundamental and systematic change in the process of investigation and the application of methodology used to examine the world. When considering how Western society began to see itself, the writings and thoughts of Copernicus (1473–1543), Galileo (1564–1642) and Newton (1642–1727) are foundational, along with the philosophy of Francis Bacon (1561–1626) and René Descartes (1596–1650). In terms of method, Bacon championed inductive reasoning, Descartes did the same for deductive reasoning, while Newton merged these two approaches to knowledge. Since a society is constructed by a group of individuals united in a common way of seeing themselves, it is easier to consider the paradigm shift as a large-scale change of framing. Western society through the Enlightenment abandoned one framing metaphor based on mysticism and magic to accept a new way of approaching the world based on a metaphor of mechanism and clockwork. The shift to a mechanistic viewpoint led the way for empirical observation and rational thought that are at the heart of modernity. The Industrial Revolution was a literal representation of changes in philosophical and scientific knowledge based on rational, scientific thinking. The new mindset also introduced an attitude that meaning, based in either nature or human thought, can be known. This attitude lies at the root of *technical rationalism*.

Pattern-based framework

The first rational architectural design method was produced by Jean-Nicolas–Louis Durand (1760–1834) and published in his book *Précis of the Lectures on*

Architecture,[16] which was produced for students of the École Polytechnique between 1802 and 1805. What was significant about Durand's textbook was that it addressed architecture as an issue of design rather than a set of construction details and practices.[17] It was not only the first method of architectural design based on the rational thought process of Descartes but also conceptual in nature, rather than a practical pattern book, making it intellectually different to the popular volumes of Vignola[18] and Serlio.[19] Understanding architecture not as the building, but as the thought process that creates the building, was a critical shift. Étienne-Louis Boullée (1728–1799), Durand's teacher, had declared a generation earlier: 'What is Architecture? Shall I join Vitruvius in defining it as the art of building? Indeed, no, for there is a flagrant error in this definition. Vitruvius mistakes the effect for the cause. In order to execute, it is first necessary to conceive.'[20] Boullée stressed that architecture was not an object to be constructed but a type of thought that had its effect in building. This idea was reinforced by Viollet-le-Duc when he proposed, to paraphrase from the quote at the beginning of this chapter, that one cannot *design* if one does not have *intentions*.[21] It is important to understand that the rise of methodology in architectural design was paralleled with an understanding that design was about intentionality that created form rather than form by itself.

Durand believed that 'architecture has as its object the composition and execution of buildings, both public and private'.[22] He introduced his thoughts originally for students of the École Polytechnique as an efficient way to produce competent designers. He had very little time to teach engineering-focused students to be sensitive to architecture. When he introduced this method, he was in conflict with the majority opinion of architectural designers of the early 1800s. Durand was working against the current poetic fashion of Romanticism as a designer who believed in a rational, scientific approach to architecture. He was also interested in the composition of a building's programme as the primary concern of the architectural designer. Poetic expression and Romanticism prioritized the public effect of the façade yet a shifting social expectation began to focus design intentions towards the performance of a building. The effect was to focus architectural design on providing interior comfort and a strong relationship between the use of a room and its formal composition rather than the social broadcasting of the exterior.[23] These shifting priorities affected Durand's belief system that constructed a definition of architectural design. As a rational approach, Durand focused on the tools available to the designer, avoiding any difficult translation between desires that were *outside* of architecture and beyond interpretation of those desires into an architectural language. This was easy for him as the core of his values was based in the composition of the interior volumes – how they were scaled, arranged, and ordered. Because of this, Durand's method allowed the idea of composition and the application of known patterns of spatial use to dominate through the application of rules-of-thumb. If, instead, had Durand believed, as Viollet-le-Duc did, that architecture was a complex negotiation between programme, client, and site not quantifiable by rules, then patterning methods might not work the best. Or, if he had believed that the most important part of the architecture was how it expressed itself visually to its surroundings, his method would not have produced a result considered successful as the method did not use elevation content as a primary tool. However, Durand did not believe this, and nor did enough members of the society he was addressing. He believed that architecture was to be pursued from small elements to final building and through the application of rulesets. Considering architecture as a series of elements to be combined in a rational way introduced a series of tools – the axis, grid, and plan. The focus on efficiency and economics introduced a value system – a way to make design decisions in order to arrive at a proposal. The value system he applied to design was based on efficiency and economics, which used formal knowledge of past projects as a guide. The use of past projects from which successful patterns and characteristics of spatial use can be identified and classified is called *typology*.

While Durand's *Précis* outlined one of the first modern architectural design methods, his process is no longer followed because societal values that judge success in architecture have changed. This doesn't mean that the underlying framework of his approach is now invalid, only that his explicit process has been abandoned. What is important in studying Durand's method is understanding how he believed that the core of architectural design was the application of *patterns* and *rulesets* – that architecture is fundamentally about the composition and arrangement of elements in space. The belief is held because patterns, in this case, are seen by the designer to hold the best type of information to allow for relevant outcomes for the final design, and those patterns could create compositional rules. A framework focusing on pattern application then limits the tool selection as well as structuring how decisions would be made and what type of information would be available to the designer. Composition and typological approaches allow the designer to work by prioritizing formal information, limiting attention on cultural and social use of space. Cultural and social content is still present, but it is held in the patterns rather than applied independently as part of the design process. A continuation of

Durand's application of patterns and rulesets to drive design decisions is found in aspects of Christopher Alexander's work on *pattern language* in the 1960s. Patterns and typology also became the core of a postmodern approach to urban design, used by New Urbanism and developed by the theoretical discussions of Raphel Monao, Anthony Vidler, Alan Colquhoun, Aldo Rossi, and Colin Rowe.[24]

Durand's method presented a formalized process to apply composition to architectural design. It is not the only way patterns are used in architecture, nor is a pattern-based framework by any means the only basis for methods found in architectural design. The use of patterns and rulesets as a primary organizational focus for a method has, though, gone out of vogue in contemporary architectural practices. Instead, there are two other major frameworks that frequently occur today, each with long historical foundations. They are more acceptable in our present cultural climate because these two sets of working methods align more closely with the values we hold for how design should operate. It is important to remember that these values are culturally constructed – they are real because they are accepted by a large number of people, not because they have any connection to a universal or fundamental truth.

Force-based framework

The second major framework for architectural design is based on forces. Although this approach differs conceptually from the application of pattern-based rules, it developed from the same rational, scientific approach as the one detailed by Durand. The force-based framework focuses on systems thinking and the negotiation of complex forces conceptualized as pressures, assets, constraints, and flows. The point of the framework is to make those forces accessible and ordered so a designer can act upon them. Systems thinking avoids the construction of pre-existing rules and sees the design of the physical environment as the result of forces and the application of principles. A systems approach doesn't believe that objects can be reduced down to simply the sum of their parts. Instead, objects are parts of a system which has structural and behavioural relationships as well as interconnectivity. Any change in the relationships ultimately changes the nature of the entire system. As a design process, the system – which includes our built environment, our social interactions, our natural environment, our financial structures, and our bodies in space – can be seen as a series of forces which have attributes, qualities, and preferred arrangements. Depending on what we wish to do, those forces can be seen either as beneficial to the process (an *asset*) or as an obstacle to the final proposal (a *constraint*). Architectural design is approached using this framework when design is understood as the negotiation of relationships between forces in a system. Negotiating relationships is seen as the way that decisions can be made and the best way to access information that is relevant to the design proposal. The force-based framework has a large degree of flexibility in terms of final outcomes depending on how the architectural designer selects initial content and to which forces attention will be paid. Regardless of content, the general framework for the design process remains the same.

While many contemporary processes of architectural design are based on the *force-based* framework, it is not a contemporary invention. We can trace documentation of the implied framework back to the writings of Eugène-Emmanuel Viollet-le-Duc (1814–1879). Viollet-le-Duc was the author of several important books on architectural theory, such as the *Dictionnaire raisonné de l'architecture française du XIe au XVIe siècle* (*Dictionary of French Architecture from the 11th to the 16th Century*; 1854–1868) and the *Entretiens sur l'architecture* (*Discourses on Architecture*; 1858–1872). He was committed to developing a rational approach to architecture and to the education of architects. While the *Dictionnaire raisonné* and *Entretiens* are Viollet-le-Duc's best-known writings, and his most influential works in the English-speaking world, they are not his clearest writings on the design process. Viollet-le-Duc was frustrated in his attempt to introduce his ideas into the major school of architecture of that period, the École des Beaux-Arts. Ultimately, he abandoned the attempt to educate students there and turned, instead, to a younger, and what he hoped would be a more influential, audience. This was done through writing story-based books about architecture and design. These popular books, such as *Histoire d'une maison* (*The Story of a House*; or *How to Build a House*), *Histoire de l'habitation humaine depuis les temps préhistoriques* (*The Habitations of Man in All Ages*), and *Histoire d'un dessinateur, comment on apprend à dessiner* (*Learning to Draw; or the Story of a Young Designer*), were all narratives in which his knowledge, theory, and views were embedded. It is in *The Story of a House*, which follows a young boy learning about architecture, that we find the description of a force-based architectural design process.[25]

In *The Story of a House*, an experienced architect walks his younger cousin Paul, who is sixteen years old, through the design process for realizing a house for his sister, Marie. In the process, Paul is taught to construct a programme for a client; examine the siting of the building for positive and negative qualities; arrange rooms for mutual advantage; consider view and light as aspects of interior space; construct a plan-based composition of all the formal elements; project a plan into a section in order to consider roof geometry; and, finally, construct elevations which are based on programmatic need. There are some strong similarities with Durand's process, particularly the sequence of design that uses first plan, then section, and finally the detailing of elevation. This process, once again, stressed interior distribution of programme over other architectural qualities. However, where Durand focused on patterns, rulesets, grids, regularity, efficiency, and order, Viollet-le-Duc applied the positive and negative relationships between elements, allowing irregularity to occur if it made logical sense based on those relationships. Although he did not use contemporary terminology, Viollet-le-Duc's approach introduced the idea of systems thinking. This was accomplished by considering human activities and environmental events as pressures or forces interconnected in an environment. Those forces, in turn, were used to shape and arrange architectural spaces for maximum comfort, efficiency, and best qualities for their use and habitation. Viollet-le-Duc didn't believe that rules were useful in design as 'ninety-nine times out of a hundred you find yourself dealing with the exception and have no use for the rule'.[26] The arrangement of the building programme was constructed through a complex relationship between spatial need, traditional use, social patterns, climatic conditions, sequencing of procession, public–private relationships, and environmental qualities such as light, wind, and exposure.[27] Architects will recognize this as a standard design process in terms of service to a client and sensitivity to a context and landscape.

Forces, as a basis for architectural design, are also behind Louis Sullivan's mantra of *form follows function*. Sullivan related architecture to organics in his writing and defined organics as the relationship between a 'pressure of a living force and a resultant structure or mechanism whereby such invisible force is made manifest and operative'.[28] 'Form follows function' can be rephrased as *function is a force or pressure that shapes form* to make it a little clearer. Frank Lloyd Wright, as a disciple of Sullivan, took the notion further. For Wright, the exterior of a building was the result of the forces of the interior[29] and his discussion of revisions to the standard kitchen was based on the forces of needs, air movement, and environment which then shape the space.[30] For all these architects, and many working today, architectural form is the result of the resolution of forces, whether physical, environmental, or social.

The premise of the methodological studies of Christopher Alexander, found in his books *Notes on the Synthesis of Form* and the more famous *Pattern Language*, is based in the resolution of forces. Alexander addressed the underlying idea of resolving design problems when he proposed that form is the result of a force, and if one examined the force then the form could be predicted.[31] This is an attitude borrowed from biological study of morphology (the study of the form and structure), a concept that originated in the late 1700s and was popularized by D'Arcy Thompson's studies in the early 1900s. In *Notes on the Synthesis of Form*, Alexander introduced mathematical set theory as a graphic tool for designers.[32] This was an attempt to diagram the forces for greater visibility and quality of architectural design resolution in order to deal with problem-solving in a complex systems-based environment. *Pattern Language* resolved forces by applying patterns and spatial rules. While that book might initially seemed to be typologically based since it prioritizes patterns, the method illustrated uses patterns only to determine judgement criteria in relation to identified forces, constraints, and opportunities.

On a process level, architectural form is the direct manifestation of forces, flows, or pressures.[33] Identifying these pressures through the introduction of a series of *constraints* and *assets* allows decisions to be negotiated, moving towards a final proposal. There are many variations available when applying the framework as a method. While the examples of Viollet-le-Duc and Wright moved through phases traditional to architectural design – i.e. programme to site to plan to section to elevation – a structure of forces, pressures, constraints, and assets within a system does not need to follow this explicit phasing. A variation of this framework sets up a conflict between two or more aspects of the design context, materiality, or programme requirements in order to drive the design proposal. An example is a programme that is too large for a site (conflict in scale and massing), or a heavy element needing to be situated above something extremely light (conflict in gravity and structure). The Villa dall'Ava project by OMA used the second example, balancing a heavy mass of a pool above a glass-encased lower level to drive the design intentions. In these cases, the situations are analysed for assets and constraints focused on the generated conflict. The resultant information is then filtered and used for a design response. We find applications of the force-based framework pushed to their limits in the work of many critical practices. Offices such as OMA and its various offshoots – including REX, Foreign Office Architects, MVRDV, WorkAC, MASS Studies, Studio Gang, and BIG – use research and analysis to determine significant constraints and assets. The content generated is then explored and resolved in order to produce radical but rational innovation in their design work.

Many designers who approach their work using force-based methods tend to believe that design is a problem–solving process and that it is simply the resolution of conflicting forces. However, problem-solving does not produce a framework for architectural design, even though the idea of 'solving problems' is well embedded in the attitudes of designers.[34] Approaching architectural design strictly as an activity of problem-solving is sometimes dangerous as this attitude has a tendency overly to reduce or limit the complexity of the environment. By doing this, it can introduce errors of judgement and misalignment of priorities. That being said, there are aspects of problem-solving in force-based methods which have to do with identification of conditions, setting up relationships, minimizing conflicts, and maximizing positive aspects. These can inform the design proposal but should not replace the active role of the designer or the priorities of the method.

Concept-based framework

The third major framework for architectural design is concept-based, using a framing idea as a way of organizing a coherent architectural response. It is probably the most prevalent, least documented, most discussed (both negatively and positively), and one of the hardest to do successfully if aiming for depth and enrichment through architectural syntax. Methods generated from a concept-based framework use metaphors, analogies, questions, and the 'big idea'. Many students and practitioners talk about their *concept* for a design, that sound-bite that can be easily grasped and gives the proposal a quickly understood purpose. The concept is used, or should be used, to organize all the aspects of the architectural design into a final form that has agreement of parts and is logically connected. This is called *coherence*, or the fitting together of parts in a way that appears natural. Visual and intellectual coherence is important to how we interpret architecture as it is directly related to perceived quality. The concept-based framework revolves, then, around the creation of a central idea which is used to organize the parts of a design proposal. All aspects of the design are then judged against, and should reinforce, the central idea. Using the concept as a judgement criteria ensures the parts all 'speak the same language'.

The central concept is so persistent in architectural design that it is difficult to know the source of the original idea. It appears to be the blending of two different, but related, historical theories. The first is the analogy as a way of conceptual-izing an overall approach towards architectural design. The second is the belief that architecture should express something beyond its own physical nature as developed through the French theory of character and codified into architecture with the use of the *parti*.

Analogy, as a type of metaphor, has an extremely long history in architectural design. It has never been a method, but rather is a tool to be applied *within* a design process, and a framing device *outside* of the method. As an external framing device, analogy is used as a way of seeing architecture's place in the world. Broadly speaking, in architectural theory pre-1850, there were two main analogies used for architecture: the human body and nature. A key statement on architectural composition by Vitruvius defines proportions of buildings in terms of an analogy with the human body.[35] Francecso Di Giorgio (1439–1502), in his *Architettura*, connects Vitruvius' image of man as a measure of proportion to the composition of the city and the construction of buildings. Leon Battista Alberti (1404–1472) cements this tradition with his theory of lineaments and the analogical mapping of the composition of the human body to the construction of buildings. Alberti is supported by other Renaissance architectural theorists, such as Filarete (1400–1469) and Andrea di Pietro della Gondola (1508–1580), who is much better known as Palladio. The shift in Enlightenment architecture came from moving the analogy from the human body to the relationships between civilization and nature as a source of meaning. Post-1850, the major analogy framing architectural design intentions then became the machine, with its promise of efficiency, reason, order, health, cleanliness, and progress.[36] Analogies and metaphors, used in this way, allow the designer to approach their design work with a philosophical position to help organize their initial choices and priorities.

Character, on the other hand, developed in the French Academy of the eighteenth century and rose with a more pictorial approach to architecture. Through architectural theory, the design of buildings became about expressive qualities and more closely aligned with techniques of poetry, literature, and theatre. One of the major theorists of the period, Gabriel-Germain Boffrand (1667–1754), considered theatre, poetry, and architecture so closely associated that it was possible to take principles from one and apply them directly to the other. Architectural design of a building become synonymous with the design of stage sets expressive of a mood or creating ambience for a play, produced by its character. Character, as an emotive, expressive quality read by the observer, was blended with metaphor in the extreme work of Boullée and Claude-Nicolas Ledoux (1736–1806).[37] Under Boullée, character became a blanket overlay of simple ideas, driven by geometrical form with no concern for constructability, occupational comfort, or materiality. Ledoux extended the idea of character even further into the purely visual by developing projects as three-dimensional symbols. In the work of Boullée and Ledoux, the expression of the building was a narrative or commentary that used the visual shape of the building to broadcast its purpose, something Robert Venturi and Denise Scott Brown would later call 'building-becoming-sculpture' – or *ducks*, as they labelled this type of formal symbol.[38] While this was the extreme, the concept of character became institutionalized into architectural education through the École des Beaux-Arts of the early 1800s through the use of the *parti*, or 'what characterizes a building'.[39] *Parti* and concept continue today as a common starting position for architectural designers.

One of the issues with concept as a method is the location of the source material. Since the late 1960s, many sources for meaning in architecture have been sought from outside of the core syntax of the discipline.[40] The issue becomes, at least methodically, how to translate that content into a valid architectural response. This issue opens up two variations on the process, depending on whether the original source for the design proposal is found *inside* or *outside* architecture. If a concept is a gesture of massing, an idea for circulation, or a simplified formal composition, then there is little issue with using the source material to help arrange the parts of the project. This type of information is considered native to architecture – the tools of plan, section, elevation, axonometric, and model can be used to explore how the source will structure the whole composition. However, there are many occurrences of architectural design which do not have internal content as a central idea. If seeking a radical or innovative proposal, designers can attempt to borrow from an outside source which is not architectural, something in another domain of knowledge, as this increases the potential for novelty and innovation. The source might be a question, ideas from another discipline, or some non-architectural object or process used for inspiration. Any movement of content from one discipline to be mapped as an explainable device in another discipline is a metaphor. The structure and operation of metaphors, and variation of analogy, is based on *domain-to-domain mapping*. This is the action of moving content from one domain or area of knowledge – say, biology and the principle of sunlight tracking in sunflowers – to another area of knowledge, such as architecture. The mapping maintains the core information and value of the original source material in order to enrich the target domain. Most of the attributes or non-essential characteristics from the source domain are dropped while relationships are maintained.

The creation of a valid architectural response through a concept-based framework is not that straightforward. While concept is one of the most common starting positions for architectural designers today, it is barely understood as a framework and mostly unexamined as a design process in architecture. In order to be successful, the method needs to use the concept to create a final proposal that has a high degree of relevance and significance to its context – be it cultural, social, or formal. In any case, the results are judged based on how *meaning and expression* are transferred from the concept through the material of architecture – its interpretation and operation. This isn't easy to do well.

Methods, beliefs, and limits

What becomes clear through this brief introduction on design frameworks based on patterns, forces, and concepts is that early attitudes and values held by the designer, whether personal or cultural in origin, are critical for shaping the content that is found in the final proposal. We introduce methods based on a design framework affected by framing philosophies in order to limit our range of choices. It immediately narrows our options and starting position, creating limits rather than being open to any influence. This is important in a complex system – and the world we live and work in is indeed a complex system. It is important to understand that approaching design with such a belief system is not unusual. In fact, it is absolutely common and necessary to approach a design process with a *design framework*, a *set of biases*, and a *value system*.

It is probably easiest to think about frameworks as containers. The shape and size of the container allows certain things (and by 'things' I mean events, information, and decisions which support selection of content in design proposals; it is just easier to call these 'things') to be done easily. Suppressing other types of information allows a designer to focus and filter content. Considering how much information can be accessed for use in architectural design, and how complicated some of the testing for relevance can be, some limitation on the scope of that content is very important. Certain tools, both conceptual and physical, allow easier access to those things than others, so it is natural that we associate tools with frameworks. It is a framework, along with the flexibility of designer bias and a value system, which allows methods to operate not as mechanical, prescriptive processes but as critical structures. A critical process implies rigorous intellectual skills, analysis, judgement, exploration, and depth. All contemporary methods of design, due to their systems-based nature, need to be exploratory and critical rather than prescriptive.

The other side of introducing frameworks, bias, and value systems to focus an architectural design proposal is the issue that the designer might be absolutely wrong in their assessment of 'what matters', or the value system might be so personal that it cannot be adapted to a wider audience. The process of design cannot be automated because while we can describe general scales, tools, and structures that occur within design, a large series of decisions needs to be made as part of that process. The ability to make good decisions is ultimately based on the sensitivity of a designer or design team to read context, priorities, and terrain in order to connect them to a design framework. A method can *help* encourage good decision-making by clearly defining criteria of success, but it cannot *make* this happen.

Notes

1 Viollet-le-Duc, Eugène-Emmanuel, *The Story of a House*. Translated by Towle, George M. Boston, MA: James R. Osgood and Company, 1874: 37.

2 General intellectual history of architectural theory and art illustrates this point. See Shiner, Larry, *The Invention of Art: A Cultural History*. Chicago: University of Chicago Press, 2003; and Gelernter, Mark, *Sources of Architectural Form: A Critical History of Western Design Theory*. Manchester and New York: Manchester University Press, 1995.

3 Kant, Immanuel and J. H. Bernard, *Kant's Kritik of Judgment*. London and New York: Macmillan and Co, 1892: Section 1.48: 193.

4 A good point to start this understanding of art's changing role in Western society is Beardsley, Monroe C., *Aesthetics from Classical Greece to the Present: A Short History*. 1st edn. New York: Macmillan, 1966.

5 The process that moved all the arts from looking for absolute rules in nature as an imitative act to exploring imagination and intuition occurred over several centuries. Kant and Hegel were instrumental in providing the philosophical framing in the later stages but earlier key texts in aesthetic and architectural theory were by Gabriel-Germain Boffrand (*Book of Architecture*), Marc-Antoine Laugier (*An Essay on Architecture*), Alexander Gerard (*An Essay on Taste*), William Hogarth (*The Analysis of Beauty. Written with a View of Fixing the Fluctuating Ideas of Taste*) and Archibald Alison (*Essays on the Nature and Principles of Taste*). The idea of taste played a seminal role and the Picturesque Movement in England

as well as the rise of Structural Rationalism were alternative effects of the shift to intellectualize architectural design.

6 Beardsley, Monroe C., *Aesthetics from Classical Greece to the Present: A Short History*. 1st edn. New York: Macmillan, 1966: 222.

7 Bhatt, Ritu, 'Christopher Alexander's *Pattern Language*: An Alternative Exploration of Space-Making Practices.' *Journal of Architecture* 15, no. 6 (2010): 711.

8 Bruno Latour presents a good discussion on the dangers of divisional thinking in Western society. See Latour, Bruno, *We Have Never Been Modern*. Cambridge, MA: Harvard University Press, 1993.

9 The discussion of the idea of embodied cognition and the fallacy of the philosophical mind–body separation can be found in many disciplines currently. The strongest advocates for this position of continual feedback between thinking and our senses can be found in Richard Rorty (politics/philosophy), Mark Johnson (aesthetics/philosophy), Steven Pinker (evolutionary psychology), George Lakoff (cognitive science), and Mark Turner (cognitive science). The following may be of interest: Lakoff, George and Mark Johnson, *Metaphors We Live By*. Chicago: University of Chicago Press, 1980; Lakoff, George and Mark Johnson, *Philosophy in the Flesh: The Embodied Mind and its Challenge to Western Thought*. New York: Basic Books, 1999; Lakoff, George and Mark Turner, *More than Cool Reason: A Field Guide to Poetic Metaphor*. Chicago: University of Chicago Press, 1989; Pinker, Steven, *The Blank Slate: The Modern Denial of Human Nature*. New York: Penguin, 2003; Pinker, Steven, *The Stuff of Thought: Language as a Window into Human Nature*. New York: Viking Adult, 2007; Rorty, Richard, *Philosophy and Social Hope*. New York: Penguin, 1999; Rorty, Richard, *Philosophy and the Mirror of Nature*. Princeton, NJ: Princeton University Press, 1979.

10 Kruft, Hanno-Walter, *A History of Architectural Theory: From Vitruvius to the Present*. London and New York: Zwemmer/Princeton Architectural Press, 1994.

11 Vitruvius Pollio, Marcus and Frank Stephen Granger, *Vitruvius, on Architecture*. The Loeb Classical Library. Cambridge, MA: Harvard University Press, 1962: Book I, Chapter 2: 1.

12 Vitruvius Pollio, Marcus, M. H. Morgan, and Herbert Langford Warren, *Vitruvius, the Ten Books on Architecture*. Cambridge, MA: Harvard University Press, 1914: Book I, Chapter 3: 2.

13 Vitruvius Pollio, Marcus and Frank Stephen Granger, *Vitruvius, on Architecture*. The Loeb Classical Library. Cambridge, MA: Harvard University Press, 1962: Book I, Chapter 3: 2.

14 Dupré, Louis K., *The Enlightenment and the Intellectural Foundations of Modern Culture*. New Haven, CT, and London: Yale University Press, 2004.

15 The entire shift didn't occur overnight. In fact, developments took several hundred years and are still continuing. The Enlightenment (roughly seventeenth and eighteenth centuries) was the major engine for this change, but those attitudes developed through the Renaissance and humanism, starting in the twelfth century. At the core of this shifting view of our own cultural identity is the rise of a belief in science and reason, and the introduction of scientific methods of enquiry, investigation, and analysis.

16 Original French title: *Partie graphique des cours d'architecture faits à l'Ecole royale polytechnique depuis sa réorganisation*. Durand, Jean-Nicolas-Louis, *Précis of the Lectures on Architecture; with Graphic Portion of the Lectures on Architecture*. Translated by Britt, David. Los Angeles, CA: Getty Research Institute, 2000.

17 Picon, Antoine, 'From "Poetry of Art" to Method: The Theory of Jean–Nicolas-Louis Durand.' In Durand, Jean-Nicolas-Louis, *Précis of the Lectures on Architecture; with Graphic Portion of the Lectures on Architecture*. Translated by Britt, David. Los Angeles, CA: Getty Research Institute, 2000: 1–68, at 1.

18 Vignola and Branko Mitrović, *Canon of the Five Orders of Architecture*. New York: Acanthus Press, 1999.

19 Serlio, Sebastiano, *The Five Books of Architecture: An Unabridged Reprint of the English Edition of 1611*. New York: Dover Publications, 1982.

20 Boullée, Étienne-Louis, '"Architecture, Essay on Art"'. In *Papiers de E.-L. Boullée in the Bibliothèque Nationale, Paris*. Translated by de Vallée, Sheila. Edited by Rosenau, Helen. London: A. Tiranti, 1953: Vol. MS. 9153: 82–116, at 83.

21 The American version of the novelette referred to the experienced architect simply as 'the cousin' while the British edition named him 'Eugène' making the book more autobiographical. Viollet-le-Duc, Eugène-Emmanuel, *The Story of a House*. Translated by Towle, George M. Boston, MA: James R. Osgood and Company, 1874: 36.

22 Durand, Jean-Nicolas-Louis, *Précis of the Lectures on Architecture; with Graphic Portion of the Lectures on Architecture*. Translated by Britt, David. Los Angeles, CA: Getty Research Institute, 2000: 77.

23 Etlin, Richard A., *Symbolic Space: French Enlightenment Architecture and its Legacy*. Chicago: University of Chicago Press, 1996: 129–130.

24 Colquhoun, Alan, 'Typology and Design Method'. *Perspecta* 12 (1969): 71–74; Moneo, Rafael, 'On Typology'. *Oppositions* no. 13 (1978): 23–45; Rossi, Aldo,

The Architecture of the City. Translated by Ghirardo, Diane and Joan Ockman. Cambridge, MA: The MIT Press, 1984; Vidler, Anthony, 'The Third Typology'. *Oppositions* no. 7 (Winter 1976): 1–4.

25 M. F. Hearn has written excellent analyses of the theory of Viollet-le-Duc, and I am indebted to his writing for extending my understanding. For further background on Viollet-le-Duc and his extensive theoretical writings, see Hearn, M. F., *Ideas that Shaped Buildings*. Cambridge, MA: The MIT Press, 2003; and Viollet-le-Duc, Eugène-Emmanuel, *The Architectural Theory of Viollet-Le-Duc: Readings and Commentary*. Edited by Hearn, M. F. Cambridge, MA: The MIT Press, 1992: 141–166.

26 Viollet-le-Duc, Eugène-Emmanuel, *The Story of a House*. Translated by Towle, George M. Boston, MA: James R. Osgood and Company, 1874: 74.

27 Viollet-le-Duc, Eugène-Emmanuel, *The Architectural Theory of Viollet-Le-Duc: Readings and Commentary*. Edited by Hearn, M. F. Cambridge, MA: The MIT Press, 1992: 141–166.

28 Sullivan, Louis, *Kindergarten Chats and Other Writings (Documents of Modern Art)*. New York: Dover Publications, 1918/2012: 48.

29 Wright, Frank Lloyd, *The Natural House*. New York: Horizon Press, 1954: 39.

30 Ibid.: 88–89.

31 Alexander, Christopher, *Notes on the Synthesis of Form*. Cambridge, MA: Harvard University Press, 1964: 15–16.

32 Alexander introduced mathematical set theory into architecture as his first attempt to produce useful tools for design in his 1964 book *Notes on the Synthesis of Form*. This volume preceded his work and book on pattern language, which was a critique of his first approach as much as it was a continuation of the application of patterns in architectural design.

33 While common terminology is *force*, as developed by Viollet-le-Duc and Sullivan, Steven Groak used the term *flow*. He considered buildings to be manifested by flows of matter and energy, including money, space, and time. See Groak, Steven, *The Idea of Building: Thought and Action in the Design and Production of Buildings*. London: E. & F. N. Spon (Taylor & Francis), 1990.

34 The idea that the purpose of design is to solve problems seems to have come in with the rise of a scientific approach to all types of knowledge in Western society. However, this attitude can be found as far back as Sebastiano Serlio in his eight numbered books (nine in total) of the *Architettura*, which started their publication in 1537. In these books, Serlio includes solutions to the problem of

housing poor workers. It isn't until the Enlightenment, however, that we find problem-solving as an explicit activity in design, rather than the final piece of architecture as the solution. Durand stated explicitly in his *Précis* in 1802–1805 that the purpose of architecture was to solve a problem based on the idea of cost. Rationalism and scientific method have reinforced the attitude that design solves problems; in the case of architecture, these problems vary greatly from programme conflicts to culturally derived issues.

35 Kruft, Hanno-Walter, *A History of Architectural Theory: From Vitruvius to the Present*. London and New York: Zwemmer/Princeton Architectural Press, 1994: 27.

36 Ibid.: 364–392, 398, 419.

37 Ibid.: 158–165.

38 Venturi, Robert, Denise Scott Brown, and Steven Izenour, *Learning from Las Vegas: The Forgotten Symbolism of Architectural Form*. Rev. edn. Cambridge, MA: The MIT Press, 1996: 87.

39 Cret, Paul P., 'The École des Beaux-Arts and Architectural Education.' *Journal of the American Society of Architectural Historians* 1, no. 2 (1941): 12.

40 Gelernter, Mark, *Sources of Architectural Form: A Critical History of Western Design Theory*. Manchester and New York: Manchester University Press, 1995.

Chapter Four

Placing theory and philosophy in architectural design

Now I approve of theorising also if it lays its foundation in incident, and deduces its conclusions in accordance with phenomena. For if theorising lays its foundation in clear fact, it is found to exist in the domain of intellect, which itself receives from other sources each of its impressions. So we must conceive of our nature as being stirred and instructed under compulsion by the great variety of things; and the intellect, as I have said, taking over from nature the impressions, leads us afterwards into truth. But if it begins, not from a clear impression, but from a plausible fiction, it often induces a grievous and troublesome condition. All who so act are lost in a blind alley.

Hippocrates[1]

This chapter addresses ideas of theory and philosophy in terms of architectural design. Rather than discussing intellectual history or key arguments in architectural theory over the past decades and centuries, the focus will be on how theory and philosophy relate to disciplinary structure and how they are used as part of a process of design – their location in methods.

Theory tends to be a touchy subject in architecture. It is mostly treated as ideology, a belief system representing values of a group. This belief system, one that is not testable or refutable and is often based on fashion or trend, is then used to create class divisions and sub-groups within the discipline. In addition, another division is created between architectural designers based on what they hold to be true or important and whether they identify with being 'theory-based' or 'practice-based'. However, the division between theory and practice is artificial and mostly imaginary – it is also ultimately detrimental to architectural design as a whole. It is not possible to divide theory from practice when engaging design as they are not separate and equal 'things'. This becomes very clear when considering architectural design from the point of view of methodology.

To start with, the idea of philosophy needs to be untangled from the concept of theory. I was at a symposium a few years ago on issues of philosophy in architecture. The room was occupied by philosophers, mostly those working in the field of aesthetics, and by architectural theorists. Both groups used the terms *philosophy* and *theory* interchangeably. When I asked for a definition of the two terms, one that presented a difference in use (otherwise why should there be two different words?), no one could offer one. It seemed, for these two separate disciplines of architecture and philosophy, that the terms *theory* and *philosophy* meant the same thing. But the issue is – and the reason for the symposium was – no one could seem to make theory *written* about architecture useful for *making* architecture. It was great for *interpreting* architecture – theory produced a series of interesting ideas. But it wasn't connected to any stable knowledge that would allow a designer to understand why *doing this* might *make that happen*.

Since the terms *theory* and *philosophy* are used interchangeably, and seem to mean the same thing, when one speaks of architectural theory, are we really speaking about the philosophy of architecture? If architectural theory is really the philosophy of architecture, how should its purpose be understood? More to the point, how are theory and philosophy to be *used* by an architectural designer?

The role of philosophy in disciplines

How is philosophy used in applied disciplines? Barnett Newman is famously quoted as saying, 'I feel that even if aesthetics is established as a science, it doesn't affect me as an artist. I've done quite a bit of work in ornithology; I have never met an ornithologist who ever thought that ornithology was for the birds.'[2] The statement was later shortened to 'aesthetics is for the artist as ornithology is for the birds', as a criticism implying the uselessness of philosophy for a practitioner of art. Newman believed that art was produced without the need of a philosopher, just as birds seemed to do perfectly well without access to the knowledge developed by the discipline of ornithology. Now, we might argue that Newman was talking about the philosopher in particular and not about philosophy in general. However, the quotation was adapted as a criticism of the knowledge developed by philosophy to be used in science. Steven Weinberg, a Nobel laureate physicist, wrote, 'I've heard the remark (although I forget the source) that the philosophy of science is just about as useful to scientists as ornithology is to the birds.'[3] Both quotes are clear attempts to make knowledge focused on the same topic (art, for example, or physics, or yeast) by different disciplines mutually exclusive and irrelevant to each other in application. They are also examples of disciplinary snobbery and the defence of a boundary of knowledge. This attitude, in view of how disciplines operate, would mean that knowledge developed in the domain of philosophy would have no use as knowledge in a domain of art, or science, or architecture. In return, the particular practice of these disciplines is proposed to be of little concern to the philosopher. Newman's implicit position was that the artist was a creator of reality and was disconnected from the general public. He seemed oblivious that the origin of this view had been inherited from the philosophy of Immanuel Kant, Georg Hegel, and German Idealism. Philosophical ideas and discussions have a long shelf life and can take years or even decades to filter into general public opinion. Once there, they persist for generations and centuries, often merging with or adapting to new ideas rather than being replaced. The way we think about everything – from concepts of beauty to how meaning is constructed – has a philosophical basis, often centuries or millennia old.

Philosophy is a discipline in the same way that architecture, medicine, or physics is a discipline. It has a boundary, a discourse and a syntax. However, philosophy differs from other disciplines in a significant way – the core of its general concern centres on issues of knowledge, reasoning, reality, values, truth, and human nature. Many of these concerns can be found in almost every other discipline – hence, they are called trans-disciplinary concerns – but they are core concerns for philosophy. Philosophy as a discipline is organized into major branches that focus these concerns. Logic approaches questions in terms of valid reasoning and is concerned with the structure of arguments. Epistemology questions the nature and extent of knowledge – where does it come from, how it is acquired and what can be known? Metaphysics questions the nature of reality, be it normative or extraordinary. Ethics examines human actions in terms of proper reasoning. Politics, as a philosophical field, is concerned with liberty, justice, concepts of property, rights, and law. Aesthetics studies sensori-emotional values, what are commonly known as judgements of taste and human appreciation. As such, it is concerned with the arts, including poetry, literature, painting, music, sculpture, theatre, and architecture.

From the above list, we can see the various fields of philosophy are organized not only by approaches to knowledge but also by application to other disciplines, such as fine arts, law, medicine, politics, and architecture. So what is the core syntax of philosophy? What does it own as a discipline?

A good general definition of philosophy comes from Branko Mitrović, an architectural historian and philosopher, who describes it as the study of 'rational arguments and reasons used to acquire beliefs independent of the views of other people'. He points out that looking at philosophy in this way makes it not about specific intellectual problems but 'a way to approach various problems by insisting on the analysis of arguments and their logical consistence'.[4] This general definition – which avoids the creation of fields based on the study of knowledge, reality, and value – considers philosophy simply as a set of intellectual tools which are critical in nature, and a producer of knowledge which is relevant to every aspect of human existence.

Philosophical tools, such as logic, are very powerful as they do not generally need any form of translation between domains of knowledge in order to be used in different disciplines. An example of one of the strongest tools of philosophy for use in architectural design is the concept of *first principle reduction* or *returning to first principles*. A first principle is the most basic proposition that can be developed in any enquiry. It cannot be reduced any further. This technique is applied in various locations in a method. It occurs when a designer wishes to refocus a design intention by stepping away from a particular pattern or form to consider the principles at work behind the form. It is also the tool at the basis of knowledge transfer between domains.

Probably the most important role of philosophy, when seen from the point of view of a practitioner, is its ability to tackle problems that are outside the reach of the practitioner's discipline. This is an issue of syntax and scope. Philosophy is capable of engaging questions that are beyond another discipline's boundaries as well as questions which that other discipline's syntax cannot answer by itself. Those questions generally revolve around issues of knowledge, meaning, and value at a societal level and their concern spans disciplinary boundaries. Philosophical thinking introduces significant cultural content and priorities into other disciplines through this action. The philosophy of science, for example, tackles questions related to science that deal with epistemological (knowledge), metaphysical (reality), and ethical (rightness) issues. These are issues that are often not relevant to the immediate needs of a practitioner involved with applied investigations.

They do, though, have larger implications to society, how we live, and how we define ourselves. Introducing philosophical issues and engaging trans-disciplinary questions will often change policy, approaches, and selection of study.

Ethics is a good example of a philosophical concern which has larger ramifications within a discipline. It is an issue at the core of a definition of a society. In recent decades, a controversy has arisen in medical genetic research around the use of human embryonic cells in stem cell research. While the discipline is genetics, the issue of whether it is correct or not to use a particular type of cell is not a practical one; it is philosophical and involves consequentialist and deontological ethics. The discussion around use of human embryonic stem cells includes definitions and attitudes towards murder – not something geneticists are able to deal with in their disciplinary syntax. The outcome of this discussion, a societal decision about what is right and wrong, would make certain lines of cells inaccessible. The genetic researcher's research methods might not be directly affected by the source of the stem cells, but new methods might be introduced because of the ethical concerns, or because of a search for new, ethical sources of stem cells.

If the ability to engage ethical questions is not found in the disciplinary syntax of genetics, it is equally absent in the syntax of architecture. There is nothing in our traditional tools or content that can engage ethics *directly*, especially on a broad, societal level. This doesn't mean that ethical discussions are never held by architectural designers, only that when they take place, they originate in the domain of philosophy.

Philosophical discussions, concerns, and positions can be translated into disciplinary concerns. Sometimes, philosophical arguments enter the practice of a discipline without anyone's knowledge. As Mitrović wrote: 'Practicing architecture means facing philosophical questions daily, although one may not always be aware of it.'[5] The Sustainability Movement of the early twenty-first century is an example of ethics and ethical arguments entering into architecture. It is a discussion focused on how our society believes it should live and what values we hold. There are more examples of intentional philosophical positions being adapted by an architectural designer. These include the early influence of René Descartes's rationalism and the more recent architectural flirtation with the philosophies of Jacques Derrida, Jean Baudrillard, Martin Heidegger, and Gilles Deleuze. Semiotics, the study of signs and sign systems, is another example of how philosophy can start to influence disciplines such as architecture.

The study of semiotics grew from John Locke's original philosophical definition of a 'doctrine of signs'[6] in the late seventeenth century. As a development in a philosophy of language, the work of Charles Sanders Peirce and Ferdinand de Saussure in the late 1800s and early 1900s built the framework for a new discipline of semiotics to be practised as a social science, separate from the philosophy of language. While semiotics became extremely important in literary theory from the 1950s onwards, the translation into architecture didn't occur until the Postmodernist architectural theory of Robert Venturi and Denise Scott Brown in the 1970s.[7]

If the statements by Newman and Weinberg are any indication of the opinions other disciplines have about philosophy, it is interesting that the one discipline that is critical when dealing with societal and cross-disciplinary concerns – philosophy – is the one that is often denied any such importance. It might be that philosophical concerns are so persistent that they are almost invisible. It might have something to do with the time-line for influence: philosophical ideas can take decades to grow in importance, with the origin obscured by the time they have. It also has to do with terminology. When philosophical concepts and explorations can be addressed from within a disciplinary boundary, their discussion tends to be called *theory* instead of *philosophy*. However, theory isn't the same as philosophy. It has different responsibilities.

Theory as an intellectual tool

The role of theory, regardless of the discipline, is to be the primary tool of the discourse of that discipline. As philosophy addresses large-scale understandings that cross disciplinary boundaries and define society, theory addresses the discipline itself. We can find general philosophical issues and disciplinary theoretical issues next to each other, parallel but at different scales of content. Theory is used to examine the content found within the boundaries of a discipline, to define those boundaries, to defend ownership over areas of knowledge, and to annex adjacent domains of knowledge in order to expand the territory of the discipline. It might move outside the boundaries to attempt to pull new material back inside, but the theory of a discipline will always be engaged with discipline-specific concerns.

As it affects how we can use theory in methods, it is worth noting that the role of theory in architecture has changed dramatically over the last century. Most of the changes centre on a societal shift to Postmodern thought. This same shift occurred in many other disciplines as well, but it is more visible in those disciplines that are naturally occurring and have long histories. The study of architectural design generally involves about 5000 years of influences – many of which are still debated, such as Classicism – expressions of truth, and the role of the experience. When we read a book of architectural theory that was written before the 1950s, we will find it is heavily involved with defining architectural practices. Traditionally, architectural theory was concerned with materials, composition, proportions, cultural expression, and construction practices. In addition, this theory was prescriptive and instructive as its role was to define (and defend) the boundaries of the discipline clearly, and to produce a discourse that tells a designer *what they should do*. Classic works from Vitruvius, Alberti, Perrault, Morris, Viollet-le-Duc, and Le Corbusier were based on this principle. Treatises were written to say 'this is inside architecture' and 'that is outside architecture'. That type of discourse produced rules, and those rules could be used directly as a method's testing mechanism (as in 'Does my design align with the tenets of Classical theory?'). With the rise of postmodern thinking, people pursuing architectural theory became less interested in defending a shared disciplinary boundary and detailing practices. Instead, they used theory to seek out new influences and to create many unique, and often conflicting or disconnected, boundaries for the same discipline in order to address a perceived loss of fixed meaning. The role of architectural theory moved away from the direct engagement with the syntax of a discipline because of the task to find new influences, new sources of meaning (interpretation), and, ultimately, new syntax.[8] Unfortunately, this made theory less relevant for an architectural designer who still needed to use the syntax of the architectural discipline in order to produce something identified as architecture.

In addition to the change in how theory is used within disciplines since the 1950s, there is a change in who is producing the theory and how that theory is being used. Our current cultural climate does not consider meaning to be stable – for example, there are always other points of view which are just as valid as the intentions of the original producer of the work. In this context, theory becomes the way to access meaning. The issue is seen perhaps more clearly by looking at Postmodern theories in literature. Literary theory has been very influential on architecture, and many of the major schools of architectural design from the last decades pull from theories in literature. However, these theories have been created for interpretation. Literary theories are an extension of the philosophy of aesthetics and are built as intellectual tools in order to analyse a work of art, whether visual or textual. Each theory is constructed around a method – a series of steps and ways of thinking – which produces the particular results that this theory is known for producing. The method used in this style of theory is analytic in nature, it examines the various parts of a whole to attempt a deeper understanding. The end result of a Postmodern theory in literature is not the generation of a work of art or design, it is an opinion. Since Postmodern theories have abandoned the concept of the universal in favour of a diversity of interpretation, we get many complementary theories, whether they are based on phenomenological, hermeneutic, gestalt, psychoanalytic, deconstructionist, or semiotic foundations. Each of these theories covers an aspect of the analysis of a work and presents a way of interpreting that work in order to discover 'how art comes about, or when it is art, or what function is exercised by art, or what are its modalities'.[9] These questions explore the idea of art as a discipline – they are questions of definition.

When we consider Postmodern theories as an intellectual tool at the disposal of a discipline, we can understand that their purpose is to reveal hidden potential and meaning, as well as to mark new territory. There are two major issues that need to be overcome for these theories to become relevant to a discipline focused on design. The first issue is that the structure of these theories is analytical in nature. It is extremely difficult to make a theory based on analysis into a direct generator for an architectural design proposal. It is like using a screwdriver to apply paint. The better way to use a screwdriver is to take the lid off the can of paint so we can get access to the paint with a brush. Analytical theories are very useful, but they need to be applied to something that already exists. The opposite to an analytical theory is a generative theory, a theory that has the ability to originate an assemblage rather than just study what is existing. The issue for architectural design, which is looking for new ways of approaching design to give a proposal significance, becomes how to use an analytical theory as a generative theory – something the analytical theory is just not built to do. The second issue has to do with the source material for the new territory. Because Postmodern architectural theories seek out extra-disciplinary content as a way to extend a boundary, there is most often a disconnection between the syntax of that other discipline and the ability for architecture to respond with any relevance. We end up with simplistic responses that fall back into visual and symbolic representation – we saw this with Deconstructivism being defined as a style rather than a philosophical approach that produced new tools for use in the discipline. Ultimately there was little permanent or significant impact on architectural design beyond being identified with metaphors of instability and fragmentation.[10] An aspect of architectural theory will most likely always be exploring beyond the borders of the discipline. This type of cross-disciplinary discourse is known to support innovative or novel proposals,[11] something valued in design culture. However, there will *always* be a need to translate this type of knowledge into an architectural syntax through methodology.

Using theory and philosophy in architectural design methods

Philosophy and theory have clear definitions when considered in terms of disciplinary boundaries, discourse, and syntax. They also have a clear relationship to architectural design methods. Both philosophy and theory are constantly used and fully integrated into a design process whether the designer is aware of it or not. The following working definition for theory will be used when discussing method: theory is *the process of determining priorities by which to propose and judge design*.[12] We can break this statement into two halves – the priorities of proposing design and the priorities of judging design. The break is necessary as these two processes are located in different places in relation to methodological structure (Figure 4.1). Processes of determining priorities by which to propose design occur *before or very early in* a method, while judgement priorities occur *within* a method.

For the way an architectural designer works, we can include philosophy as part of the first definition of theory. Theory and philosophy are confused as being the same thing in architectural design because they are both used as part of the set-up approach to a design process. When architectural designers seek out philosophy as an *active* part of the design process, as opposed to being generally influenced by philosophical positions found as part of society, they are looking for something as inspiration to help set values and priorities. Philosophy, along with exploratory theory, is one way to help the designer think differently about the world. Andrew Ballantyne said it well when discussing the thinking of the French philosophers

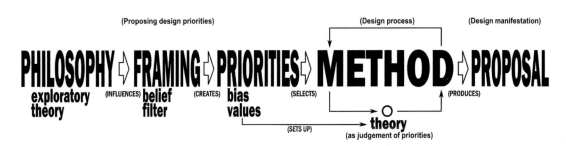

Figure 4.1: Locating the relationship of philosophy and theory to design methodology

Gilles Deleuze and Félix Guattari. The designer does not read the philosophical writing of Deleuze and Guattari for direct application to architectural design. Ballantyne writes that the text produces 'ideas in me that I would not have had by myself'.[13] Philosophy and theory allow an exploratory thinking which creates possibilities of richness before a design process even starts. They do not ensure richness; it is up to the designer to make the connections between the ideas held in these explorations and the production of meaning and relevance in the design proposal. When an architectural designer has accessed philosophical or theoretical thoughts as the foundation of their process, they might call them 'my belief' or 'my attitude' or 'my philosophy'. This is a large-scale orientation of thinking that needs to be focused into a design intention in order to be usable.

As part of an architectural design method, it is confusing to call the process of determining priorities by which to propose design a *philosophical position*, a *theoretical position*, or a *belief system*. These terms are too generic and imprecise. Instead, a philosophical position is translated so as to allow a designer to approach their work with a *frame* or a *framing effect* – a focused way in which the designer sees the world or applies their belief system. Framing 'refers to the process by which people develop a particular conceptualization of an issue or reorient their thinking about an issue'.[14] This isn't exclusive to designers, but involves all humans. It is often called a *point of view*, and colours our interpretation of events, information, and actions. Framing sets up a *starting bias* which will generate a *starting state* for the design process. The starting state is usually the first phase of a design method. Framing effect, starting bias, and starting state are a type of filtering. They limit boundaries, focus decision-making, and produce a way of interpreting information.

An architectural designer might start a process by saying, 'My approach is to think about architectural design from the point of view of the relationship between humans and the ecosystem, and I believe that relationship matters.' First, this is an ethical statement with a philosophical grounding. The relationship between humans, landscape, natural systems, and non-human inhabitants touches on many philosophical fields, including ethics, metaphysics, epistemology, and politics. There are many directions this framing might take the designer that set up the starting bias. Our designer goes on to say, 'The way I think of this relationship is for humans to be considerate neighbours to other creatures that share our landscape.' It is a more focused statement than the framing, but is still open to various interpretations – each of which will produce a different starting state for the design proposal. However, *all* proposals based on this bias will be judged by the quality of the relationship that the built proposal supports for non-human residency. The starting bias might set up a project based on issues of types of occupation and adjacency, which are addressable by architectural syntax. There might be more examination of the 'external' content of ethics, ecosystems, and diversity. The same starting bias could set up a project based on various issues of the ecological footprint of humans, or how to minimize infrastructural impact. All are valid starting points from the same framing. Various methods can be used to generate a valid proposal. The framing and starting bias will give some clues to which method might be more successful.

Another example of a framing bias is found in Donald Schön's classic work, *The Reflective Practitioner*. In describing how his professional Quist, a master architect, thinks about his approach to design, Schön writes, 'Quist values nooks, nice views, and a softening of hard-edged forms.'[15] The nooks, nice views, and soft edges are a starting bias which flavour all decisions made in the design process. These beliefs most likely came from a sociological framing rather than from philosophy, as the framing seems to be about human interaction and interpretation of the environment. As part of a design method, Quist could connect his value for nooks into any of the three method types discussed previously. A pattern-based method could be used to analyse successful past nooks for their spatial patterns and then reapply those patterns on the current site. A force-based method could look at the qualities of the nooks instead of the nooks themselves, as well as the qualities and location of views. The constraints and assets of the qualities of nooks and views could be combined with context, occupation, and circulation to form a proposal. A concept-based method could redevelop the entire project based on scaling and application of nook qualities, reinterpreting areas where the nook is not normally considered but could be successfully translated.

The examples above show that framing and bias are necessary to begin thinking about design, but they are disconnected from the actual method. What the framing and starting bias do is identify what the designer believes to be the most relevant way to think about architectural design. They allow the design intentions to be accessible and identify the priorities which will be used for judgement criteria. However, the intentions still need to be connected to a framework, used to identify relevant methodological tools, and applied to specific phases of a particular method to be useful.

The most important tool developed by framing and bias is the one that sets priorities to judge design. This is the point where theory takes on its more traditional definition of being a *set of principles which are continually tested for falseness.*[16] If a designer, like Quist in the example above, wanted to base a design on the social aspects of the nook, then there need to be some criteria that let the designer know that what they intended and what they proposed are related to each other. The judgement criteria form the bridge between intentions and proposal. It is the judgement criteria, generated from the framing and starting bias, that enable decision-making to occur with coherence in the design method. The judgement criteria ensure a level of coherence in the final proposal by aligning decision-making towards a consistent target, creating a consistent relationship between parts. In the case of architectural design, coherence is how the various elements, events, forms, occupations, materials, voids, circulations, shapes, textures, colours and masses address the major intentions of the design proposal. Design decisions, based on the judgement criteria, are able to be aligned towards the same purpose and reinforce each other.

Judgement criteria usually take the form of general statements or principles, generic enough that they can be applied at various scales but particular in application of design intentions. In the example about a shared landscape, judgement criteria will be based on the quality of the relationship between human and non-human factors. The judgement criteria will lead to decisions that select forms for human occupation sensitive to factors beyond solely human needs (Figure 4.2). Each line of design investigation will develop possibilities that are

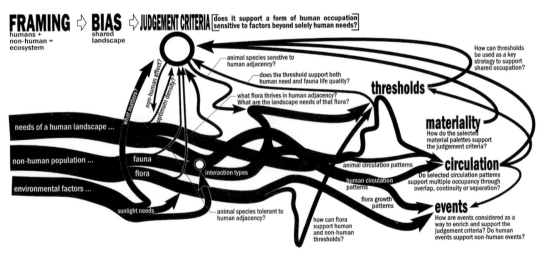

Figure 4.2: Fragment of a design process showing the role and location of judgement criteria in developing coherence when based on multiple primary factors

checked against how they address the judgement criteria. In the example of the nooks, the judgement criteria could be around ideas such as intimacy, screening, noise reduction, and indirect circulation. This information would come from initial investigation into how nooks operate and then would be used to organize all aspects of the design proposal.

Belief to effect

One of the difficulties in 'doing' architectural design is the process of decision-making and the transference of a framing philosophy into a usable form. The major type of information needed to make decisions in architectural design is based on human interpretation of spatial qualities, elusive qualitative aspects, or effects that are not absolutely repeatable. Architectural proposals often only create the probability or potentiality of something occurring or being interpreted. It can not generally *make* something happen; nor can it produce behaviour or behaviour patterns. Theory and testing are used to get closer to the intentions. In this way, architecture is not deterministic – it cannot be exactly predicted – because humans are not deterministic. We have a sense through observation, trial and error, and precedent review that there is a connection between a certain formal composition and a certain interpretation or quality of occupation. This is the difficulty with testing: a solid basis of knowledge is needed to understand what has potential and what contradicts or opposes intentions. It could be said that this is where intuition is introduced but, in this context, intuition means experience, perception, and study.

In order to illustrate how a philosophical belief creates a framing effect which sets up starting bias, a judgement theory, and a structure for decision-making, an example can be explored using the idea of truth. The belief that truth is important as a way of approaching the world is a philosophical position. One way in which the idea of truth has been translated into architectural design is as the belief that materials should be used truthfully as an expression of their essence. The basic concept can be traced from Aristotle to nineteenth-century British Socialism and French Structural Rationalism influencing Modernist architectural positions. Aristotle's philosophy proposed that all things had within them an essence, which was the nature of what they are and should be. It was truthful to use a thing in the way it was intended based on this essence. The writing of John Ruskin echoed Aristotelian philosophy when he expressed the belief that the honest use of materials was an ethical concern and necessary as part of architecture.[17] Viollet-le-Duc paralleled the thinking of Ruskin about the truth of materials as a core principle when he wrote: 'To build, for the architect, is to make use of materials in accordance with their qualities or their own nature – all this with the preconceived idea of satisfying a need by the simplest and solidest means; of giving to the thing built the appearance of duration, and of giving it appropriate proportions in accordance with the human senses, human reason, and human instincts.'[18] In twentieth-century Modernism, truth to materials and honesty of construction was one of the tenets of work by Mies van der Rohe, Walter Gropius, Le Corbusier, Frank Lloyd Wright, and Louis Khan. It was part of their philosophical framing, how they interpreted events in the world.

Truth is important to architecture. Yet, how is it used as part of a design process? Materials by themselves cannot be honest; nor can buildings, as they can only be assigned honesty by human interpretation. A society decides that an unpainted panel of wood is truthful, or that a panel of wood that is sealed but expresses the wood grain is truthful. This is not an idea that is found within architectural syntax, as there isn't any aspect of architectural syntax that can directly address ethics and honesty. Instead, a philosophical position (*truth and honesty are important*) produces a framing position (*architecture should express truthfulness and honesty*), which sets up a starting bias (*materials and construction processes will express truth*), and develops the beginning of a theory of truth that is used as a testing mechanism and judgement criteria (*this is the way materials and construction are truthful*).

At this point, a design method has not even been identified, but everything is in place to set up and judge elements in a design proposal. There are various directions the design process could go from this point, depending on the identification of the major framework – patterns, forces, or concept. Experienced designers tend to construct methods from frameworks that are most aligned with the particular needs of the situation they are addressing. Several framing positions can be blended as nested frameworks within the major framework – a fairly common occurrence. The example of truth is only one aspect of a Modernist philosophical framing. In addition to the framing position of truth, there were several other major values at play, including framing that addressed space as a plastic element, attitudes towards utopia, technology as the saviour of social problems, and attitudes towards historical continuity. Master Modernist designers used all of these values to make different decisions in different aspects of the project – space planning, material selection, façade representation, massing, and landscape integration. What is important is that they held a value system that they used to engage architectural design as a way to set up testing, judgement, and decision-making.

The belief that architectural design can be pursued without preconceptions or bias is non-productive. On the contrary, identifying framing and bias is the first tool of a designer. Understanding interest and how it shapes decisions are variables used in the design process. Framing and starting bias will always shift along with how a culture judges significance and relevance as part of its mythology. Decades ago, relevance was a dialogue with social equity through public space; today it might be about energy balance and the representation of 'greenness'. Relevance is a point of entry of fashion and cultural peer pressure into design. Framing, starting bias, and judgement criteria do not *change* methods; they exist as factors associated with methods, identifying what is considered an important belief. The same context can be approached with the same programme and the same method but with a variation of starting bias or judgement criteria. When this happens, the same method could be followed but the final proposal will be radically different. This does not invalidate the structure of the method; variance through flexible application is a natural part of the system.

Notes

1 Hippocrates, 'Praeceptiones (Precepts) 1.' In *Hippocrates Collected Works*, edited by Jones, W. H. S. Cambridge, MA: Harvard University Press, 1957 [1923]: Vol. 1: 313–315.

2 Newman, Barnett, 'Remarks at the Fourth Annual Woodstock Art Conference.' In *Barnett Newman: Selected Writings and Interviews*, edited by Newman, Barnett and John P. O'Neill. Berkeley: University of California Press, 1992: 242–247.

3 While the original quote is often attributed to Nobel laureate physicist Richard Feynman, it has almost moved into being an urban myth as there is no record of where and when it was said. Weinberg, Steven, *Facing up: Science and its Cultural Adversaries*. Cambridge, MA: Harvard University Press, 2003: 8.

4 Mitrović, Branko, *Philosophy for Architects*. New York: Princeton Architectural Press, 2011: 14.

5 Ibid.: 11.

6 Locke, John, *An Essay Concerning Human Understanding*. London and New York: J. M. Dent/Dutton, 1961: 4.21.4, 175.

7 Venturi and Scott Brown focused on iconography and the sign systems of buildings. The later discussion of this framing attitude can be found in

Koolhaas, Rem and Ulrich Obrist, 'Re-learning from Las Vegas, Interview with Denise Scott Brown & Robert Venturi.' In *Content*, edited by Koolhaas, Rem and Brendan McGetrick. Köln: Taschen GmbH, 2004: 150–157. The classic work addressing sign systems is Venturi, Robert, Denise Scott Brown, and Steven Izenour, *Learning from Las Vegas: The Forgotten Symbolism of Architectural Form*. Rev. edn. Cambridge, MA: The MIT Press, 1996.

8 Archigram is an example of the cultural shift, academicization of architecture, the search for new syntax and new sources of influence for architecture, including attempting to redefine purpose. Developing alongside other cultural vectors of critique and protest in the 1960s, Archigram initially set out to address the disciplinary syntax of architecture as a way to engage early Modernist principles but protesting the drift of Modernism into sterility and orthodoxy. The group, centred at the Architectural Association in London, England, was polemical but did not manage to build any projects in their initial form. They did have a huge effect on the next generations of architectural designers, including Richard Rogers, Norman Foster, and Will Alsop. See Cook, Peter, *Archigram*. New York: Princeton Architectural Press, 1999; Crompton, Dennis, Barry Curtis, William Menking, and the Archigram Group, *Concerning Archigram*. 3rd edn. London: Archigram Archives, 1999; and Sadler, Simon, *Archigram: Architecture without Architecture*. Cambridge, MA: The MIT Press, 2005.

9 Iser, Wolfgang, *How to Do Theory*. Malden, MA: Blackwell, 2006: 8.

10 Allen, Stan, 'The Future that is Now.' In *Architecture School: Three Centuries of Educating Architects in North America*, edited by Ockman, Joan. Cambridge, MA: The MIT Press, 2012.

11 Research has shown that one of the advantages of cross-disciplinary research is the need to translate knowledge out of deep disciplinary syntax in order for that knowledge to cross disciplinary boundaries. The act of syntax reduction often brings associations and observations that would not normally be visible. See Cummings, Jonathon N. and Sara Kiesler, 'Collaborative Research across Disciplinary and Organizational Boundaries.' *Social Studies of Science* 35, no. 5 (October 2005): 703–722; Lakhani, Karim R., Lars Bo Jeppesen, Peter A. Lohse, and Jill A. Panetta, *The Value of Openness in Scientific Problem Solving*. HBS Working Paper No. 07-050. Cambridge, MA: Harvard University Press, 2007; Lakhani, Karim R. and Jill A. Panetta, 'The Principles of Distributed Innovation.' *Innovations: Technology, Governance, Globalization* 2, no. 3 (Summer 2007): 97–112.

12 Versions of this definition can be found in the following books: Gelernter, Mark, *Sources of Architectural Form: A Critical History of Western Design Theory*. Manchester and New York: Manchester University Press, 1995; and Johnson, Paul-Alan, *The Theory of Architecture: Concepts, Themes and Practices*. New York: Van Nostrand Reinhold, 1994.

13 Ballantyne, Andrew, *Deleuze and Guattari for Architects*. Thinkers for Architects Vol. 01. London and New York: Routledge, 2007: 19.

14 Chong, Dennis and James N. Druckman, 'Framing Theory.' *Annual Review of Political Science* 10, no. 1 (2007): 104.

15 Schön, Donald A., *The Reflective Practitioner: How Professionals Think in Action*. New York: Basic Books, 1983: 135.

16 Popper, Karl, *The Logic of Scientific Discovery*. Abingdon: Routledge Classics, 2002.

17 Ruskin, John, *The Seven Lamps of Architecture*. New York: J. Wiley & Sons, 1884: 31.

18 Viollet-le-Duc, Eugène-Emmanuel, *The Foundations of Architecture: Selections from the Dictionnaire Raisonné*. 1st edn. New York: G. Braziller, 1990: 106.

SECTION II

THINKING TOOLS

Chapter Five

Thinking styles

> Invention, it must be humbly admitted, does not consist in creating out of void, but out of chaos; the materials must, in the first place, be afforded: it can give form to dark, shapeless substances, but cannot bring into being the substance itself.
>
> Mary Shelley[1]

Learning how to do architectural design is, first and foremost, learning how to think. This isn't meant in terms of intellectual capacity or ability – being smart doesn't necessarily make one a good designer. Thinking, in this context, means becoming skilled at applying *different styles of thinking* within the same process and towards the same goal. Thinking styles are complementary and not exclusive – everyone has the capacity to perform different styles of thought as they are all part of our human mental processing. Still, most people will find one approach to thought more comfortable or easier than another. That approach tends to define how a person is considered by others. As an example of an extreme, when someone is considered *too stiff* or *too dreamy*, this is a description of that person's dominant thinking style. Stiffness and dreaminess refer to how that person approaches the world – which paths of thought they encourage, which ways of thinking come more naturally to them and which ones are resisted. A 'stiff' person might notice small technical details by constantly analysing their surroundings while a 'dreamy' person might be jumping from general ideas to set up situations that are only loosely based on their surroundings. Neither of these approaches can be judged as being right or wrong. Thinking styles don't work in that way. Of course, two people with different dominant thinking styles might not appreciate each other, but this is a different issue altogether. What matters, for us as designers, is that different thinking styles produce different approaches to knowledge. They give us access to different options and conclusions. One style can also engage with another to generate movement through a design method by providing content and assisting decision-making. While not methods themselves, thinking styles are the core building blocks of any architectural design process. The ability to link different thinking styles together – and then to focus them by bias, scale, and topic – is the foundational capacity to produce architectural design.

There are other important conceptual tools used in architectural design besides proficiency with the core thinking styles. Decisions are a critical aspect of designing, with hundreds of choices being made inside every design method. While decisions cannot be automated by design methods, decision-making can be considered in terms of its type and boundary. The type of decision-making used in architectural design is based on being *good enough* rather than perfect, applying *judgemental heuristics* and the concept of *satisficing*. The boundary of architectural decision-making is to be considered in terms of domain knowledge. Along with decisions, other tools related to innovation and lateral thinking approaches can be identified. One is *first principles reduction* or *returning to first principles*. This tool suspends immediate judgement and steps back from known conclusions while still addressing core principles in the design context. Another is not a single tool, but the set of tools used in *domain-to-domain transfer*. This collection of tools is used to move knowledge explicitly from one domain or discipline into another while maintaining important relational content. Both first principles and domain-to-domain transfer address structural content (what it does or how it performs) rather than attribute or surface characteristics (what it looks like) as a way to develop depth while maintaining relevance.

Models, methods, and thinking

Many models have been proposed over the past sixty years for 'the' design process, including studies in creativity and problem-solving. Although not an exhaustive review, it is worth considering here the conceptual basis of some of those models in order to extract any shared content. The original purpose of most of these models was to describe a single comprehensive and essential design method, covering *all* types of design.

Models of the design process usually involve three to five stages which describe the activities of generation, exploration, comparison, selection, and representation.[2] There are frequent references to problems, problem-solving, and solutions, as well. For example, Edward Banfield's rational planning model starts with the identification of a problem and the definition of goals. These generate a series of options or alternative approaches which are then analysed for their potentials. Out of the group of options, one is chosen and then this is refined into a design solution.[3] Another simple model that is more directly connected to architecture originated from the studies of education and architectural design in Denis Thornley's work of the 1960s. Thornley's model includes examining the brief or programme, using this as a focus to explore meaning and find forms, then moving on to developing and refining the design proposal.[4] We find in this model the core of professional service – programme, space planning, and building proposal. The outline was adopted as a general description of architecture by professional societies such as the Royal Institute of British Architects (RIBA) and the American Institute of Architects (AIA).[5] The less specific, but more complex, architectural design model of Tom Markus and Tom Maver involves the stages of analysis, synthesis, evaluation, and decision in three phases of outline, scheme, and detail design.[6] While otherwise a linear process, an allowance is presented between evaluation and synthesis for an iterative loop in each phase. This begins to address the *test–retest* action as an aspect of design, developed elsewhere by other models. Peter Rowe, in his summary of design models, describes the iconic model of Morris Asimow as analysis, synthesis, evaluation, and communication in a spiral moving from abstract to concrete.[7] Moving out of the architecture domain, Boehm's Spiral Model of design, used in software and industrial design, follows the steps of determining objectives, identifying and resolving risks, developing a proposal, and testing.[8] The process loops through these three stages at least four times, evolving the *product* in each of the loops in phases of refined prototypes (Figure 5.1).

The problem is that while these models are general descriptions of the design process, they are not actually a design *method*. Trying to apply them to an active design process would be like baking a cake based on a general model. We can describe the process of baking as being three steps, such as deciding on flavour, mixing ingredients to form batter, and baking the batter to present a product. Generally, this is true – this is always the broad outline for baking a cake. But in practice, this list of steps is impossible to apply without more details, decisions, and context – the recipe.

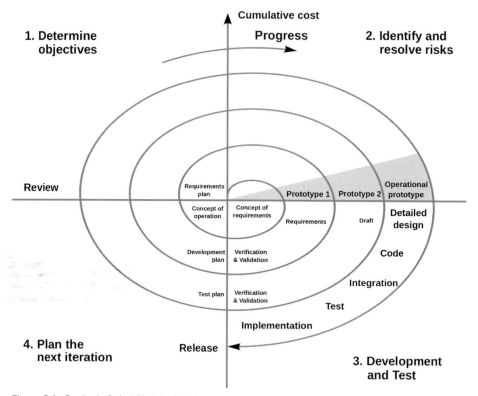

Figure 5.1: Boehm's Spiral Model of design

Source: Conrad Nutschan/Wikimedia Commons

Looking outside the design disciplines for other models that are based on creativity can help clarify shared characteristics in applied design methods. While creativity and design are not equivalent, it might also be argued that there is very little difference between them. The lines are blurred because creativity tends to be defined in terms of innovative output – some sort of physical or virtual product – which could also be said to be the result of a design process. Other disciplines which actively pursue creativity rather than design, such as research sciences and business, are clear that the result should have 'novelty [...] and some form of utility – usefulness, appropriateness, or social value'.[9] Two of the major models based on creative problem-solving are Osborn-Parnes's *Creative Problem-Solving Process* (CPSP)[10] and the Soviet inventor Genrich Altshuller's *Teoriya Resheniya Izobretatelskikh Zadatch* or *Theory of Inventive Problem-Solving* (TRIZ).[11]

There are parallels between models of innovation, such as CPSP and TRIZ, and models of architectural design. CPSP and its many variations have six steps divided into three phases. The phases are *Explore the Challenge, Generate Ideas,* and *Prepare for Action,* in which are found the steps of identifying the general goal, gathering relevant information, clarifying the problems, generating ideas to solve the selected problem, moving from ideas to applying a solution, and, finally, setting up a plan of action. TRIZ is focused on inventiveness based on contradictions between two or more elements involved in the problem generation. The process seeks to resolve the conflict without compromising any of the factors, and draws on past knowledge from other innovative solutions. For our purposes, the importance of TRIZ is its use of four phases that describe the transformation of the problem. The phases move linearly, starting at defining a specific local problem and looking to a matching general TRIZ problem found in a different domain of knowledge or as a general principle. The process then moves to a specific TRIZ solution through domain transfer, and attempts to apply that specific solution to the original problem, producing an innovative local solution. While this seems quite different to the other methods discussed, it involves the same familiar steps of problem definition and goal-setting (local problem), options and alternatives (general TRIZ problem), application and testing of alternatives (specific TRIZ solution), selection of chosen option, and refinement of solution (specific local solution). What makes TRIZ different from the other models discussed above is its algorithmic nature based on pattern identification, the use of domain-to-domain transfer of knowledge, and first principles reduction embedded as part of the phases.

Simplified to their foundational operations, these models present important information to a designer. The models describe either stages of work focused on products (schematic, programme analysis), as Lawson notes,[12] or represent a blend between thinking activities (exploration/analysis/synthesis) and outcomes (communication). The correlation between all the models is their implication that there is a stage that is about figuring out what to do (analysis/programme review/ client intention), a phase that is about putting those things together (synthesis/ schematic design), and a phase that decides whether what is done makes any sense (evaluation/review). This can be said in another way – design requires exploration, exploration requires selection, and selection requires relevance. Exploration, selection, and relevance all use different styles of thinking to be successful. These thinking styles are traditionally called *divergence* and *convergence,* terminology that

originated in the studies of human intelligence by the American psychologist
J. P. Guilford. Both Jones and Rowe used the terms 'divergence and convergence'[13] in their studies, but other designer researchers call the thinking styles
'ideate' and 'evaluate',[14] 'imaginative and logical',[15] 'generate and explore',[16] or the
'generation of variety and the reduction of variety'.[17] In the end, these all refer to
the same mental operations. It is the incorporation of these thinking types into a
framework which allows design to be both imaginative and analytical at the same
time.

Design involves generating ideas through exploring situation, context, and/or
content for opportunities, issues, or concerns. Exploration and generation engage
a style of thinking called *divergent thinking*. It might also be called imaginative,
expansive, generative, or exploratory thinking. The basis of divergent thinking
is the ability to explore as many diverse ideas around an aspect of the design as
possible. This occurs not only at the beginning of a design process but many times
throughout the process. While the starting state of design is the introduction of
divergent thinking into the process, this thinking style recurs through a design
method at various scales. Any time possibilities and options are sought, divergent
techniques based on exploratory thinking are engaged. These divergent techniques
generate all the content which will be used in the design. More robust exploration
creates more possibilities with which the designer can work. In contrast, without
an uninhibited exploration of possibilities, an exploration which is non-judgemental and non-critical, there is little material from which a designer can develop
a rich proposal.

The counterbalance to divergent thinking is a type of thinking that involves
synthesis, evaluation, testing of alternatives, or reduction of content. All these
concepts engage a style of thinking called *convergent thinking*. Convergence is the
act of bringing things together, and this style of thinking is analytical, critical,
and evaluative. For example, synthesis, a core thinking activity in design, is an
act of convergence. Synthesis is about combining elements that engage with
each other to produce a unique and new entity. While synthesis is generative
because it makes something new, it is a reductive process. It reduces complexity
by selecting elements, organizing relationships, and eliminating other possibilities.
Convergent techniques of evaluative thinking look at what has been generated by
the exploratory thinking through divergent techniques, highlighting some options
as having potential and eliminating most others. After every evaluative act, there is
a decision to be made, a selection of what is abandoned and what moves forward.

The decision uses judgement criteria as a testing mechanism to help narrow the results of evaluative thinking.

All convergent techniques are about classification, analysis, and sorting, while divergent techniques are about imagination and idea generation. The two families of techniques, along with the exploratory–evaluative thinking styles they introduce, are complementary. A situation is explored, the results are sorted, options are identified, and then the choices are tested against the judgemental criteria in order to make a selection.

The terms used in this book for these two fundamental styles of thinking and their associated tools will be *exploratory* thinking using *divergent* techniques, and *evaluative* thinking using *convergent* techniques. This terminology will hopefully separate the style of thinking from how its techniques are applied in order to generate architectural design. The application of thinking styles is the engine behind the design process, but they only work if they are put into a context. Thinking styles are not phases or steps in design; they are conceptual tools that operate within a phase. Sometimes there is only divergent or convergent thinking present, but more often both thinking styles are used in a given phase. They generate and analyse possibilities. A framework focuses the thinking styles using disciplinary syntax, representational tools, and scales of application. There is no scale or content in thinking styles by themselves – the same thinking style can be applied at multiple scales from the cultural to the detail level, and to multiple layers of content. While inexperienced architectural designers tend to use thinking styles in single or limited threads of content as part of a method (limited complexity), experienced designers might use the same method but run multiple parallel threads applied to different elements, at different scales, intersecting in complex ways. Moving from novice to mastery in architectural design is gaining experience and skill at applying more layers, elements, and scales of thinking in architectural design work.

Divergent techniques of exploratory thinking

Exploratory thinking is a process of extending the boundaries of possible solutions by engaging the creative and imaginative process using divergent techniques. There are a few principles to remember when applying this thinking style. First, judgement is always deferred during a divergent technique. This means that while a topic, starting state, or aspect of the design is being explored, no decisions should be made nor any ideas censored. Ideas should not be considered in terms of what is liked or disliked. There are no bad ideas during exploration. Nothing (at this moment) is stupid, silly, or crazy. No matter the insanity of the ideas that these techniques generate, the purpose at the moment is just to document them. Part of the way innovation and creativity works is by extending how people think the world works (what they know) to encompass new information or ways of doing things (what is really possible) that still align with the context in which that work is situated.

In addition to deferring judgement, issues should be examined as broadly as possible. It is important to generate as wide a range of options and possibilities as quickly as possible. Divergent techniques are not looking for the single perfect position or approach. Judgement is not built into the structure of the tool; the purpose of this thinking style is to generate possibilities. Threads of ideas are followed to new ideas which are, in turn, expanded into new chains of associations. While quality of the generated content is as important as quantity, the convergent techniques will, most likely, abandon 99 per cent of the generated ideas from the divergent techniques.

The most common technique of exploratory thinking is the divergent technique known as *brainstorming*. This term was coined by Alex Osborn in his 1953 book *Applied Imagination*, based on his successes using creative thinking as a Madison Avenue advertising executive.[18] The practice of brainstorming follows the principles above – start on a topic, problem, issue, or position, then generate as many unbiased responses as possible. While the original idea of brainstorming was based on group work, it is also successful (and some studies have found it to be more successful) as an individual activity. The basic premise is to approach the topic in a relaxed way, letting ideas generate other ideas and following those paths as far as you can. Each thread in the brainstorming session should generate new possibilities, and while there might be drift from the starting position, some of the generated ideas could be relevant. In this way, brainstorming supports lateral thinking by connecting things whose interrelationships may not be immediately obvious or strictly logical.

There are many variations of the brainstorming technique, and many people use the term as an alternative to divergent thinking. The basic method of brainstorming can be performed by the tool of *mind-mapping* (Figure 5.2). This is a diagrammatic technique of brainstorming that starts with a single topic, problem, issue, or position to be explored, written on a large, blank sheet of paper (analogue or digital). This becomes the centre of the diagram. Starting at this centre, elements of free association and branching ideas start to surround that idea. These can be single words, sentences, or graphics. The layout of the elements on the page is intuitive; branches and connections should be graphically shown and made as unselfconsciously as possible. There is also no analysis or judgement at this point. The idea is that natural groupings will occur by the way in which the information is arranged, something that will be used by a convergent technique to evaluate the brainstorm and render it into useful information.

The *trigger method* brings more structure to the standard mind-mapping technique and limits some threads of exploration. Trigger starts out as a standard brainstorming session. However, once a first round of content has been developed, the results are scanned to identify the ideas that seem important or significant. While judgement is not generally part of exploratory conceptual tools, it is used in trigger to filter some of the quantity to focus on quality. The selected ideas become 'triggers' that become the foci for the next rounds of the brainstorming session. Once triggers have been identified, just those ideas are explored in a non-judgemental way. This variation allows for more depth in particular threads rather than a large mass of 'noise'.

Rather than free association of ideas in a standard brainstorming session, *variable brainstorming* focuses the brainstorming session by basing the process on an outcome variable or goal. Something that is desired or deemed necessary is identified as a variable, and becomes the focus for the divergent technique. In architectural design, this might be related to an aspect of programme, circulation, massing, interpretation, or experience; or it might be based on a conflict, a difficulty, or an ambition. Taking the meditative space as an example, circulation might be identified as an important aspect to the design. The general idea of circulation

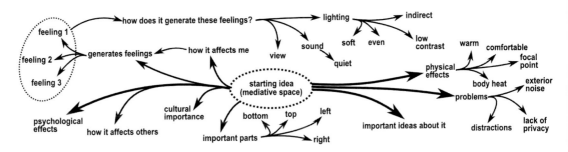

Figure 5.2: Divergent technique of mind-mapping (brainstorming)

would be narrowed to a variable that is considered important to the quality of space, such as how to arrange movement to support the idea of meditation in the architectural proposal (Figure 5.3). The first step is to list all the different types of movement that would occur as part of the proposal, from human locomotion to vehicles and mechanical movement. Elements that work against the desired variable would also be listed, such as interruptions and resistance caused by particular circulation interactions. The initial variable limits the original field of options to filter the brainstorming, thereby helping to maintain some quality at the expense of quantity. The brainstorming is still expansive but variable brainstorming introduces only those threads which seem to relate to the initial variable.

Another strong exploratory tool for divergent thinking is to ask questions. All forms of questioning are based on abandoning assumptions to look at a situation with fresh eyes. It might be that the way we see things is simply because that is the way they have been seen. An exploratory process which suspends expectations and sees the situation in a new way could reveal another approach. There are several techniques to help open our view to possibilities.

Challenge starts from a situation which might be a central topic, problem, issue, or position. The first step in the technique is to write down all the assumptions about that situation and its parts. This is done in order to examine normative assumptions towards that situation, giving the designer a sense of 'the way things are'. The purpose of challenge is to examine these assumptions to see if the results can be achieved in a different way. Once there is a list of assumptions, each assumption is challenged systematically. Every element on the list is subjected to questions such as 'Why is this so?' and 'How else could we achieve the same result?' The questions expand into a chain of questions and answers proposing other ways to achieve the same result without using the existing process.

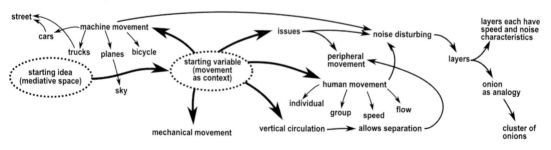

Figure 5.3: Divergent technique of variable brainstorming

Challenge can also be done with *escape thinking* rather than a challenge question. Escape thinking takes the assumptions you have listed from the challenge process and reverses their point of view. Moving down the list of assumptions, the opposite for each item is presented in place of the existing assumption and then considered for how it might affect the situation. For example, if an element is known to be always white or soft, ask what would happen if it were black or hard instead. Using the circulation example, challenge would consider the consequences of walking fast in an area that is normally slow, stopping circulation where movement is necessary, or putting conflicting circulation forms adjacent to each other to see what might happen. A list of all the effects and consequences of a reversed view is compiled and reviewed in order to challenge what is assumed. For an architectural designer, this reveals opportunities to engage design decisions. The interest is what advantages might occur by thinking about the situation and its parts in a different way.

Another form of questioning is called *questioning as the Other*. The Other is a philosophical and social science term meaning that which is not us, that which is different, or that which does not belong. It is generally used in terms of social groups and personal identity. The term, in this case, denotes a change of point of view from that normally adopted by the designer and their society. The Other doesn't look through your eyes and doesn't have your preconceptions of the world. This form of divergent thinking challenges your assumptions of how you approach the world and why you think what you think. It addresses biases which presuppose the limits of choices and ideas that can be generated in an architectural designer's work. There are several approaches to this technique, but they are all based on asking questions about the topic, problem, issue, or position from the point of view of an outsider. The classic form is that of a visitor from another culture, another time, or another planet. The Other might be an alien who has just arrived on Earth (Figure 5.4) or an exotic stranger introduced into a context radically different from their origin. It might also be someone who has travelled in time, switched ages, or switched genders. *Questioning as the Other* can also be used to examine the present by projecting back into the past or the future. The Other, in this case, would be yourself if you project from the present moment and extrapolate the effects one hundred or one thousand years into the future or past.

This technique has been used many times as a way of critiquing existing conditions, both in literature and film. *The Day the Earth Stood Still, E.T., Crocodile Dundee, Back to the Future, Peggy Sue Got Married, Tootsie, Mrs Doubtfire, Big, Freaky Friday* and *District 9* (there are too many to list) are all examples of *questioning as the Other.* They make us look at ourselves. They make us consider how we *do* act and how we *might* act. The basic method is the same, regardless of the nature of the Other. All these motifs are really just a way to approach a context without predetermined assumptions. They provide an easy way to put yourself into a different thinking structure. The questions then become, 'What do you think of this [situation, topic, problem, issue, or position], and what would you do?' Responses to these questions should be presented with an explicit naivety, and extended into one or several chains of questions and answers.

The final divergent technique is *SWOT analysis.* The technique can be used either to generate new content or to refine existing content. SWOT stands for Strengths, Weaknesses, Opportunities, and Threats. As a divergent technique, the analysis takes a topic, problem, issue, or position and details the factors which will make that thing possible or impossible to achieve. The idea is to generate as much critical content as possible from exploring the strengths, weaknesses, opportunities, and threats around the particular situation selected (Figure 5.5). The results can then be examined using a convergent technique which will reduce the volume and identify key factors for the design to engage. By focusing on creating a large volume of non-judgemental information, the method increases the potential to make connections between aspects of the situation which are not at first apparent, such as a relationship between certain threats to success and other things considered to be strengths.

Questioning: Alien as the Other

A: Welcome to Earth
   Q: What is this place?
A: Earth or this building?
   Q: Right now, where am I?
A: You are in the public library.
   Q: Is every building a library?
A: No, there are lots of kinds of buildings. A library is just one of them.
   Q: What makes this a library?
A: There are books here.
   Q: What is a book?
A: It is printed material, bound, and read.
   Q: You are here and you are not a book.
A: I came here to meet my book group.
   Q: Is that a stack of books?
A: No. It is a group of people that get together and discuss a book. Its theories, validity, the story and message it talks about.
   Q: The book talks?

A: Kind of. As you read it your mind is submerged in the world it creates. You have an internal dialogue about its message.
   Q: Is this a bad world? Should I get out of here? It sounds like no one wants to be here.
A: No. It's not a bad world. It is nice to imagine something new and fun that is different than your everyday life.
   Q: Soo... all these people here are trying to escape from their lives?
A: Some are. Some are here to learn or exchange ideas, like me. Some are here because it gives them a place that is quiet. There are some here that don't have access to the information in these books or the internet any other way.
   Q: Everyone is here because they want something that they can't get anywhere else? Nowhere else on Earth has these things?
A: You can find things like this other places. Discussions at lectures and schools, information on-line, quiet in your home. Here they find all of those things and can decide what they want to do, what is interesting to them for free.
   Q: What does interesting mean?
A: Interesting... attractive, motivating, exciting, out of the ordinary. People need diversions.
   Q: Free, you mean they don't pay anything to be here? With so much offered why don't they make money on stuff?
A: Not everyone has money to pay for these things but as a society we have decided information and communication is important. It doesn't matter if you agree with all of it or even if it is a subject you want to read. I hate romance novels but some people love them and it is important that they have access to them.
   Q: So everything ever written is here?
A: No. They can't get everything in here. Some things are too rare. Some aren't deemed 'acceptable'. Most libraries around here will try to get what you need through library exchange and find things on-line.

Figure 5.4: Divergent technique of questioning – an alien asks about a library

Courtesy of Erin Smith

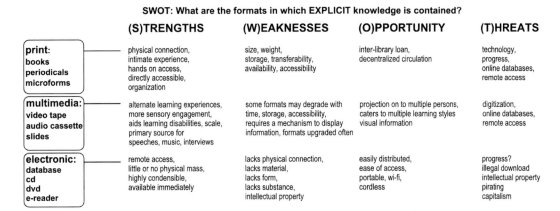

SWOT: What are the formats in which EXPLICIT knowledge is contained?

	(S)TRENGTHS	**(W)EAKNESSES**	**(O)PPORTUNITY**	**(T)HREATS**
print: books periodicals microforms	physical connection, intimate experience, hands on access, directly accessible, organization	size, weight, storage, transferability, availability, accessibility	inter-library loan, decentralized circulation	technology, progress, online databases, remote access
multimedia: video tape audio cassette slides	alternate learning experiences, more sensory engagement, aids learning disabilities, scale, primary source for speeches, music, interviews	some formats may degrade with time, storage, accessibility, requires a mechanism to display information, formats upgraded often	projection on to multiple persons, caters to multiple learning styles visual information	digitization, online databases, remote access
electronic: database cd dvd e-reader	remote access, little or no physical mass, highly condensible, available immediately	lacks physical connection, lacks material, lacks form, lacks substance, intellectual property	easily distributed, ease of access, portable, wi-fi, cordless	progress? illegal download intellectual property pirating capitalism

Figure 5.5: Divergent technique of SWOT analysis – physical access to knowledge formats

Courtesy of Brendan Cagney

For architectural designers there are also several divergent techniques which are graphic and physically based. Architects speak of delaying decisions, trial-and-error models, sketching and doodling, the use of collage, montage or narratives, reverse massing (where solid becomes void and vice versa – a physical version of challenge/escape thinking), and unexpected combinations, such as programmatic spaces, public–private collisions, or massing conflicts (shaking expectations).[19] There are many techniques and variations, but they all are based on the same principle – opening the field of enquiry to increase possibilities for evaluation, decision-making, and design directions. They will always be followed by evaluative thinking applied through a convergent technique.

Convergent techniques of evaluative thinking

Evaluative thinking uses convergent techniques in order to organize, analyse, and clarify the content that was generated using divergent techniques. As the process of exploration should create a large volume of information, it is necessary to apply convergent techniques to filter that mass. All convergent techniques apply evaluative thinking in order to sort, combine, and organize content. The purpose is to narrow the number of possible solutions, identify paths by which to move forward, and set up the decision-making process.

The main tools for sorting large volumes of information are based on *clustering*. Clustering or cluster analysis organizes the content of a divergent process into groups and categories. Those groups will have some similar characteristic that provides the logic for the organization. Of course, it is up to the designer to decide what that similarity should be as implied by the starting bias and project intentions. Once there are smaller collections of information, it is possible to start to see patterns or themes in the content. The organization will reduce noise and help highlight priorities and possible directions for the architectural proposal. In addition, clustering can be performed with or without explicit bias, depending on the attitude and needs of the designer. After a large collection of ideas has been documented, for example around the idea of a library as a cultural institution, clustering techniques can be applied to that collection (Figure 5.6). Scanning the mind-map starts to develop groups of common associations. In this case, while there are many different threads of ideas, there are only three major groups identified: the need for cultural broadcasting, the interest in flexibility, and the priority of publicness. As part of clustering, the group with the largest set of associations or items would be considered the most important. This topic would set the design direction. The end result of the clustering is a reduction, it clarifies a large mass of information by creating categories based on shared relationships. The major clustering tools are the *snowball technique*, *affinity diagramming*, and *highlighting*.

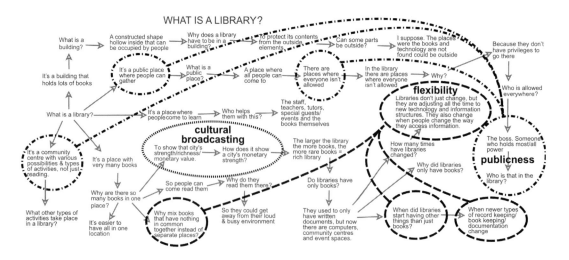

Figure 5.6: Convergent technique of clustering grouping elements into categories

The *snowball technique* is the basic clustering tool. The technique can be performed either digitally or on paper. The important factor is being able to move the information around. The basic operation in snowball is *like-with-like organization*. It begins by breaking up the results from the exploratory technique into individual items, otherwise known as *chunking* (Figure 5.7). The results are then arranged so elements that seem to be associated are grouped together, or elements that are alike are collected as a category. The categories can be titled once there are enough elements grouped to give a theme, but the title should be assigned naturally as part of the process. Titles and group composition should not be decided before the convergence starts as the process should be emergent rather than predetermined. If an element seems to belong in two categories, then that element is duplicated and listed under both. The categories can then be analysed for patterns and relationships, creating a second layer of grouping. The categories are then assessed for strength and ranked hierarchically. Decision-making and selection are based on choosing the strongest category in relation to the intentions of the architectural design. The content of the category can be used to set priorities and judgement criteria and to set up the next phase of the design method.

The *affinity diagram* or *K–J Method* is a modification of the *snowball technique* created by Jiro Kawakita. The major differences are the use of nested categories

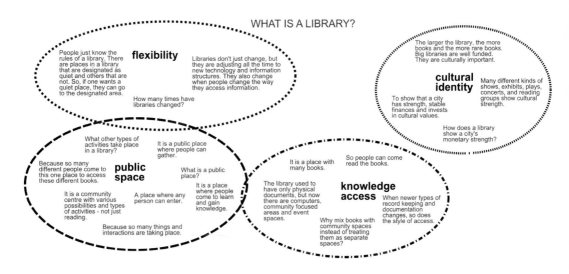

Figure 5.7: Convergent technique of snowball

rather than a single level of hierarchy, and the use of multiple passes at organization. The basic cycle of the K–J Method starts by placing each item from the brainstorming or questioning session on individual cards or another format that allows for moving the elements around individually. The cards are then shuffled, spread out, and reviewed. As in the snowball technique, a like-with-like organization is performed which organizes elements into groups. The key to the K–J Method is to be careful not to apply too much analysis at this point. Small differences between elements in the groups should not be a concern; rather, major relationships should be identified on the first pass. Oddities are also acceptable at this point as things that don't fit into any group might be very important. Each group should be identified by a title and there should not be more than ten groups. If there are more than ten, then the groups should be reviewed for shared properties. These groups can be merged or the clustering can be performed again. The groups should then be reviewed for sub-groups and super-groups. The process is done graphically, with elements arranged on large work or digital surfaces such that a pattern emerges from the spatial arrangement. The overall structure of the element layout should be explained, looking for facts and connections rather than impressions. This final step will be used to determine priorities for decisions in the design process.

Highlighting is another clustering technique, but differs from snowballing and affinity diagramming as it actively seeks to apply bias to the results of an exploratory technique. Highlighting is applied to the results of a divergent technique, focusing on screening ideas and collecting the best out of a large group of options (Figure 5.8). Unlike other clustering techniques, highlighting creates clusters only out of ideas that are felt to be interesting or intriguing – known as *hotspots*. The basic highlighting method starts with listing the ideas from the brainstorming or questioning, identifying those that seem to be intriguing or interesting. At this point, although this is an evaluative thinking process, no judgement is made as to whether the idea or element is possible. Once a collection of interesting elements has been selected from the original mess of information, the elements are sorted into clusters, or hotspots, where all the ideas seem to be related. The hotspots are reviewed for those that jump out as being more interesting than the others. These will have a special quality, an association, unusual consequences, or special implications, although they will probably need to be analysed further to explore their potential fully. If more than one hotspot is highlighted, then the convergence process ends by either combining several hotspots that are close to each other or selecting the strongest hotspot.

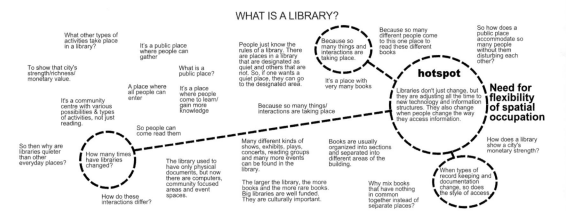

Figure 5.8: Convergent technique of highlighting presenting bias as active tool

While clustering-based techniques are good for rendering large amounts of information into organized groupings, sometimes it is necessary to do a finer-grain analysis that focuses on fewer elements. This might be at the end of a clustering process, or it might be from a question-based exploratory technique. For this, a strategic convergent technique is needed. Strategic techniques are based on determining qualities of an element or entity, looking at positive and negative aspects in order to determine strategies of development. The major technique is SWOT analysis (Strengths, Weaknesses, Opportunities, and Threats), discussed above as a divergent tool. A strategic technique can be used as both an exploratory and an evaluative tool. In the evaluative form, the results from any other divergent technique can be examined using SWOT analysis. The purpose is to clear away any noise from the subjects that have been identified as important to the design proposal or to refine content. *Strengths* are those things that are done easily or naturally. These might be obvious but they also might be side-effects. The strength of a stair might be the ability to gain height quickly while still visually connecting two datums or floor plates. *Weaknesses* are those things that are lacking, done badly, or not addressed. The stair is a point of disconnection, can be hard to navigate for those not able-bodied, and doesn't compensate for things with wheels. An *opportunity* is the identification of something that is not currently exploited but could be – usually by extending a strength or addressing a weakness. A stair's visual connection between two levels might be an opportunity to connect to another aspect of the proposal. The opportunity might be a design exploration that looks at visibility, partial broadcasting, and spatial foreshadowing using the stair to address these possibilities. Finally, *threats* are things that will continue to make performance poor or affect the overall success of the proposal. For example, a stair's limits for universal access can be identified and addressed through the threat aspect.

There are other forms of SWOT which have slightly different terminology but the same intentions. These terms revolve around groups of assets and constraints, often called advantages, limitations, opportunities, and unique features, or likes, concerns, and opportunities.

Decision-making

It is important to use divergent techniques in order not to fall into a trap of premature decision-making, or presupposing answers before investigation. Gestural or 'gut-instinct' choices are only as good as what is known by the designer as part of their experience. Relying strictly on this knowledge, although it is often used for framing, limits both the search for relevance and the possibility of any proposal to move beyond the expected and normative. There is an oft-repeated phrase that goes 'I don't know much about art but I know what I like'. The counter-proposal to this phrase is 'I don't know much about art *but I like what I know*'. We tend towards that which is familiar, something that satisfies a pattern that we recognize – a memory. However, this doesn't always (or often) make good architectural design, as it makes too many assumptions without exploration. One of the strengths of an office like OMA is very aggressive exploratory periods with multiple lines of investigation, breaking the design project down into smaller independent units; this suspends decisions.[20] When the term *research* is used by designers, it often means this exploratory investigation that examines possibilities, data, content, and options around a design situation.

Once the exploratory techniques have created tens, hundreds, or thousands of possibilities (something that occurs at multiple times in any design project), the issue becomes how is one selected to move forward? The convergent techniques are focused on reducing the content to a manageable and organized set, but from this more limited group a choice still needs to be made. Humans are not computers; we don't shift through thousands or millions of lines of a database to tabulate possibilities – our mental resources are limited in this way. But we do work with lateral, relational, and inferential thinking – things computers don't do well. As such, we will not cross-reference even a dozen indexes to identify the absolute best decision – mostly because what is *best* in terms of design is a problematic idea. As part of a system that is incredibly complex (i.e. interpreted human social space), who can say that the best decision for one aspect of the design proposal will be the best for other aspects? A structural system might be considered best for its efficiency in transferring gravitational forces, best in terms of costs, or best for material embedded energy. At the same time, if our focus is on how interior space is occupied in a particular way and with a certain quality, it might be that none of these best choices is right in this context. If fact, they may work against the proposal by interrupting the flow of space, by being positioned in a difficult way that affects other spatial compositions, or by scaling incorrectly for the intentions. What the design proposal must be is coherent; and, in order to create coherence, a stopping rule is used based on the framing bias.

The issue addressed by a stopping rule is quite simple – do we choose this selection or do we keep looking? Without taking up the heuristics debate or arguments on cognitive processing and rationality, it is possible, in a limited way, to identify how designers make decisions.[21] An architectural designer will not make an exhaustive search of each and every aspect of the design looking for a perfect selection. An approach like that would grind the project to a halt. Instead of looking for decisions that are *perfect*, architectural designers (and almost everyone else) make decisions that are *good enough*. In respect to architectural design, this is an idea that is highly relevant in the situation – a result of relational rather than rational thinking. There might be several ideas which could satisfy the criteria equality well. The term coined by Herbert Simon for this type of decision-making is *satisficing*, which connects a limited human mind with the structure of its environments.[22] Satisficing, as a decision-making strategy, is important because it allows designers to make decisions in a situation where not all of the consequences of every choice are known and where there is no single correct answer. Instead of looking for an optimum conclusion, the benchmark of success is set at a level that is acceptable. The first time that we encounter something that exceeds that measure, we stop looking for alternatives. Underlying this strategy is the belief that because no decisions are *perfect* and any decision can always be replaced by something that satisfies the needs of that content in a better way, to insist on a perfect solution would be both futile and pointless. Satisficing can also be seen as a strategy in design that makes decisions but considers them as temporary until confirmed or reinforced by other decisions.

The role of stopping rules in design methods is to make the process realistically completable within a timeframe and to reinforce coherence of the whole. The whole can be assembled from independent parts focused on their own effects, but they still need to work together toward an overall intention. As Rem Koolhaas writes, 'This impossibility triggers the autonomy of its parts, but that is not the same as fragmentation: the parts remain committed to the whole.'[23] As such, there will be various stopping rules at multiple scales, one for each of the selections to be made in the design process. These rules will run parallel to each other and the process of testing against the rules creates the looping process in design. Each stopping rule will set a level and an expectation for the results of a convergent technique, aligned by the framing and starting bias. When the analysis identifies something that exceeds the rule, then that element is chosen and temporarily pinned into place in the design proposal. The iterative aspect of design occurs when a stronger or more dominant element is chosen later in another part of the design proposal which conflicts with or isn't supported by an earlier choice. A designer will loop back to the earlier selection, adjust the selection of the stopping rule to bring it into alignment with the new information by exploring the content of the related convergent process. If nothing in the convergent output satisfies the current stopping rule, then the divergent content can be reviewed, the exploratory process can be rerun, or the stopping rule might be adjusted. Architectural design proposals are both hierarchical and systems-based. Designers look for ways that a chosen element supports multiple levels in the design context with which it engages, as well as recognizing other elements that have priority in that context. In this way, decisions are made so that the overall composition supports an intention without inconsistency (i.e. produces coherence).

Notes

1 Shelley, Mary Wollstonecraft, 'Introduction.' In *Frankenstein: Or, the Modern Prometheus*. London: George Routledge and Sons, 1891 [1831]: v–xii, at ix.

2 Stempfle, Joachim and Petra Badke-Schaub, 'Thinking in Design Teams: An Analysis of Team Communication.' *Design Studies* 23 (2002): 473–496.

3 In Banfield's own words, 'a rational decision is one made in the following manner: (a) the decision-maker lists all the opportunities for action open to him; (b) he identifies all the consequences which would follow from the adoption of each of the possible actions; and (c) he selects the action which would be followed by the preferred set of consequences'. He recognizes that a

rational process isn't rational as there are many choices, of which quite a few are appropriate for the situation. Banfield, Edward, 'Ends and Means in Planning.' *International Social Science Journal* 11, no. 3 (1959): 361–368.

4 Thornley, Denis G., 'Design Method in Architectural Education.' In *Conference on Design Methods: Papers Presented at the Conference on Systematic and Intuitive Methods in Engineering, Industrial Design, Architecture and Communications, September 1962, London, England*, edited by Jones, J. Christopher and Denis G. Thornley. Oxford, London, New York, and Paris: Pergamon Press, 1963: 37–51.

5 *The Architect's Handbook of Professional Practice*, edited by Demkin, Joseph A. 14th edn. New Jersey: John Wiley & Sons, 2008: 520–531.

6 The method of Markus and Maver is described by Bryan Lawson in his introduction to design thinking. Lawson, Bryan, *How Designers Think: The Design Process Demystified*. Oxford: Architectural Press, 2006: 37–41.

7 Rowe, Peter, *Design Thinking*. Cambridge, MA: The MIT Press, 1987: 47–48.

8 Boehm, Barry, 'A Spiral Model of Software Development and Enhancement.' *ACM SIGSOFT Software Engineering Notes* 11, no. 4 (1986): 14–24.

9 Nickerson, Raymond S., 'Enhancing Creativity.' In *Handbook of Creativity*, edited by Sternberg, Robert J. New York: Cambridge University Press, 1999: 392–430.

10 Gerard Puccio and collaborators have a very comprehensive overview of the current state of creative problem-solving in Puccio, Gerard J., Mary C. Murdock, and Marie Mance, 'Current Developments in Creative Problem Solving for Organizations: A Focus on Thinking Skills and Styles.' *Korean Journal of Thinking and Problem Solving* 15, no. 2 (2005): 43–76.

11 Altshuller, Genrich, Lev Shulyak, and Steven Rodman, *The Innovation Algorithm: TRIZ, Systematic Innovation, and Technical Creativity*. Worcester, MA: Technical Innovation Center, 1999.

12 Lawson, Bryan, *How Designers Think: The Design Process Demystified*. Oxford: Architectural Press, 2006: 36.

13 Convergence and divergence are the most common technical terms for the thinking styles. We find this terminology used by Jones in his classic work on design methods: Jones, J. Christopher, *Design Methods: Seeds of Human Futures*. London: Wiley-Interscience, 1973. Convergence and divergence are also referenced in Rowe's book on architectural design conceptual processes: Rowe, Peter, *Design Thinking*. Cambridge, MA: The MIT Press, 1987.

14 Basadur, Min and Milena Head, 'Team Performance and Satisfaction: A Link to Cognitive Style within a Process Framework.' *Journal of Creative Behavior* 35, no. 4 (2001): 227–248.

15 Lawson, Bryan, *How Designers Think: The Design Process Demystified*. Oxford: Architectural Press, 2006: 142.

16 Finke, Ronald A., Thomas B. Ward, and Steven M. Smith, *Creative Cognition: Theory, Research, and Applications*. Cambridge, MA: The MIT Press, 1992.

17 This clear statement was made by W. Ross Ashby as referenced by Horst Rittel in Protzen, Jean-Pierre and David J. Harris, *The Universe of Design: Horst Rittel's Theories of Design and Planning*. New York: Routledge, 2010: 93–119.

18 Osborn, Alex, *Applied Imagination: Principles and Procedures of Creative Problem Solving*. New York: Charles Scribner's Sons, 1953.

19 Rem Koolhaas described the process of reverse massing in the competition design for La Bibliothèque nationale de France in 1989. The building organization was developed by considering programmatic spaces as being not-building, a reverse to the usual approach. See Koolhaas, Rem, 'Precarious Entity.' In *Anyone*, edited by Davidson, Cynthia C. New York: Rizzoli, 1991: 148–155.

20 Rem Koolhaas writes extensively on the internal process of OMA in several books and articles. Good places to start are: Koolhaas, Rem, Bruce Mau, Jennifer Sigler, and Hans Werlemann, *S, M, L, XL*. New York: Monacelli Press, 1998; Koolhaas, Rem and Nobuyuki Yoshida, *Oma@work*. Tokyo: A+U Publishing, 2000; and Koolhaas, Rem and Office for Metropolitan Architecture, *Content*. Köln: Taschen, 2004.

21 As a practising designer, I have sympathy for simple heuristics as well as the bounded and ecological rationality models of human thinking – mostly because I can recognize in my own experiences the alignment of these models with the realtity of making decisions in a complex and non-linear design environment. For further reading on this topic, see Kelman, Mark, *The Heuristics Debate*. New York: Oxford University Press, 2011; Gigerenzer, Gerd, Peter M. Todd, and ABC Research Group, *Simple Heuristics that Make Us Smart*. New York: Oxford University Press, 1999; Goldstein, Daniel G. and Gerd Gigerenzer, 'Models of Ecological Rationality: The Recognition Heuristic.' *Psychological Review* 109, no. 1 (2002): 75–90; and Todd, Peter M. and Gerd Gigerenzer, 'Bounding Rationality to the World.' *Journal of Economic Psychology* 24, no. 2 (2003): 143–165.

22 Simon, Herbert A., *The Sciences of the Artificial*. Karl Taylor Compton Lectures. Cambridge, MA: The MIT Press, 1969.

23 Koolhaas, Rem, 'Bigness.' In *S, M, L, XL*, edited by Koolhaas, Rem, Bruce Mau, Jennifer Sigler, and Hans Werlemann. New York: Monacelli Press, 1998: 494–517, at 500.

Chapter Six

First principles

That from which a thing can first be known; for this also is called the origin of the thing, e.g. the hypotheses are the origins of demonstrations. (Causes are spoken of in an equal number of senses; for all causes are origins.) It is common, then, to all to be the first point from which a thing either is or comes to be or is known; but of these some are immanent in the thing and others are outside. Therefore the nature of a thing is an origin, and so are the elements of a thing, and thought and choice, and substance, and that for the sake of which – for the good and the beautiful are the origin both of the knowledge and of the movement of many things.

Aristotle[1]

First principles reduction is a thinking tool used to suspend knee-jerk responses which are focused on forms or objects. It allows alternative ways of thinking around an object, situation, or application while providing clarity to the intentions of a project. First principles can be considered a core mechanism for approaching innovation, and first principles reduction is one of a designer's strongest primary conceptual tools. The tool is adapted from philosophy, where a first principle is the most basic or foundational proposition, lying at the core of an enquiry. The first principle of any object is one that cannot be reduced any further. In architectural design, it is used to move past the formal resolution and think about the effects, needs, and actions that exist *behind* that form. *First principles reduction* allows an architectural designer to respond to what something does rather than what it looks like. It also allows access to the identified first principles by exploratory and evaluative tools, creating new opportunities for the design proposal.

First principles as a tool

One of the strengths of reducing a situation back to its fundamental principles is allowing a designer to approach that situation without a predetermined conclusion. Attention to first principles connects designers to the factors underlying forms rather than the forms themselves – it suspends known conclusions to examine sources. A first principle, then, is an abstraction of the situation being examined that represents the highest possible degree of generalization without losing the primary factors that make that situation what it is. It is generally focused on performance aspects or activities but might also include social events if those events are fundamental causes. As a foundational premise, the abstraction is not described in any particular disciplinary syntax but in general terms. It is this abstraction into general syntax that allows the generalization to be used as content in the design process without concern for the exact formal nature of the original object or situation. This is not the same as architectural design without preconceptions.[2] While it is very useful to approach design without immediate formal conclusions, attempting to design without any preconceptions is the surest way to produce nothing usable, as testing and relevance are impossible to determine.

Historically and philosophically, first principles is associated with the search for knowledge, irrefutable truth, and primary proof. Aristotle is the point of entry for concerns of being and purpose in Western society, writing extensively on the ideas of origin and causes.[3] For Aristotle,

> When the objects of an inquiry, in any department, have principles, causes, or elements, it is through acquaintance with these that knowledge and understanding is attained. For we do not think that we know a thing until we are acquainted with its primary causes or first principles, and have carried our analysis as far as its elements.[4]

First principles was instrumental in Enlightenment scientific process through Descartes, and integrated into modern Rationalism. In architecture, it was used by theorists such as l'abbé Marc-Antoine Laugier to defend aesthetic positions. As part of his narrative to place authority on Classical Greek rather than Roman sources, Laugier reduced the need for human shelter to its principles in *Essai sur l'Architecture* (1753). Through his narrative, Laugier identified shelter from sun and rain as well as exposure to light and fresh air as primary factors of habitation. Through the story of a primitive man searching for shelter that matched the needs of his body, the essence of architecture was described as the raising of fallen branches as columns and placement of more branches to create a sloped roof.[5] Laugier used the reduction to essential needs of the human body and reapplication in architectural form to prove the Classical Greek elements of column, entablature, and pediment as the basis of perfect composition and primary truth.

While Laugier used first principles to develop a theoretical position based on cultural mythology – Classical Greek aesthetics was the correct and truthful way to build – the tool is currently used as a way to remove expectations of a known outcome. The basic operation behind first principles reduction can be examined by considering an example from Christopher Alexander. The reductive process engages a focused sequence of exploratory then evaluative thinking styles to perform the abstraction. Alexander used first principles to explore the kettle and then connected the results to a force-based design method.[6] In order to suspend an immediate formal proposal of a traditional kettle, a kettle wasn't considered as a known object with a formal tradition – domed chamber, spout, handle, and lid made out of copper or enamelled steel. Instead, it was reduced to its first principles. Abstracted to its foundational premises, a kettle is simply a way to heat small quantities of domestic water to boiling, something Alexander noted when he addressed issues of ensemble, form, and context.[7] As a design situation, it might not be useful to reconsider the entirety of domestic heating or to question the requirement that a kettle must be a discrete, movable object. It was a conscious choice of the designer to limit the reduction to the kettle as an object rather than addressing a larger situation in which the kettle plays a part.

As a tool, the first principles reduction of the object of a kettle would ignore the final form and see the factors that shaped that particular manifestation of the form. In this case, there needs to be some place to hold a small quantity of water, that water should have access to a heat source, there should be some way to bring water into the holding location, some controlled way to move water out of the holding location, ease of portability, efficient thermal transfer, and resistance to heat loss. The design situation has expanded but also become much clearer. Each of these discrete events can be considered in an individual exploratory and evaluative process and then the entire results can be evaluated for connections, relationships, conflicts, and potentials. The efficient thermal transfer and thermal insulation requirements might lead to material investigations and shapes of the holding location, while another design investigation could explore how to access gravity-fed water from a kitchen tap. A third possibility would explore weight, ergonomics, and centres of gravity when addressing portability. When the various reductions are synthesized into a proposal, the result might produce a wide variety of forms (Figure 6.1). Yet the underlying factors of the original situation are maintained, providing context and focus.

While using the same foundational factors, a kettle can be designed, such as the graceful Dusi by Juliet Symes. The first principles reduction that defined the situation of the design investigation for the Dusi kettle added a parallel string of reduction based on the ritual of making tea. Social events were part of the second reduction as ritual was an important part of the design. The two sets of generalized principles merged the kettle and the teapot by mapping shared aspects of the basic operations of both objects/events, allowing for the proposal of a single object. The final form is double-walled borosilicate glass container with a base of highly conductive copper. A combined stainless-steel tea infuser and tea leaf scoop slips into the steam release opening (Figure 6.2). The final form merged the principles of boiling water and making tea by examining the foundational premise of both acts, resolving them into a highly synthesized and sophisticated product.

One of the uses of first principles is to take something that appears to be singular and break it into its multiple aspects of fundamental activities and operations. The kettle as an object was singular, but when considered as a reduction,

Figure 6.1: Variations of kettle design, all meeting the requirements developed through first principles. Left: Japanese standard kettle. Centre: Semispherical electric kettle, designed by Peter Behrens, 1908. Right: Japanese electric water boiler

Source: Wikimedia Commons

Figure 6.2: Dusi kettle and teapot

Courtesy of Juliet Symes

it had many activities within the form. Another example of the same effect is presented by Nigel Cross in his description of first principles reduction used in the design of a new steering column for the McLaren F1 race car by Gordon Murray.[8] As Cross describes, a traditional steering column consists of a standard three-quarter-inch steel bar covered in a plastic housing. The bar is traditionally used for its strength to resist torque and bending loads that occur in that location, and the housing covers the electrics and mounting. However, the bar added weight and limited the driver's feel for the road. Murray, instead of accepting the standard steel bar, reduced the design situation down to its fundamentals, which included the torque and bending loads the bar resisted as well as the need for a shell to isolate wires and mechanics from the driver's body. The result was to separate the physical forces into separate design issues. Bending loads where transferred to the column housing, leaving the bar to handle only torque loads. Moving from generalities to particulars, the shell materiality was explored with aluminium selected instead of plastic. The proposed design was lighter, stronger, and more sensitive than the original.

Architectural design and questioning

While architecture has different priorities from those of industrial design, its processes use first principles reduction in much the same way. First principles can be used on multiple scales from the analysis of programme and organization of volume to reconsidering relationships of architectural objects and forms. Joshua Prince-Ramus noted that approaching architectural design from first principles was a core strategy while working on both the Seattle Public Library and the Wyly Theater. In the former, first principles reduction was used to reduce the library programme back to fundamental relationships and occupations. A convergent technique of clustering was then applied, producing a programmatic reorganization which operated successfully but was different from expectations. In the latter, challenging the operation and massing of a theatre 'allowed [the designers] to go back to first principles, and redefine fly tower, acoustic enclosure, light enclosure and so forth'.[9] By using first principles reduction, each of the programmatic spaces could be considered for the qualities of their operation (environmental and social). This included the spatial organization which best met the needs of the programme elements based on user patterns rather than the traditional form of 'theatre' as a type.

As another example, Frank O. Gehry described the process of first principles reduction when discussing attempts at implying movement in static form. Working on developing versions of the *Olympic Fish*, he said, 'Okay, the tail and fins are hokey, so let's cut off the head, let's cut off the tail, and see how much of the kitschy stuff we can get rid of, and still get the sense of movement.'[10] By 'kitschy', Gehry meant those elements that are used to identify *fish* rather than *movement* (attributes rather than relationships). He abstracted the original event of a fish swimming to its essence through reduction (Figure 6.3). The final proposal was a generalization that implied movement only expressed in a sculptural syntax.

The same process can be used at a smaller scale. If an architectural designer were asked to design a stair, they might start by looking at treads, rises, runs, and railings. However, the idea of a stair can be explored through first principles, reducing the form to its basic operations – what makes a stair a stair – while abandoning an immediate commitment to form. As a reduction, a stair can be defined as a way to move vertically in an efficient way (short run), while using no external power source and providing a continuous, diagonal visual connection between floors. The efficiency of the treads requires significantly less space and less travel distance than a ramp. Elevators use less floor space but disconnect circulation and must be powered. Once a stair has been reduced to its fundamental premises, the design question examines if there is a way to satisfy the same premises that a stair addresses while suspending the introduction of the object of a stair? First principles reduction might lead to a redesign of the entire circulation pattern, look at reducing the

Figure 6.3: *Olympic Fish* sculpture by Frank O. Gehry in Barcelona, Spain

Photograph by Sergi Larripa/Wikimedia Commons

stress of human mobility and energy output to move vertically in a non-powered situation, or examine vertical elements that reinforce the sense of connectivity. The concluding design does not need to be a stair, nor must it be immediately recognizable as a stair in a traditional way. It would still operate as a stair, however, because it would satisfy the fundamental principles of what a stair does.

Architectural and urban designers who are known for producing innovative work make extensive use of first principles reduction as a way of reframing a situation and abandoning predetermined outcomes while addressing primary requirements. Mitchell Joachim and his non-profit design group Terreform ONE regularly use first principles as a way to propose creative projects meant to challenge existing practices. Several of their projects, such as Homeway, Fab Tree House, and Willow Balls, reduce the idea of housing to first principles in much the same way as Laugier did, although applied to very different intentions. The reduced idea of housing sets up a starting state free of traditional responses or expectations. For example, in the MATscape: Material Mosaic Triplex project, the house is examined as a node in an ecological system (Figure 6.4). The reduction breaks the house into its types of occupancy and activities, allowing the designer to connect residency to food production, climatic control, waste, and closed-loop systems. The initial reduction did not select the elements of the design or the direction of the final proposal but it did set up a starting state that brought focus to core priorities while maintaining fundamental principles.

Terreform ONE's proposal Smart DOTS + Soft MOBS – NY 2028 Environmental Mobility clearly illustrates how first principles can change the approach to a design for a new bus (Figure 6.5), blending conditions of urban and transportation design. Rather than starting with a normative idea for a bus, which follows the standard type and physical form of a road vehicle, the SOFT Blimp Bumper Bus design proposal addressed the principles that operate behind the bus. First principles reduction addressed the bus for *what it does* rather than what it looks like. Seen in this way, a bus is not a road vehicle based on the tradition of the horse-drawn cart but is simply a way to move a large group of people across an area of land in fixed patterns at standardized (low) speeds and with the ability to get on or off at short intervals. Many other mass transportation systems perform in similar ways, including subway and light rail. However, the strength of a bus system is its flexibility and lack of fixed, exclusive infrastructure – it doesn't need rails, or stations, or tunnels, or platforms.

Figure 6.4: MATscape: Material Mosaic Triplex, 50% Living House and contiguous landscape

Courtesy of Mitchell Joachim, Terreform ONE

Figure 6.5: SOFT Blimp Bumper Bus from Smart DOTS + Soft MOBS

Courtesy of Mitchell Joachim, Terreform ONE

The starting state of the design proposal became not how to redesign the object of the bus as a container on wheels but how to design for the periodic movement of people in a flexible network across a bounded landmass. The reduction by first principles moves the project from an issue exclusive to transportation design to blend with urban concerns, in much the same way as the reduction of the kettle could challenge the engineering infrastructure of the house. Ultimately, in this project, the bus is reduced to a couple of major items to focus the design investigation – the action of picking up and dropping off passengers combined with the need for constant movement. The resulting proposal suspended the seats from a floating engine (the blimp) on soft, hanging chairs. The seats, all disconnected from each other by the tethers, move at a constant speed of 15 m.p.h. The vehicle uses existing roadways but is not reliant on them or their limitations, such as traffic jams, since the main body of the vehicle hovers. The proposal stresses efficiency: the 'bus' never stops moving, and the hanging chairs eliminate the need and loss of time for the normative 'bus stop'.

It was returning to first principles which allowed the designers to consider the bus from the point of view of effects and operations rather than objects. The reduction was combined with a starting bias that stressed soft materials as transportation infrastructure in order to develop the design proposal. Opportunities are then created, and judgement criteria identified, due to changing the relationship between the human body, objects and safety.

The process of *first principles reduction* is most easily performed through questioning – either a *challenge* or a *SWOT* technique. Primary questions are based on asking how something works, why it is like that, what its purpose is, how we interact with it, and what it does. A limit for the reduction is also necessary for a clear point to stop. The limit brings focus – will first principles reduction challenge the object (bus, kettle), a part of the object (stair, steering column), or the context of the object (heating water, transportation networks)? The answers to the challenge questions can be followed back until the principles cannot be reduced any further *based on the limit*. As part of the reduction, each identified principle should be removed to see if that removal changes the fundamental nature of the design focus. If a kettle is an efficient way to boil small amounts of water quickly, then heat transfer is a fundamental principle while a spout for pouring water is not. The spout can be removed as long as there is some way for hot water to exit the heating location in a controlled way. Either the spout needs to be reduced further into a first principle or it needs to be abandoned. Developing first principle questions is a way of stepping away from the superficial symptom to address the underlying systemic cause – it is ultimately about addressing improved relevance.

First principles reduction is used in force-based methods directly, often helping to define the forces, pressures, flow, constraints, and assets. When used in central concept-based methods, it becomes a form of domain-to-domain transfer by identifying underlying relationships. First principles is central to pattern-based methods as a tool for analysis and pattern identification. Independent to the framework, first principles reduction is a strong tool to help refine a framing bias into a starting state.

Notes

1 Aristotle, 'Metaphysics.' In *The Complete Works of Aristotle: The Revised Oxford Translation*, translated by Ross, W. D., edited by Barnes, Jonathan. Bollingen Series edn. Princeton, NJ: Princeton University Press, 1984: Vol. 2: 1552–1728: 1013a.14–23.

2 Gelernter, Mark, *Sources of Architectural Form: A Critical History of Western Design Theory*. Manchester and New York: Manchester University Press, 1995: 273.

3 According to W. D. Ross, the translator of *Metaphysics* in the Jonathan Barnes-edited volume, the word *origin* in Greek can be translated as *source, first principle, rule*, or *office*. See Aristotle, 'Metaphysics.' In *The Complete Works of Aristotle: The Revised Oxford Translation*, translated by Ross, W. D., edited by Barnes, Jonathan. Bollingen Series edn. Princeton, NJ: Princeton University Press, 1984: Vol. 2: 1552–1728: 1599fn.

4 Aristotle, 'Physics.' In *The Complete Works of Aristotle: The Revised Oxford Translation*, translated by Hardie, R. P. and R. K. Gaye, edited by Barnes, Jonathan. Bollingen Series edn. Princeton, NJ: Princeton University Press, 1984: Vol. 1: 315–446: 184a10–15.

5 Laugier, Marc-Antoine, *An Essay on Architecture* [*Essai sur l'Architecture*]. Translated by Herrmann, Wolfgang and Anni Herrmann. Los Angeles, CA: Hennessey & Ingalls, Inc., 1977 [1753]: 11–13.

6 Alexander, Christopher, *Notes on the Synthesis of Form*. Cambridge, MA: Harvard University Press, 1964.

7 Ibid.: 17.

8 Cross, Nigel, *Design Thinking: Understanding How Designers Think and Work*. New York: Berg, 2011.

9 Prince-Ramus, Joshua, *Joshua Prince-Ramus on Seattle's Library*. Long Beach, CA: TED, 2006. http://www.ted.com/talks/joshua_prince_ramus_on_seattle_s_library.html.

10 Friedman, Mildred and Frank O. Gehry, *Gehry Talks: Architecture + Process*. New York: Universe Publishing, 2002: 48.

Chapter Seven

Domain-to-domain transfer

I am an enemy of symbols. Symbol is too narrow a concept for me in the sense that symbols exist in order to be deciphered. An artistic image on the other hand is not to be deciphered, it is an equivalent of the world around us. Rain in Solaris is not a symbol, it is only rain which at certain moments has particular significance to the hero. But it does not symbolize anything. It only expresses. This rain is an artistic image. Symbol for me is something too complicated.

Andrei Tarkovsky[1]

Architecture is a discipline and it has a domain of knowledge. As a discipline, there is knowledge that is found inside and outside of its domain. Outside knowledge cannot be used *directly* in architectural processes and proposals. There will always need to be a form of translation which mediates non-architectural knowledge into an architectural response. Outside knowledge can be very useful in developing an architectural design proposal as part of the designer's initial framing, influencing the starting bias, or helping to make the proposal significant by connecting formal ideas to social and cultural content. While it might be easier to pretend that it is possible to do strictly formal design, it is really next to impossible. This is because anything formal, a shape in space, is still made, seen, interpreted, and judged by a human. No formal move can be made without being interpreted as an act of human cognition. When a line is marked on the ground and given a certain weight, length, and mass, it involves thinking and decision-making. The designer considers that line with all its associations, and an inhabitant engages with that line responding to the latent value based on human and personal experience. Engaging human experience, as an embedded aspect of architecture, means that all architectural form contains relationships, memories, and sensations. Architecture as a social act addresses content based on human psychology, physiology, evolutionary biology, mythology, language, 'politics, social conditions, cultural values and the like'.[2] Architectural composition is based on an internal syntax that incorporates its own knowledge, but it also infers external knowledge.

In order to use external knowledge in architectural syntax, it needs to be translated through an operation of domain-to-domain transfer. Otherwise, the proposal will risk being considered not-architecture. This is true not only for architecture, but for all disciplines. For example, a business group might take inspiration from biology to affect how they think about organizational structure. The external content uses its own particular language, which needs to be translated into a business model in order for it to be operational in the business environment. Ultimately, while the source material might speak of emergence, complexity, biospheres, and biocoenosis (language native to biology), the final form of whatever is proposed will be executed in terms of economics and human resource management (language native to business). In architecture, the native language (syntax) is formal and includes surface, massing, shadow, texture, sequence, pattern, presence, colour, occupation, and materiality, amongst others. External content accesses ideas derived from literature, poetry, mythology, biology, politics, economics, and other disciplinary domains of knowledge. The basis of this transfer is to enrich the proposal with additional layers of content that reinforce the architectural content. The use of external content is one of the hardest skills to acquire as an architectural designer, as it is easy to produce superficial and shallow work counter to the intent of enrichment and depth.

Technically, all domain-to-domain transfers could be called *inference transfers*. To infer, or to draw an inference, is to reach a conclusion based not on what was explicitly said but what was implied. This act could also be called 'reading between the lines'. As used to describe the movement of knowledge from a *source domain* to a *target domain*, an inference is basing the truth (or relevance) of a proposition, a statement, or a judgement not on the explicit content of *what is there*, but on associated content *that is implied*. The selected content is brought forward from a source domain, mediated through a transfer frame, and then implied in the target domain. The validity, quality, and significance of the content in the target are dependent on the relevance of the relationship between itself and the content from the source. There are other more common terms for this activity – it is called an analogy, a metaphor, a homology, or a simile. Regardless of the terms used, which have different nuances in different disciplines and bring their own history and baggage, the basic action is the same. There is an association of the two domains of knowledge so that the richness, familiarity, and complexity of the source domain can be used to add quality, comprehension, and organization to the more obscure target domain.

The structure of domains

A useful theory of domains and transferring information for application to architectural design comes from the original psychological and cognitive science work on analogies by Dedre Gentner.[3] Gentner views a domain as a system made of objects, object-attributes, and relations between objects (Figure 7.1). It is important to understand the distinction between these three aspects of a domain. An *object* is described as something that is discrete and identifiable within the system. Using an example of a rabbit, Gentner makes the point that an object might be an entity (the rabbit), part of a larger object (a rabbit's ear), or a larger collection of objects that are combinations of the same type (a colony of rabbits).[4] The important point is that an object functions as a whole – it can be identified as separate to its context.

The concept of objects in the architectural domain works in exactly the same way. An object can be a stair (entity), a riser of a stair (component part), or a multi-storey circulation system (sequence of objects in a coherent whole). *Object-attributes* is the term used to describe an object and that object's characteristics. It is sensory information that refers to properties such as the object's colour, scale, texture, shape, luminosity, and mass, along with qualities of taste, sound, and smell. The stair could have attributes of grey, concrete, rough top surface strips, smooth sides, non-reflecting, and the appearance of weight. Or it could have attributes of orange, plastic, smooth, shiny, and the appearance of lightness. While attributes require an object and are about the object itself, the object can be identified independent of the attributes. When two or more objects and their attributes are associated, relational information is produced. *Relations between objects* contain structural content which describes how an object is arranged in regard to other objects in a system. Relations occur between dissimilar objects and key attributes. The stair example would have a series of relational qualities that have to do with

Composition of a Domain

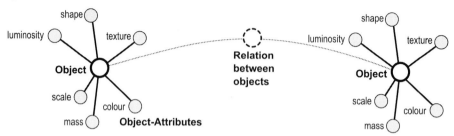

Figure 7.1: Domain as a system of objects, object-attributes, and relations between objects

how the stair is positioned with respect to entrances, roof systems, walls, windows, and doors (as other objects). Through these relations, the stair could take on interpreted qualities of exposure, visibility, prominence, edge, slippage, grandness, or shaft. Qualities involved as part of relations between objects are not about the object itself but about the relationship of the object to other objects and their attributes in the context.

The three aspects of a domain – objects, attributes, and relations – are important because they affect the ability to make strong connections between domains when inferring content for use in design. Transfer of content across domains is vital to communication, assisting innovation and deepening meaning. When looking at this transfer, we see there is a significant difference between relationships and attributes (Figure 7.2). Relations have the ability to transfer deep meaning, while attributes are limited in their richness of associations and even have the ability to confuse disciplinary content if present in quantity.[5]

Although both attributes of objects and the relations between objects can be used as information to be mapped between domains, it is the relational content that strengthens communication. We can see this using a basic example of standard metaphor. When we say *a cloud is like a sponge*, the information about what is known regarding sponges is used to describe something that might not be known about clouds. That information is primarily relational in nature. The domain-to-domain mapping takes the relations between the sponge objects – fibrous material, empty space, swelling action, and the sticky nature of water molecules – as the content to be mapped from the source domain. The relationship between space, material, and water holds the instructional content. A rich transfer of relational information allows a deeper understanding of clouds by using something that is

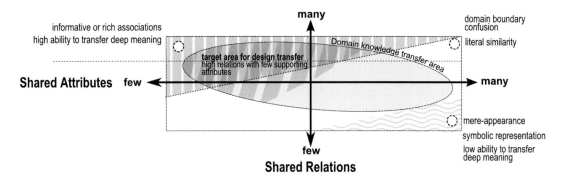

Figure 7.2: Graph of different opportunities in cross-domain mapping based on volume of shared relations and attributes

Source: Adapted from Gentner and Markman (1997)

not a cloud. Through the mapping of a sponge (source domain) to a cloud (target domain), the cloud is understood as a container that collects water, holds it, then releases it. Like a sponge, the cloud can be visualized as mostly empty space of loosely packed fibres, even though physically a sponge and a cloud are dissimilar.

The transfer mapping can be extended even further, should it be desired. Knowledge of sponges might produce a visual of a hand squeezing a sponge to press out water, an action that maps to the cloud dropping rain on a landscape. This basic example contains only information about relations between objects and no directly mapped attributes (Figure 7.2: upper left of graph). The richness of a relational mapping can be contrasted to an attribute mapping. If the same example of a cloud is used but attributes rather than relations are mapped, the domain-to-domain mapping produces something like *a cloud is like a marshmallow*. This mapping uses the attributes of soft, white, and, possibly, fluffy. While the mapping has been used to help visualize the appearance of the cloud, there is little ability to use the attribute mapping to develop a deeper understanding of its operation.

It is possible to construct a strong mapping of information between domains using few or many relations, as well as some supporting attributes. The marsh-mallow–cloud example illustrates the difficulty of achieving any deep meaning using only attributes. When only attribute content is mapped between domains, it is called a *mere-appearance transfer* (Figure 7.2: lower right of the graph). In architectural design, this would be considered symbolism. The 'duck' of the Venturi/Scott Brown critique is a mere-appearance transfer, 'where the architectural systems of space, structure, and program are submerged and distorted by an overall symbolic form'.[6] Symbolic form is a transfer of many attributes with little or no relations involved in the mapping. Venturi and Scott Brown went further than this and argued that symbolism through attributes displaced the architectural syntax without translation into architectural concerns. Attribute mapping has little relationship to structural content found in the architectural domain (programme, circulation, occupation, void/solid, etc.) as it is focused on surfaces and appearance. The end proposal results in a visual or symbolic expression that takes on literal meaning (an icon) rather than implied meaning.

Relations between objects should always be hierarchically more prominent if the desire is richness of internal syntax rather than overlaid imagery. When attributes are transferred, they should support relations between objects that have been mapped between domains. While the presence of many attributes with few or no relations creates symbolism, the presence of many attributes with many relations also creates issues. Too many shared attributes, along with many shared relations between domains, begins to blur disciplinary boundaries (Figure 7.2: upper right of the graph). This is called a *literal similarity*. The more shared elements between the external domain and the architectural, the greater the possibility that the external domain is misinterpreted *as* architecture. We see this issue between architecture and the domain of sculpture. Many of the objects, attributes, and relations align between sculpture and architecture but the overall priorities are very different. Often, we find sculptural concerns are introduced as architectural concerns.

The work of Frank O. Gehry often slips into literal similarity. While Gehry Partners has a strong architectural practice, Gehry himself makes clear statements that his design interests align with artistic priorities and the exploration of artistic concerns in architectural syntax.[7] Many of those concerns centre on expressing movement in a static object, a concept that sets the starting bias for Gehry's work. The approach to this concept is influenced by artistic priorities of surface, representation, and painterliness. Implied movement is explored through the transfer of surface attributes and formal relationships based on sculptural priorities. The domination of the artistic domain of knowledge over architectural syntax (occupation, circulation, sequence of bodily movement) is one of the reasons why Gehry's work is often accused of being sculpture rather than architecture. The priority and starting state of the Walt Disney Concert Hall (1999–2003) was to have the building appear to 'flutter' as if it were a sail caught with the wind momentarily on both sides of the fabric (Figure 7.3). Gehry attempted to transfer this quality from his interest in sail boats and the work of seventeenth-century Dutch painters.[8] The attributes for luffing sails were transferred with little translation into architectural concerns, making a one-to-one mapping of sail surface characteristics to sculptural elements. The result is not inference but literalness. While the project can still be considered successful (as it met the artistic expectations of the designer), the question becomes whether it is architecturally enriched. Other projects, including the Bilbao Guggenheim, use fish and liquids as starting points to map knowledge between domains – sources selected by focusing on creating the impression of movement in the unmovable through mapping attributes without engaging relations between architectural objects.

Figure 7.3: Walt Disney Concert Hall by Frank O. Gehry

Courtesy of Carol M. Highsmith Archive, Library of Congress

First principles reduction as domain transfer

While primarily a tool for opening up alternative ways of thinking around an object, situation or application, *first principles reduction* is at the core of how information is moved between domains. The act of reduction begins to abstract an object or situation away from a particular disciplinary application to a more general statement. The abstraction decreases the reliance on deep disciplinary syntax where the object can be seen only as part of a single discipline. A tree, as an object, is part of the biological domain, but if reduced to its operational factors, such as the nature of its shading function or as a system for conducting nutrients, these fundamental principles can be accessed by other domains, such as architecture or engineering. When used as domain transfer, the process does not end at the identification of fundamental principles. Once a general understanding of principles, with their forces and effects, has been achieved, it is relatively easy to move those general principles across disciplines *if the principles are shared between domains*. The generic, generalized factors that are the result of a first principles reduction are not coded in any disciplinary language. They can be associated with a new domain and then expanded back to a particular application by applying deep discipline syntax (Figure 7.4). There does still need to be relevance between the source and the target mappings that comes from the sharing of principles by both domains. The target will work using the same principles as the source even though it is housed in a different domain. Its appearance should be significantly different, however, due to the influence of disciplinary syntax.

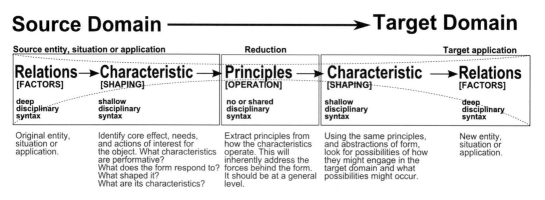

Figure 7.4: Diagram of cross-domain mapping through first principles reduction

The concept behind first principles reduction as domain transfer can be examined by using the example from the PBS animated children's series *Curious George*.[9] It might seem interesting to use children's educational programming about a curious monkey to explain conceptual techniques for architectural design, but a four-year-old is taught first principles reduction and transfer as a basic thinking skill in their mental development. In the episode 'Snow Use',[10] Curious George wanted to build a snowman on the hottest day of the year. Of course, there was no snow, so George investigated crushed ice cubes, mud, and rocks as ways to make a 'snowman'. The ice melted, the mud didn't hold its shape, and the rocks were too heavy. George considered his options and decided that sand was the best material with which to build a snowman in the summer.

While the episode had the educational objective of exploring 'the results of mixing different natural materials with water', the real value to the narrative is learning how to reduce a situation to its principles and to transfer those principles to a new situation. How and why did George decide that sand could operate as a substitute for snow? George reduced the idea of the snowman to its foundational principles – snowmen are made from physical particles that can aggregate, adhere (the particles stick to each other), and have plasticity (they can be shaped). In order to build a snowman in summer, the principles of aggregation, adherence, and plasticity would need to be found in a new material, while that material's reliance on cold environmental conditions would need to be abandoned. Ice could aggregate but it wasn't plastic, and nor was it stable in the hot temperatures found in the new situation of summer. Mud could aggregate and was plastic but the particles weren't sticky enough to form a stable shape. Rocks could aggregate and were stable in heat but didn't adhere or have plasticity. The ultimate choice of sand was selected because it met all of the conditions of the reduction. Sand could aggregate, it was sticky when the correct percentage of water was added, it could be shaped, and it was stable in hot temperatures. George's reduction of the snowman allowed a mapping to occur between two very different situations (winter to summer) using a transfer between domains of knowledge (snow hydrology to soil mechanics). This action enabled George to transfer the principles of a snowman to a condition where it is not natural – summer. He is innovating by reducing to first principles and moving knowledge between domains.

Curious George's reduction was fairly simple, although it required a precision of thought. The same activity can be shown operating in a more complex way by looking at examples that move knowledge from biology to architecture. Both biology and architecture are physically based domains. The two domains share areas of interest, such as morphology, kinetics, health, and responses to environment that include thermal properties, light, and air movement. As both knowledge domains address these factors, it should be possible to identify the principles in any of these shared concerns in order to move those principles between domains. The need is to identify a shared principle in order to perform a transfer. If the principle is not shared then the resultant transfer will most likely default to a visual representation – a symbol – with limited depth and richness.

A tulip can be used as an example of how biology can generate knowledge that can be used in architectural design. A tulip is a biological organism that manages a complex environment while maintaining its own internal equilibrium. Tulips operate through several principles with some of the most interesting found in the operation of the petals and leaves. The operational factors found in this complex mechanism are photonasty, nyctinasty, turgidity, osmosis, and auxesis. These terms are all found in the deep disciplinary syntax of botany. However, the principles they express are physical and environmental, which means that although the *terms* are specific to biological deep domain syntax, the *ideas* behind them are likely to be transferable. As an aspect of architecture can be considered as being concerned with internal consistency against external pressures using building skins, there should be points of relevance for a domain-to-domain transfer.

There are several different opportunities to transfer principles using the mechanisms found in the tulip. One example, in an investigation guided by Dale Clifford of Carnegie Mellon, focused on the photonastic principles of the tulip, concentrating on the mechanical reaction to light exposure and heat.[11] The starting point was the movement of the petals as a performative event (*relations*). The interest for the architectural designers was in the opening and closing of the petals that responded to the environmental effect of light. When the petals were examined for their operation, it was found that there is cellular action driven by the increase of cell size in two directions without the addition of new material. In botany, this is called auxesis or having auxetic principles. The petals also respond to sunlight at a cellular level, which is a photonastic principle (*characteristics*). This information was used as the point of first principles reduction. The principles are clearly identified but still in shallow disciplinary syntax. Auxesis and photonasty, which are botanical terms, needed to be translated into more general statements that could move across disciplinary boundaries. Models were created in order to study ways of reproducing the principles operating in the tulip's mechanical response systems

(Figure 7.5). As a reduction, the principles focused on studies of hydraulics and convection as well as expansion and elasticity (*principles*). Particular attention was paid to cyclical events as the principles reduced from the tulip required the ability to expand and then contract back to an original form. This led the designers to look at joints, folds, kinetic reactive materials such as shape-memory alloys, composites, and lamination.

Once removed from the particular domain syntax of botany, exploration of principles was brought into the architectural domain using shallow syntax (*characteristics*). Moving from basic studies of joints, hydraulics, convection, morphology, and materials, the explorations prototyped several different paths of development. While several responses were investigated simultaneously, they all responded to principles grounded in a kinetic reaction to light and volume change without material addition (Figure 7.6). In shallow architectural syntax, mechanical responses to the presence of heat and light were mapped to how they might affect air movement. The modelling illustrated a strong connection of shared principles between the botanical and architectural disciplines, implying the ability to make a successful domain-to-domain transfer.

The design process, using a method based on a force-based framework, increased in complexity and specificity as it moved further into the disciplinary deep syntax

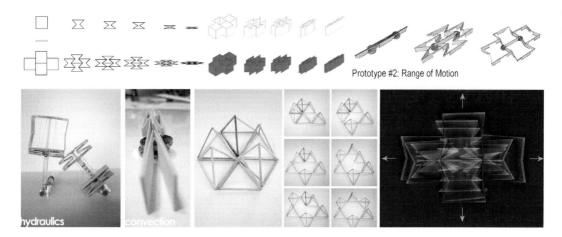

Figure 7.5: Discipline neutral investigations of principles operating in photonastic and auxetic events

Courtesy of Kathryn Grube, Lauren Hetzel, Amanda Joseph, Jia Liu, Ryan Mccourt, Rana Salah, Erica Sanchez, and Raman Shamoo

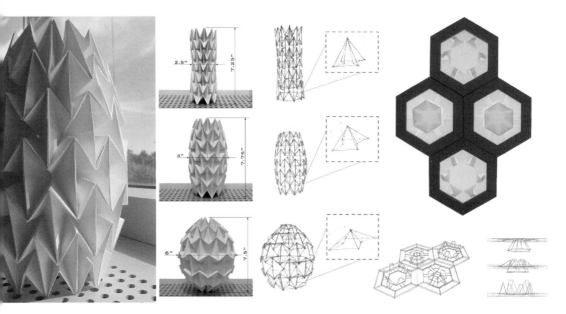

Figure 7.6: Shallow architectural syntax-based diagrams and models of auxetic principles

Courtesy of Kathryn Grube *et al.*

of architecture. The final architectural response transferred the biological operations from the tulip's petals to an architectural façade module that expanded based on light levels and changes in heat. The automatic response to environmental effects allowed for passive cooling and the reflection of indirect light (Figure 7.7). The scale of the module was increased to develop into a prototype wall system (*relations*; Figure 7.8).

A different set of initial principles could be selected as part of the starting bias. A second investigation focused on how a tulip maintained homoeostasis while under a large range of exterior conditions, such as extreme temperature changes and drought.[12] Initial research highlighted the complex internal resource management and energy storage of the tulip that became the focus of the first principles reduction (*relations*). Investigations then focused on the use of water to create structure, store energy, and regulate the tulip's internal and external factors (Figure 7.9). The core operation of how water is used at a cellular level is based on the principles of osmosis and turgidity (*characteristics*). Osmosis was reduced to the passive movement of liquid across a membrane, and turgidity to the state of being distended by internal pressure.

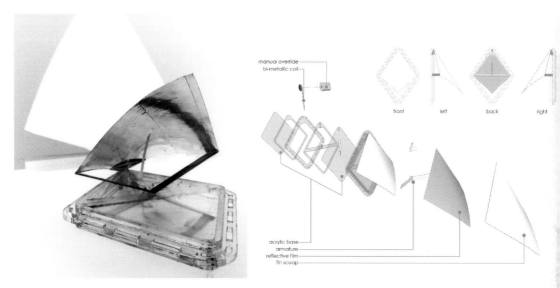

Figure 7.7: Architectural module based on the tulip including elements which swell and open using light sensors

Courtesy of Kathryn Grube *et al.*

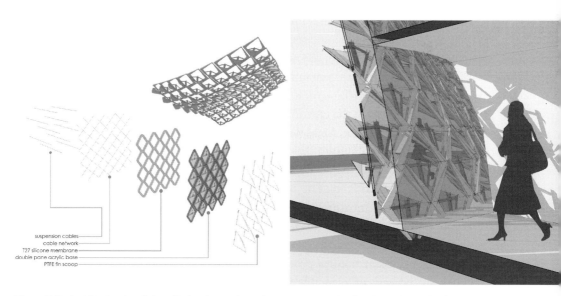

Figure 7.8: Architectural wall installation focused on air movement and reflective indirect lighting

Courtesy of Kathryn Grube *et al.*

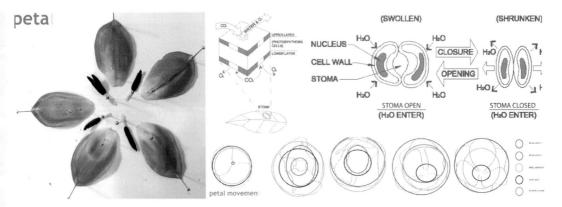

Figure 7.9: Transfer of a tulip to architecture based on principles of osmosis and turgidity – the tulip flower dissected and cellular operations examined focusing on the movement and storage of water

Courtesy of Eric Henry, Tomos Karatzias, Quang Lam, Jason Rostar, and Erin Smith

The ability to move water across membranes and the use of water to create distended but rigid structure became the focus for the architectural exploration. The principles were modelled and explored in a generic or shared-domain syntax looking at wicking, absorption, evaporation, and material properties (*principles*). After many explorations, one line of the investigation moved into material studies that combined the wicking rates and holding capacity of sheet- and volume-based material. This combination seemed to meet the requirements of storage and release of energy based on bio-hydraulic variants. The reduction was mapped to climatic control in shallow architectural syntax. Moisture could be related to an interior environment through the creation of a micro-climate generated by air-borne water absorption and release (*characteristics*). An open-mesh, polyester membrane was developed, using imbibition balls as a moisture battery. The membrane allowed for a high range of wicking while the open mesh increased exposed surface area for evaporation (Figure 7.10). The final proposal became a self-supporting, open–wall system integrated into grey water recycling. Internal environmental quality was regulated through moisture absorption and release through air convection (*relations*).

While the two examples above had different outcomes, they used the same domain-to-domain transfer process to achieve their proposals. In both examples, the basic process of principle identification, abstraction, and mapping can be identified. Once the principles had been extracted and basic mapping occurred, they were made more specific in the new domain.

Figure 7.10: Architectural proposal of wall system for passive temperature and humidity control

Courtesy of Eric Henry *et al.*

Structure-mapping as domain transfer

Structure-mapping is a more complex form of transfer through first principles reduction. It is the basis of how analogies and metaphors can be used legitimately in architectural design. In structure-mapping, the interest is in identifying strong relations between objects in the source domain in order to enrich the content of the target domain (architecture). A selected aspect of the source domain – which is a context, an event, or a situation – is 'exploded' into its component parts. This will include objects of the source domain, the attributes of those objects, and the relations between those objects. The source domain is selected based on the framing, starting bias, hypothesis creation, and filtering of the designer. Once a source has been identified, there are three major steps: moving from a source frame through a transfer frame and on to a target frame (Figure 7.11). The source frame holds content in a particular syntax, the transfer frame moves that content into general principles, and the target frame translates the general principles back to particular syntax but in a different domain of knowledge.

The source frame contains the objects and attributes in a set of relationships. It is the relationships in the selected content that will be used primarily for translation into architectural syntax. The process of moving from the source frame to the target frame is a process of reduction through first principles and reapplication of those principles to related architectural content. Much of the source content will

121

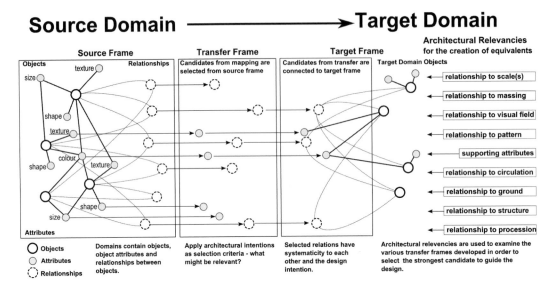

Figure 7.11: Diagram of cross-domain mapping through structure-mapping

be discarded as the process of transfer moves from the source to the target. There should be as much content as possible in the source as it will increase the chances to identify something which is a strong candidate for transfer. While the content of the source frame is being developed, architectural objects can be explored at the same time in the target domain. They should be tentative placements at first, generated through thinking about the priorities in the design situation. Like all design processes, there is an iterative nature to structure-mapping. The process moves from the left and right edges to meet in the centre and then loops to verify selections.

Once a strong set of objects and their relational connections have been identified in the source frame, and architectural objects have begun to be lightly connected in the target frame, possibilities for mapping can be listed in the transfer frame. Only the strongest, most relevant, and most systematic elements should be passed forward into the transfer frame. There will be another reduction of content from transfer to target frames, so selections should be identified based on potential for an architectural response with the willingness to abandon any that do not support a strong mapping. Relational aspects should always be prioritized, but some supporting attribute content can also be pulled forward to reinforce the relationships. As in the transfer through first principles, the content of the transfer frame is connected to relationships and supportive attributes in the architectural domain using deep architectural syntax. Architectural objects are confirmed and the relationships between those objects guided by the content of the transfer frame. As the process moves from source to target frames, there should be a decrease in the visibility of the relationships and attributes. This decrease is necessary because the target domain borrows content from the source, *inferring* that content to add richness to the target rather than representing that content. Explicit content from the source domain should not be literally present in the manifestation of the target domain.

The application of a structure-mapped process can be thought about as a network of related first principles reductions moving from particular to general then back to particular. The process can be illustrated through a couple of examples. One of the easiest transfers to do is the mapping of fluid dynamics to human circulation. These two domains share many aspects, but they are far enough apart for there to be no confusion about their boundaries. Rather than just general fluid dynamics, the source frame can be focused by looking at the movement of water in a river, which has rich variations and imagery to help in its use as a design source. This would be considered a metaphor – movement in the building is like the flow of a river. However, the point is not to map visual characteristics so the circulation *looks like* a river, but that circulation *acts like* the principles of movement in water. This example will show how relationships are transferred while most attributes are abandoned (Figure 7.12). This is a limited example; a full process would include many more objects, relationships, and attributes.

The aspects of fluid movement in regards to environmental objects becomes the focus to filter the source frame when considering mapping fluid dynamics of a river to architectural space. Several relationships in the source frame can be named based on their performance, such as an eddy, a sink, a hole, a pool, a pillow, a chute, and a drop. All of these words are descriptions of the interaction of water with river banks, obstacles (rocks), and the river bed. In addition, all of the relationships have to do with changes in speed of movement or changes in level. Considering the movement of a river in this way reduces its relationships to a set of first principles. These principles are strong candidates for transfer into architecture, since the architectural domain has access to a related syntax through circulation, architectural objects, and datum. Moving from the source frame, the transfer frame would reduce the relationships to their principles so that they

Source Domain ⟶ Target Domain

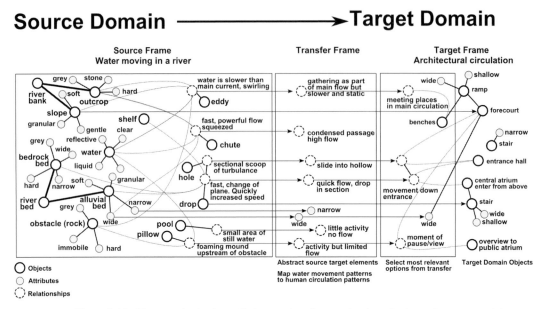

Figure 7.12: Diagram of a basic applied cross-domain mapping transferring water movement to architecture

might be connected to architectural syntax. The final move into the target domain would engage those relationships with architectural objects. There might be some direct mapping between source objects and target objects to help organize the relationships if there is a very strong relationship between their principles and operation.

At the moment, the example is fragmentary and little more than a sketch. The architectural elements are still vague, and need to be focused with a context, site, and programme. What is important is the transfer of content between domains that allows for new ways of organizing existing architectural syntax, as well as suggesting possible novel relationships. The connection of relationships in river dynamics might allow the designer to consider the placement of architectural objects as ways to slow down movement, moments that are then reinforced with the placement of gathering or meeting areas. The nature of the target object is flexible, but constrained to a connection with the underlying principles. While this example uses circulation objects and rooms, it could use smaller, less specific elements as well (wall, ceiling, column) or sensory information (shallow, pattern, light). Any element of architectural syntax is possible for the final domain objects as long as there is access to the type of information held in the transfer frame and there is coherence between the parts.

Structure-mapping and transfer through first principles are generally done without elaborate diagrams. An experienced architectural designer is used to thinking in terms of objects, attributes, and relationships, even if the exact terminology is different. The designer will make connections between principles based on experience, although, as architecture is a discipline dominated by the visual, it is easy to fall into attribute-only transfers. The diagram is a useful tool to make sure the initial moves are as expansive as possible and to ensure that relationships are stressed over attributes. The source frame should explore as much of its territory as possible, the transfer frame is used to reduce, abstract, and focus, while the target frame is about expanding principles back into deep disciplinary syntax and decision-making.

Another example of an applied structure-mapping process is available in the built work of Steven Holl, a master at using metaphoric content to create rich architectural responses. Holl is known to work through external source material as well as phenomenological qualities of light and perception as the basis of his architectural proposals.[13] As described by the architect, the House at Martha's Vineyard (1984–1988) is on 'a hill overlooking the Atlantic Ocean as it meets Vineyard Sound. Strict code determines that the house be set back from the marshland [which is classified as] […] a no-build zone and it should have a 1-story elevation when viewed from the beach.'[14] The situation of the house, including the history of the area, literary references to the island, and the hill site all influenced Holl's conceptual starting point for the design. His early watercolour shows a low-slung building floating on the dunes with a stick-framed, ribbed covered walkway leading to the entrance (Figure 7.13). The house appears to emerge from the sand with foliage encroaching on all sides. Holl placed a 20-cent stamp representing Herman Melville, author of the literary classic *Moby Dick*, on the bottom of the watercolour. Melville provided the source material for the house's design.

Martha's Vineyard inspired Melville as a location and source material for his classic novel, *Moby Dick*. The whaling tradition of the island as well as its real-life residents informed the atmosphere and events in the book. Holl, in turn, used events in Melville's writing as metaphors to respond back to the location of the island, a transfer of knowledge from the literary domain to the architectural. A passage in the book sketching the use of a beached whale skeleton by a local Indian tribe was the starting point for the design. The passage describes 'a great Sperm Whale, which, after an unusually long raging gale, had been found dead

Figure 7.13: Steven Holl's watercolour sketch showing the design intentions for the House at Martha's Vineyard

Courtesy of Steven Holl Architects

and stranded, with his head against a cocoa-nut tree, whose plumage-like, tufted droopings seemed his verdant jet'.[15] Once the body was stripped of its flesh, the bones were pulled into a glen away from the water by the Indian tribe and the 'ribs were hung with trophies; the vertebrae were carved with Arsacidean annals, in strange hieroglyphics; in the skull, the priests kept up an unextinguished aromatic flame'.[16] Holl suggested that the Indian tribe would 'stretch skins over [the skeleton], transforming it into a house',[17] while Melville described the relationship between the bones and the foliage as

> the great, white, worshipped skeleton lay lounging – a gigantic idler! Yet, as the ever-woven verdant warp and woof intermixed and hummed around him, the mighty idler seemed the cunning weaver; himself all woven over with the vines; every month assuming greener, fresher verdure; but himself a skeleton. Life folded Death; Death trellised Life; the grim god wived with youthful Life, and begat him curly-headed glories.[18]

These impressions became the source frame for the House at Martha's Vineyard.

As a source frame, the whale skeleton is part of a larger set of relationships, including the proximity to the water, the Native American population, the natural decay of organic material, landscape, and plant growth. The response by Steven Holl was to propose a house as an inside–out balloon frame suspended over the cresting dune. The stick framing echoes the skeleton of the whale while supporting a veranda within its perimeter. The wood frame also acts as a stage for native vines to wrap the lines of the house, a parallel to the passage by Melville, where the whale carcass becomes a trellis for vines, returning the bone structure to nature. It is possible to reconstruct the possibilities which map these relationships to their successful transferal in the final target response (Figure 7.14).

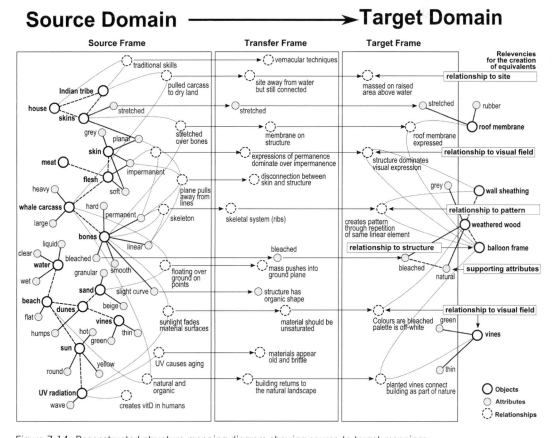

Figure 7.14: Reconstructed structure-mapping diagram showing source to target mappings

Figure 7.15: Completed project of Steven Holl's House at Martha's Vineyard

Courtesy of Paul Warchol Photography

Rather than being simply a mere-appearance transfer of the remains of a beached whale, the metaphorical process of domain-to-domain transfer translated relevant relationships between objects in the events described in the *Moby Dick* passage. A few attributes are also transferred to reinforce those relationships. The source domain contained an association of the skeletal structure with the ground, supporting a mass through a series of point connections to the ground. The structural expression, as a reduction, was mapped to the architectural while the skeleton, as an object, was abandoned. The skeleton was translated as a materiality and a rhythm – an underlying systemic pattern between objects – rather than the superficial image of bones. In the architectural domain, the balloon frame was the primary equivalent to the skeleton, allowing for the expression of rhythm, the relationship to the ground, the lines to express structure, and support for vines identified in the transfer frame. The bones and flesh of a carcass were reduced to a relationship between permanence and impermanence, informing a play between structure and cladding. The building site, although acting as an essential constraint dictated by code, reinforced the relationships mapped and strengthened the overall proposal. Materially, wood was dominant. As a natural material, it would express weathering, react to the ageing process, and associate the architectural proposal deeper into its context. It does this not by blurring the distinction between building and landscape but as the whale skeleton would – overlapping, intersecting but still discrete and separate. As did the whale, the house is both extending the landscape and resting on the landscape. In the final architectural proposal, the original event of the whale carcass and Native American use dissolved completely – they are no longer found in the final work. Only the structural relationship mappings remain present, addressed in the syntax of the target domain (Figure 7.15). The metaphor is mapped not as an image or a symbol but as a way to strengthen relations between architectural objects and enrich the final proposal.

Notes

1 Andrei Tarkovsky interviewed by Brezna, Irena, 'Ein Feind der Symbolik.' *Tip* 3 (1984): 24–31. Translated by Sewen, Adam at http://people.ucalgary. ca/~tstronds/nostalghia.com/TheTopics/Symbols.html.

2 Eisenman, Peter, *Diagram Diaries*. New York: Universe Publishers, 1999: 37.

3 The fundamental theory of how analogies are structured and how information is transferred can be found in Gentner, Dedre, 'Metaphor as Structure Mapping: The Relational Shift.' *Child Development* 59, no. 1 (1988): 47–59; and Gentner, Dedre, 'Structure-Mapping: A Theoretical Framework for Analogy.' *Cognitive Science* 7, no. 2 (1983): 155–170. A good, accessible summary of the research is found in Gentner, Dedre and Arthur B. Markman, 'Structure Mapping in Analogy and Similarity.' *American Psychologist* 52, no. 1 (1997): 45–56. Further reading and applications are in Gentner, D. and C. Toupin, 'Systematicity and Surface Similarity in the Development of Analogy.' *Cognitive Science* 10, no. 3 (1986): 277–300; Gentner, Dedre and Robert M. Schumacher, 'Use of Structure Mapping Theory for Complex Systems.' Presented at the Panel on Mental Models and Complex Systems, IEEE International Conference on Systems, Man and Cybernetics (1986); Falkenhainer, B., K. D. Forbus, and D. Gentner, 'The Structure-Mapping Engine: Algorithm and Examples.' *Artificial Intelligence* 41, no. 1 (1989): 1–63; and Gentner, Dedre, Keith James Holyoak, and Boicho N. Kokinov, *The Analogical Mind: Perspectives from Cognitive Science*. Cambridge, MA: The MIT Press, 2001.

4 Gentner, Dedre, 'Structure-Mapping: A Theoretical Framework for Analogy.' *Cognitive Science* 7, no. 2 (1983): 156.

5 Gentner, Dedre, 'Metaphor as Structure Mapping: The Relational Shift.' *Child Development* 59, no. 1 (1988): 47–59.

6 Venturi, Robert, Denise Scott Brown, and Steven Izenour, *Learning from Las Vegas: The Forgotten Symbolism of Architectural Form*. Rev. edn. Cambridge, MA: The MIT Press, 1996: 87.

7 Isenberg, Barbara, *Conversations with Frank Gehry*. New York: Alfred A. Knopf, 2009.

8 Friedman, Mildred and Frank O. Gehry, *Gehry Talks: Architecture + Process*. New York: Universe Publishing, 2002.

9 Curious George was created in 1939 by Hans Augusto Rey and Margret Rey as a character in the children's book *Cecily G. and the Nine Monkeys*. The first book that starred George as the main character was published in 1941 after the Reys had fled Paris. Curious George has been a continuous staple in the experience of childhood, especially in the United States, for the last seventy years.

10 *Curious George*, Season 3, Episode 2. Originally aired 2 September 2008 on the Public Broadcasting Service (PBS) in the United States.

11 This master's-level project was developed at Lawrence Technological University by Kathryn Grube, Lauren Hetzel, Amanda Joseph, Jia Liu, Ryan Mccourt, Rana Salah, Erica Sanchez, and Raman Shamoon in a studio guided by Dale Clifford of Carnegie Mellon University. The support faculty comprised Jake Chidester, Matthew Cole, Beverly Geltner, Mary Cay Lancaster, Ralph Nelson, Philip Plowright, Chris Schanck, and Tod Stevens.

12 This master's-level project was developed at Lawrence Technological University by Eric Henry, Quang Lam, Tomos Karatzias, Jason Rostar, and Erin Smith in a studio guided by Dale Clifford of Carnegie Mellon University.

13 Steven Holl writes and publishes on the ephemeral, spiritual, and phenomenological aspects of architecture as well as on light and spatial quality. See Holl, Steven, *Parallax*. New York: Princeton Architectural Press, 2000; and Holl, Steven and Lebbeus Woods, *Steven Holl: Architecture Spoken*. New York: Rizzoli, 2007.

14 Holl, Steven, 'House at Martha's Vineyard.' http://www.stevenholl.com/ project-detail.php?type=&id=25.

15 Melville, Herman, *Moby Dick, Or the Whale*. New York: Charles Scribner's Sons, 1902: 387.

16 Ibid.: 387–388.

17 Holl, Steven, 'House at Martha's Vineyard.' http://www.stevenholl.com/ project-detail.php?type=&id=25.

18 Melville, Herman, *Moby Dick, Or the Whale*. New York: Charles Scribner's Sons, 1902: 388.

SECTION III

FRAMEWORKS AND METHODS

Chapter Eight

Patterns

In every country, the orderly art of building was born from a pre-existing seed. Everything must have an antecedent; nothing whatsoever comes from nothing, and this cannot but apply to all human inventions. We observe also how all inventions, in spite of subsequent changes, have conserved their elementary principle in a manner that is always visible, and always evident to feeling and reason. This elementary principle is like a sort of nucleus around which are assembled, and with which are consequently coordinated, all the developments and the variations of form to which the object was susceptible. Thus did a thousand things of all sorts reach us; and in order to understand their reasons, one of the principal occupations of science and philosophy is to search for their origin and primitive cause. This is what ought to be called type in architecture as in every other area of human invention and institution.

Quatremère de Quincy[1]

The use of patterns to model composition and geometry can be found at the heart of numerous approaches to architectural design. Many architects maintain a belief that 'architectural design is essentially pattern making'[2] and that a 'central purpose of architecture is to bring order to chaos: to create recognizable patterns of material construction that might allow the meaning of habitation to emerge'.[3]

As developed through the history of the discipline, composition through patterns is about the application of rules based on the relationships between architectural elements of various scales. It is better to think of the rules as general principles broadly applied, or *guiding rulesets*, rather than 'letter of the law' directions. This distinction is important as the type of repetition used by designers is fuzzy. Fuzzy repetition allows variation in application while still maintaining adherence to core principles. Quatremère de Quincy, the late Enlightenment theorist, described the rulesets as *types*. He considered a type as a pattern that detailed the essence of an architectural situation and contained a set of principle relationships between the parts. In architecture, the most prominent source of these rulesets is the extraction of relationships from previously successful projects and naturally occurring events through the analysis of precedent or case-studies. The way people use a space creates an identifiable structure between the parts – a *pattern*. If that pattern is successful in supporting a particular use of a space, it should be found over and over again in the same context, thus becoming a *type*. The repetition of successful patterns is the basis of traditional approaches to design. When used as a vernacular, the patterns are not at an active level of awareness. However, patterns and types can be used consciously to give architectural designers access to the social use of space through fundamental spatial configurations. Patterns are repeated in composition because they work in the context where they are found.

Patterns in architectural design embed social information in formal composition – how a space is used by a person is expressed in its shape, volume, adjacency, qualities (light, sound, textures, atmosphere), and distribution (where elements are found within the space). If the formal aspects of a space are a strong reflection of the use – the space supports specific rituals such as eating, sleeping, or gathering – and the use is not unique, then there is little need for active decision-making on the part of the designer. The reproduction of the same composition should bring the same successful type of occupation and social use. The space is not duplicated exactly, but the formal principles of the space are extracted and reapplied in a fuzzy repetition. Instead of applying judgement criteria based on framing or starting bias, the designer can focus on developing a proposal based on 'geometric schema'.[4] Geometry is directly accessible by the tools architects use, such as the drawing techniques of plan, section, and elevation, or models and formal diagrams. Architectural tools have been developed to provide direct access to the core type of content that is found in architectural design, such as mass, void, texture, colour, shape, adjacency, grid, light, volume, rhythm, procession, and circulation. Tools such as plans generally respond to grids, circulation, and rhythm; sections address volume, voids, and vertical relationships; elevations represent massing, texture, and shape; and diagrams detail adjacencies and intangibles such as light, sound, or view.

A pattern-based framework is considered to be an *internal* method as it does not require the transfer of content between domains of knowledge. Methods based on a pattern framework might have external content embedded into spatial configurations, such as cultural values and vernacular practices. As a design method, only the spatial relationships are used explicitly; everything else is ignored. This process assumes that all activities and events are reflected in how a space is arranged. For example, a designer must develop a space for several small groups of people to gather at the same time in order to discuss sensitive information. Social content might include a need for privacy, a light quality that supports a sense of intimacy, discrete (and discreet) entrances and exits from the location, and a sense of ritual and solemnity. In terms of architectural spatial configuration, this might translate into patterns that include several small, convex spaces that support the need for gathering, indirect light coming from high on a wall for soft light levels, circulation paths that allow movement into the space from multiple directions, and a certain isolation of the interior spaces from each other. The spatial configuration can be diagrammed in its generality and its patterns identified, including the relationship between parts of each pattern. Once the patterns and their components are identified, the spatial configuration can later be reapplied in the same type of context without needing to address the social forces that originally formed it explicitly.

The history of patterns as a source for architectural design stretches very far into the past. Pattern-based approaches have been present since the earliest treatises of architectural design, existing as a series of rulesets and best practices communicated to other architects. Vitruvius, in his *De Architectura*, or *Ten Books of Architecture*, identified patterns for use in architectural design on various scales when he gave instruction on how to locate a city, lay out healthy streets, site public buildings, configure temples (e.g. column placement), and design and construct houses.[5] When Vitruvius discussed the design of a farmhouse and instructed that 'the kitchen be placed on the warmest side of the courtyard, with the stalls for the oxen adjoining, and their cribs facing the kitchen fire and the eastern quarter of the sky',[6] he was communicating a generalized and repeatable pattern of spatial configuration. There was no discussion of why the oxen should face the fire, or why the kitchen belonged on the warmest side – these decisions were embedded in the rulesets. Vitruvius' rulesets for a farmhouse kitchen can be easily diagrammed using architectural tools. Starting to design a new farmhouse, the patterns of spatial composition can be extracted and applied without ever worrying about the cultural mythology that places belief in the fact 'that oxen ought to face only in the direction of the sunrise'.[7] The same approach was updated for the twentieth-century architect by Christopher Alexander, although in a much more sophisticated way in order to accommodate complexity. Alexander addressed the application of pre-existing formal relationships when he wrote:

> it makes the most sense to think of the inside as a FARMHOUSE KITCHEN, with a big table in the middle, chairs around it, one light hung over the center, a couch or armchair off to one side [...] When I start to imagine this, and imagine entering it, I realize that it is more important than I realized to keep it back, slightly, from the door, to make something out of the ENTRANCE ROOM that lies between.[8]

The FARMHOUSE KITCHEN is a pre-existing set of relationships between architectural elements. The relationships are not exact – the size of the table, the distance from the table to the comfortable sitting area 'off to one side', the style or intensity of the light – none of these elements is explicit. However, the relationship represents a pattern that can be repeated.

Information used in a pattern-based framework is generally addressed as *typology* or the study of types in architectural design. A type is created by a 'process of reducing a complex of formal variants to a common root form',[9] which basically means that a large collection of architectural objects with common relationships can be understood by their shared characteristics regardless of individual differences. Rafael Moneo says it more clearly when he notes the fact that architecture 'belongs to a class of repeated objects, characterized, like a class of tools or instruments, by some general attributes'.[10] A repeated object is identified by the core characteristics of its formal composition. A hammer is a hammer because there are core and persistent compositional characteristics found in each and every manifestation of the hammer. When it comes to describing the root form of the hammer, that which makes it not a screwdriver, an axe, or a pick, a relationship can be identified between a handle and a head with at least one flat striking area. The handle could be longer or shorter but there will be a range that is common (finishing hammer to sledgehammer). The head might have two striking surfaces or one with a claw, pick, waffle, or other variation. Material, or even colour, has not entered the description of the hammer type as these are non-critical. The handle might be wood or steel, wrapped in rubber, painted, varnished, or left bare; the head might be steel, wood, or rubber – all depending on the application. Every variation is still a *hammer* because it satisfies the essential pattern of relationships between elements (handle attached to flat striking head). A new hammer can be designed by applying the hammer type to the context in which it is to be used. The type will repeat the basic relationships between parts, the context will allow modification of those relationships to fit the purpose. This is what is meant by fuzzy repeatability – common set of relationships is satisfied while the particular application allows for variations to occur *as long as they do not break the core relationships*.

In the same way as a hammer can be considered as a formal pattern identified as a type, architecture contains patterns which are types. These are standardized patterns of relationships among architectural objects found over and over again within our inhabited spaces. An architectural object can be at various scales – from an element, such as a column, to a building, such as a courthouse. The key factor is understanding architectural types not as the object but as the relationships the object represents in architectural syntax. As such, the core of an architectural type will be found in the spatial configuration (circulation, gathering, public/private, entrance), the articulation of the surface (transparency, translucency, opacity, solidity), and the structural systems (span length, volume, void) as these define the core information of any formal composition. Patterns and types in architecture will always be defined by *internal* characteristics of formal features, such as dimension, distance, massing, surface quality, aspect ratio, and scale. These formal features set up a situation that allows a space to be washed with a certain quality of light, or that projects a particular psychological atmosphere.

Patterns and types do not tend to be supported as a design process in current architectural design practice because it seems to be difficult for designers to separate formal principles (how things are arranged) from aesthetics (how things are represented). When designers do support typologically based design, it generally comes with representational and ideological values. The designer identifies the source of the design's content as pulling from existing patterns by making the architecture look historical, usually from Roman or Greek source material. This is part of a large and long-running argument as to whether 'traditional' or 'modern' design is better. Yet this argument is disconnected from method. This disconnection is possible because the principles – the relationships among the elements and how they are organized – are independent of their representation. A type-based approach can appear to be modern or Classical depending on material or massing choices that occur *after* the patterns have been applied. Proposals based on patterns do not have to be vernacular in their conclusions. There are ways to use pattern-based methods to produce innovative work by treating the process as a resolution of systems rather than an application of symbolism.

Structural framework

While patterns as type was developed as architectural theory by Quatremère de Quincy at the end of the eighteenth century, the process of accessing patterns for use in architectural design was first documented as a rational method in the early nineteenth century by J-N-L Durand. As different eras and contexts in history and culture have introduced different value systems for designers, information that occurs before method (framing, starting bias, context, values, and decision-making) radically affect the appearance of the final composition of an architectural proposal. Even so, the same design framework is often used, with the framing and bias producing a variation of method. While Durand's design method isn't followed currently, the underlying framework of pattern extraction and reapplication is still very much in use today.

Durand lived at a point in history when a scientific mindset and belief in methods had been fully integrated into Western society. Rational thought was valued highly and France, where Durand lived, was recovering from the Revolution of 1789 which had suppressed ostentatious displays of wealth and upper-class taste. Against this backdrop, function-driven rationalism dominated the teaching at the École des Beaux-Arts and École Polytechnique in the late 1700s and early 1800s. Students broke away from the Classical as it had a political relationship to the class structure. The change in value judgement challenged the late eighteenth-century focus on decoration as the focus of architectural design. Efficiency became valued over visual display and there was a greater interest in producing buildings prioritizing human comfort. In terms of disciplinary tools, the change in attitude shifted the primary graphic tool of architects from the elevation focused on decoration and public presentation to the plan embodying comfort, fitness of use, and efficient spatial distribution.[11] It was this *framing* effect that was found at the core of Durand's method, producing a *starting bias* based on 'fitness and economy'.[12]

Fitness included the good use of materials, structural soundness, creation of a healthy environment, and a strong relationship between the parts of the building and its purpose. The plan was the first tool to be engaged, with the grid used to organize the spatial composition rationally. The plan was important to fitness as it allowed issues of quality and comfort in the distribution of interior space to be a major design influence, setting up *judgement criteria*. Economy affected *decision-making* in terms of efficient spatial arrangements. For example, where Durand's method supported symmetry, it was not primarily for the aesthetic effect or structural soundness. Instead, symmetry was valued because it was less expensive than irregular shapes. Walls were to be continuous throughout a site because they were cheaper to build this way. Irregular sites were 'corrected', creating efficient geometry, such as pure squares, rectangles, circles, so as not to be 'highly inconvenient for use'.[13] These are the values that drove the organization of Durand's approach. The framework that Durand used to design, regardless of these values, was a typological process based on extracting and applying patterns to particular use and context. While contemporary Western society might not share Durand's values towards efficiency and cost as a driving purpose of architectural design (although this discussion would not be out of place in the building industry today), the structure of a framework is independent to framing, bias, and judgement criteria.

Whereas Vitruvius wrote a set of directions for the proper way to arrange certain building types, Durand produced a series of rulesets based on composition as part of his method. The rulesets are presented in a scientific, categorical way in four dimensions: material choices, building elements, building parts, and building types. Durand's method integrated these four dimensions into an analytical, inductive design process[14] based on constructing a final proposal by combining building elements to create a whole. Architectural meaning would be generated not by decoration but by architectural composition using only internal syntax. Specifically, the method required attention: '(1) to the objects that architecture uses, that is, the elements of buildings; (2) to the combination of these elements, in other words, composition in general; and (3) to the alliance of these combinations in the composition of a specific building'[15] (Figure 8.1). Elements of building, as defined by Durand, are walls, piers, pilasters, doors, windows, columns, beams, floors, roofs, and vaults. These could be combined into parts of a building with a series of best practices and rulesets. Parts of a building were porticoes, porches, vestibules, staircases, rooms, galleries, and courtyards. Each of these parts related to a building type and to the expression of the building through its character.

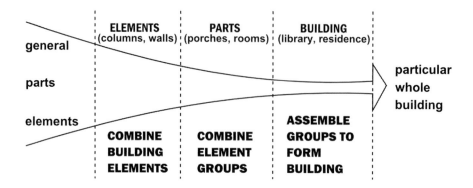

Figure 8.1: Overview framing of Durand's architectural design method

In his lecture on 'Composition in General',[16] Durand separated his process into horizontal (plan) and vertical (section) combinations, making the latter dependent on the former. The plan was to be designed first, the section developed second. Elevation was considered the result of the plan and section. The core tool used in the process was the axis.[17] An axis is simply a line used as a reference. Axes that are arranged perpendicular to each other create a grid and an interaxis is the space between two axes. The placement of the major axes, secondary axes, and interaxes controlled the location of the elements and the relationship among the parts (Figure 8.2). Durand's *Précis*[18] described this part of his process as starting with horizontal disposition (plan). Parallel and equidistant axes would be placed on the plan and then a grid made using secondary axes perpendicular to main axes, spread equal distances apart. *Rulesets* were used to lay walls on axes separated by the appropriate number of interaxes. The axes were also used to arrange the placement of columns, pilasters, and piers. Doors, windows, and arcades were located by bisecting interaxes to make a new grid, again using rulesets. Once the horizontal had been determined, the architectural designer would move to vertical disposition (section). Vertical combinations of elements would be derived from horizontal dispositions, allowing for variation. Variations are chosen based on fitness and economy, as represented in rulesets. Finally, the elevations were developed from the horizontal and vertical dispositions.

Durand's method can be identified as one based on applying patterns incorporated in rulesets to make decisions, focusing on developing a whole from parts. The rulesets hold the patterns, and the patterns contain the judgement criteria.

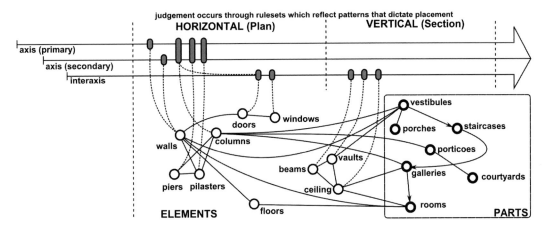

Figure 8.2: Durand's compositional method for arranging building elements into parts

Judgement criteria are the ideas which hold the values for the project and are used to test options in order to make selections. For example, Durand wrote:

> the rise of the steps is generally one-half of their width or tread. If a staircase leads to a large number of rooms on a single floor, it is surrounded by galleries. Sometimes it consists of a single flight and sometimes of two. Each of these simple stair forms may be combined with another of the same kind; in which case a vestibule is placed between the two.[19]

Here, Durand was describing relations between architectural objects that could be defined as a pattern. The pattern described how the second floor of a building was entered and the different compositional arrangement of public and private spaces. The relationship between the stairs, galleries, rooms, and vestibules created a pattern that had been developed through past applications and could be repeated. That pattern contained many factors, including how the spaces were to be used, social expectations, cultural norms, qualities of light and air, visibility, and safety. However, since the only information needed as a formal designer was the spatial composition, the judgement criteria could be simplified to whether the relationship of rooms on the second floor to the stair was public or private in its use.

Patterns are found in Durand's method at three different scales: relationships between building elements with their proper distribution for proportion and visual pleasure; sequences between building parts depending on social use; and the overall arrangement of major building types. All of these patterns could have been shown graphically as diagrams, which is important. As Christopher Alexander comments, 'If you can't draw a diagram of it, it isn't a pattern.'[20] For a pattern to be *real*, it must be able to be described, reproduced, and communicated. Durand did not provide isolated diagrams to describe the rulesets. Instead, students were to study his drawings of completed buildings in order to extract formal compositions and then reapply those patterns in their own work. Ultimately, patterns are not rigid rules or detailed instructions. They are rough sketches that address a set of general spatial relationships which have been shown to have a potential effect on human occupation.

Durand's method could be accused of being prescriptive or mechanical in nature, and that would be a legitimate charge. However, the description of assembling elements to parts through rulesets is only a fragment of a larger process. This set of instructive steps was meant for students who are learning composition to follow, thereby allowing good composition to be achieved with the minimum of effort and the maximum of efficiency. A high degree of success was expected through connecting current spatial composition to historical use. The phases in the method were arranged in such a way that the values held by the designer are reinforced. Durand's method offers a good example of how tools control access to information and engage the designer's priorities. Moving from plan to section and then finally to elevation meant interior spatial qualities would be a primary focus. The design of the building would be based around the layout (disposition) of the rooms. If the starting point was elevations and then axonometric, section, and finally plan, a completely different set of priorities would be present in the design. Instead of prioritizing the arrangement of the programme, the design would focus on the way the building was seen from the outside streets. The plan would be compromised for the qualities of the elevation, something of which Durand was very critical. In order to reinforce the qualities of interior space, the patterns found in the rulesets contain instructions biased towards plan-based information.

Durand's full design method integrated the *building elements into parts* process within a larger framework for building composition. The method allowed decisions to be made in regard to the grid arrangement, the site, the building needs, and the cultural requirements (Figure 8.3). Through this process, the designer could understand where and why the axes were arranged, and how elements should be arranged on those axes to achieve a desired effect. It also allowed for a large degree of designer bias, which affected the final proposal, while maintaining the principal concerns that the method supports – good efficiency, economy, and distribution. All these were affected by priorities of function that occurred in two ways in nineteenth-century French architectural design. First was the idea of *character*. Character was the *rightness* of the expression of the building,[21] an expression of truth and ethics still found in many aspects of architectural design. The second functional concern was the layout of programme. This meant that while the composition component was inductively based, moving from the part to the whole, the requirements of nineteenth-century French architectural theory required larger patterns to guide the shape of the smaller ones.[22] The legacy of character and large pattern representaton is found in the *parti*, the architectural tool used to represent the essence of a design proposal's strategy concisely in either a formal diagram or a brief statement. The term 'parti' most likely came from the French expression *prendre le parti de*, meaning 'to assume a position between several choices', which has been shortened to *parti pris*, meaning 'a strong, assumed position'. In its original application as an École des Beaux-Arts tool, the parti would be developed from the study of programme or building type, expressing that which 'characterizes a building'.[23] Character, through the parti, would be used to help organize the rooms and axes to create a *croquis*, or guide. In Durand's method, character and parti were both tools to help composition by pattern.

Durand's method can be analysed to identify the area of framing, starting bias, thinking styles, scale of focus, and use of patterns (Figure 8.4). When the core of

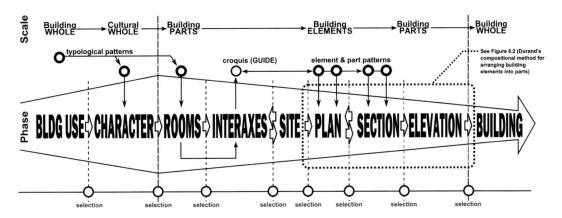

Figure 8.3: Diagram of Durand's 'Procedure to Be Followed in the Composition of Any Project'. The full process introduced use, site, and expression to composition by ruleset

Durand's process – as well as the central theory of typology – is examined, the process is seen to be concerned with the identification of underlying patterns based on existing use of space and the reapplication of variations of those patterns in order to aggregate into a new whole. Variations of patterns are selected based on site, character, and scale, allowing formal drift to occur through non-exact reproduction. The final whole, as a reflection of the pieces, should meet the overall criteria of its use since it meets the criteria of all the individual elements. In Durand, the issue is forced slightly with the introduction of character as a way to order the overall proposal, blending his typological approach with a concept-based aspect.

All pattern-based methods start with objects or events of cultural mass, which is basically a way of saying there has to be repetition of a pattern enough times to make it significant. This can be seen when Durand explored past use and known expression to set up the *starting state* and the major *judgement criteria* in his first two phases. Those phases were also the point of exploratory thinking when large-scale choices were made affecting the disposition of rooms and the spatial configuration of the interior. After this point, most of the thinking styles found in the method were evaluative and analytical, based on selecting and applying predetermined forms to meet the objectives, rather than exploring alternatives and innovative solutions. Even the construction of the rulesets was mostly analytical, comparing existing examples to reduce them to a common root form of fundamental relationships – that information which allows a type to be constructed.

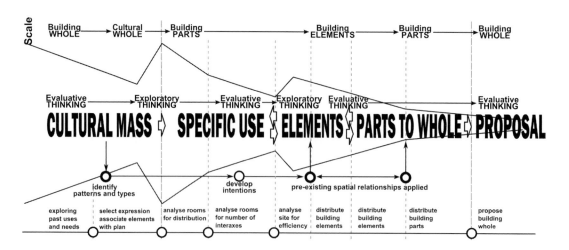

Figure 8.4: Durand's method based on thinking styles, thinking scales, and disciplinary focus

Durand identified nine phases in his complete method, each containing activities and tools driven by his framing and bias. Cultural shifts stressed the disposition of rooms and human comfort while architectural theory prioritized character as an initial design. Building use, character identification, and room analysis (programme) were then the first tasks for an architect to determine, representing the first three phases. The belief in the importance of spatial distribution and rational order created the order for the next five phases. Patterns were applied first to arrange interaxis, then site, plan, section, and, finally, elevation. Durand's bias and framing of programme distribution, efficiency, and cost was used as the judgement criteria in the phases of interaxis, room analysis, and plan. His method, while peculiar to his historical context in terms of priorities, can be reduced to a more general framework (Figure 8.5). Initial phases are about context and culture, moving to apply predetermined formal characteristics from a small scale (elements) to create a larger composition (building). There were really only four major phases in Durand's process:

1. identification of formal patterns from existing types, spatial relationships, and drawn examples;
2. identification of particular needs and uses based on occupation and context;
3. selection and application of building elements; and
4. aggregation of building elements to building parts, and of building parts to the whole building.

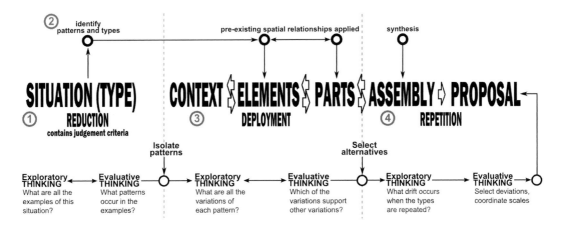

Figure 8.5: Generic framework of a pattern-based design process including thinking styles

The core process can be modified slightly by locating thinking styles as they are found in design. The strength of a design process, as a unique activity, is the combination of a thinking pattern that moves from exploration (divergent) to evaluation (convergent) to decision (selection). This chain of thinking is found at various scales and parallel investigations in a single method, occurring wherever a decision needs to be made. The generic framework from which methods are developed applies formal properties to create elements, which are then aggregated into a larger whole through exploration, variations, and repetition.

While Durand was prescriptive about the application of patterns, twentieth-century explorations into typology by Aldo Rossi, Rafael Moneo, Giulio Carlo Argan, Alan Colquhoun, and Anthony Vidler,[24] as well as typomorphology by Saverio Muratori, M. R. G. Conzen, Anne Vernez Moudon, and George Baird, interpreted the process, allowing for greater flexibility.[25] The flexibility came from the fact that a pattern is a reduction of a particular situation, much like *first principles*. In fact, the core of a pattern-based framework could be considered as a variation of first principles that focuses on formal properties rather than operational factors. Aldo Rossi recognized this when he wrote that 'typology presents itself as the study of types of elements that cannot be further reduced, elements of a city as well as of an architecture'.[26] In the same way that a first principles reduction describes a general situation rather than a particular application, a typological pattern holds the core content of spatial configuration, structural logic, or surface articulation but without specific details. Once the simplified formal properties of a pattern have been identified, those properties can be explored in order to associate specific applications with the general rules. For example, if there is a pattern found in a building typology that has a long-span structural relationship (30'-0" to 200'-0"), the exact structural element does not matter. The pattern requires only a long, clear span free of vertical load transfers. In application, the form that satisfies this pattern might be a joist, beam, parallel cable structure, pneumatic arch, hinged frame, or truss system. Bay dimensions could be explored as part of the design investigation, or the different merits of form, vector, section, or surface active systems. This would be part of the exploratory thinking. A selection of one of the options that satisfies the rule of long span would be made and applied to the design proposal. The application leaves a lot of room for variation. Any form that satisfies the pattern will work, allowing for a fuzzy repeatability – meaning that while there might be a recognizable typology, each proposal might have a different structural system meeting the long-span rule.

Applied methods

Since there are many different patterns at work in any architectural design proposal, the strength of the design comes from associating patterns which together can strengthen each other – what is called *synthesis*. As part of the evaluative thinking aspect of the design process, the variations of a pattern would be examined not by themselves, but in relation to other patterns that also occur in the same proposal. While the long-span pattern can be satisfied by many particular applications, it may be possible to use that long span in ways other than structural. If the proposal also includes another kind of pattern that requires an even natural light across the long space and a shift in floor plane, then those long-span structures that allow for such possibilities in light and changes in section can be the focus of selection (see Example 2, below). This cuts down the amount of choices, making decision-making easier, and also improves the integration of the architectural elements. While the process might appear linear, it is actually extremely iterative. A pattern would be selected and then reinforced by another pattern, while all previous selections at various scales are checked for fit. Often a variation of a pattern can be applied, only to be discarded later and another variation of the same pattern selected based on the applications of a later pattern which is determined to be more dominant or important for the overall proposal.

There are many ways to apply variations of this framework, running from straightforward to extremely complex. The designer can focus on large-scale patterns of occupation and movement applying repetition as an application of the general type, components and modules creating repetition within the project, integrate multiple scales of spatial configurations, develop patterns based on occupational relationships, or even transfer patterns from one typology into another if characteristics match. These are all starting biases which will affect the type of information and the selection of the patterns. The content of the method will be found within the architectural syntax as there is no domain-to-domain transfer in this process.

Comparative case-study analysis

The big question is: where do the patterns come from? While some theorists, such as J-N-L Durand and Christopher Alexander, have presented packaged descriptions of spatial logics (patterns), they are in the minority. Most architects are wary of predetermined content, even when it describes only a basic level of relationships. In fact, throughout the resurgence of interest in typology in the 1970s and onwards by architects focusing on urban design, such as Aldo Rossi, Leon Krier, and James Sterling, only general discussions of type theory can be found. Books dedicated to composition in architecture do not identify persistent spatial relationships which support occupation and use of space, even though they discuss the principles of formal architectural design.[27] It is rare to find documentation in architecture of underlying formal relationships that are repeatable and independent of their representation and particular context. The closest might be the *Time Saver Standards for Architectural Design* or *Graphic Standards* series of reference books – though these address more exacting dimensions than patterns require. There seems to be resistance to developing and communicating set patterns as this feels deterministic, conflicting with the perception that design should produce novelty based on individual genius in an unidentifiable process. However, patterns are used constantly in architecture. The tool that is used to develop patterns for use in design is in the precedent or case-study, in either the individual or comparative form.

The case-study has a long history of use in architectural design. The study of previous works of architecture is a strong part of the design culture of the discipline. However, when an architectural designer looks to previous work for *inspiration*, it is not to duplicate exactly what has been done before by borrowing stylistic elements, material, or colour schemes. Instead, the work should be analysed for how it *operates*, recognizing how particular concerns have been approached and identifying novel applications which address underlying principles (spatial, technological, and social). The core of this operation is the extraction of underlying compositional or formal patterns that advance this end.

The standard approach to case-study analysis tends towards examining a single project, or to assess projects individually as parts of a series. However, if the goal is to look for a pattern *which is a type* then it is necessary to compare many case-studies. As discussed above, a type is a reduction which presents a rule. All members of the type group should satisfy the rule. It is difficult to know if there is a type if only a single project or a single instance is examined. This might be the single exception to the rule that is confused as being the rule. Comparative case-study analysis can be used to reduce architectural projects down to their shared principles. This process looks across multiple examples of a building type or urban space, comparing variations to identify the patterns present. Those patterns create principles and then those principles can be reapplied in new relationships of the same building or context type.

Typology can be found at all different scales in architectural design, from the larger urban compositions to the organization of small rooms. There are many different factors that can be used as part of the analysis but they will mostly fall into the categories of spatial configurations, massing volumes, structural systems, social densities, and surface qualities. These are all factors that can be described by the language and tools used in architecture, making its use easier than having to transfer information across disciplinary boundaries. There will be some variation of priorities in the factors used for analysis depending on the major concerns of the designer. For example, when some architectural and urban designers, such as Léon Krier, argue for the strength of urban rather than suburban development, they are identifying typological patterns based on plot–boundary relationship, private–public differentiation, and order reinforcement.[28] The scale is larger than a single building, and focused on the relationship of the building massing to the surrounding space. There is no discussion of interiors, programmatic elements, structure, or other smaller architectural factors. Instead, the focus is on property lines and how individual plots or blocks aggregate into larger compositions. This focus implicates political and policy issues since it involves land ownership, division, and regulation. Krier brings his own framing and starting bias to the process, as he values historical pre-industrial European development patterns. The framing and bias affect which patterns he supports and also how the projects are represented. How an urban pattern is determined can be illustrated by taking a random sample of urban and suburban locations from Paris, Berlin, London, and Rome (Figure 8.6).

Similarities are already visible even before a reduction, but these can be made clearer. Using the analytical priorities of plot–boundary relationship, private–public differentiation, and order reinforcement, the figure-ground of the examples can be isolated. There are some clear patterns that appear in just the formal massing and its relationship to the property line (Figure 8.7). The first things that jump out are the similarities and differences between the two sets. The masses in the top row, the urban examples, all have very strong boundaries with hollow centres. The property line and the massing of the building are close together. The masses in the bottom row, the suburban examples, present almost the opposite, with the massing pulling away into the centre of the area defined by the property line and a lack of edge definition.

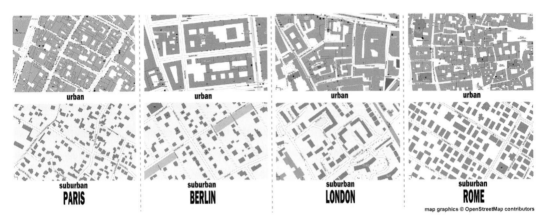

Figure 8.6: Generic methodological framework of a pattern-based design process including thinking styles

Base data from OpenStreetMap

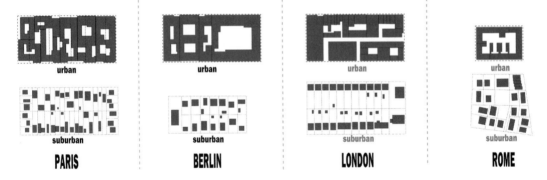

Figure 8.7: Urban massing typologies for major European cities

When this is considered as a rule, the basic operation can be diagrammed, using the priorities of boundary and massing (Figure 8.8). For pattern analysis, any single city could have been considered to have derived its urban and suburban formal rules. However, the rule identifies a type if we can find a pattern that is shared across cities – what makes a city a city and a suburb a suburb.

For architects, type patterns at the urban scale can provide massing information which includes basic size, shape, volume, and relationships to other buildings. This can either reinforce a continuous whole (street wall) or create objects in a field (suburbs). In the case of an urban pattern based on historical development, the

Figure 8.8: Urban versus suburban typological patterns based on urban grain/property line reinforcement

massing reinforces the property edge while providing significant interior void space for privacy, natural light, air movement, and green space. Suburban development produces rules which inverse these relationships.

Massing and property line are not the only aspects of our built space that can be used as part of the analysis. Urban case-studies can be reduced by looking for relationships that affect architectural placement and massing relative to urban grain patterns, urban hierarchy, green infrastructure, circulation, general materiality, street furniture, types of use, and social focus points. Urban grain patterns would include the size of blocks, property dimensions, height, scale, and spacing of buildings. Urban hierarchy looks at the relationships between buildings based on social prominence (Figure 8.9); green infrastructure would include the relationship between parks, fields, boulevards, street trees, and lawns. Circulation analyses automotive, mass transit, industrial, and pedestrian patterns of movement (Figure 8.10). Patterns in urban palette (colour, texture, and materiality) would be identified in materials such as brick, stone, vinyl, or wood as dominant materials. Street furniture looks for underlying rules in the occurrence of smaller-scale urban elements, such as lighting or benches. Types of use generally follow zoning ideas of residential, commercial, or industrial. Focal points identify vistas, nodes, attractors, or other items of social weight (Figure 8.11).

The study of existing layers of activity reduced to formal patterns allows access to reapply those patterns as part of an architectural or urban proposal. The patterns might suggest the importance of a site as a nodal point, a stitch in the urban fabric, or a contrast as a circulation anchor. Typological analysis provides substantial

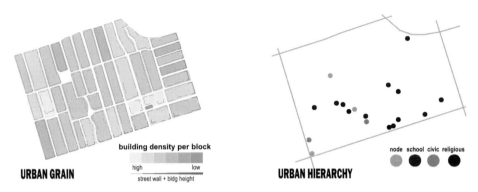

Figure 8.9: Urban grain and hierarchy typological analysis

Courtesy of Zachary Verhulst

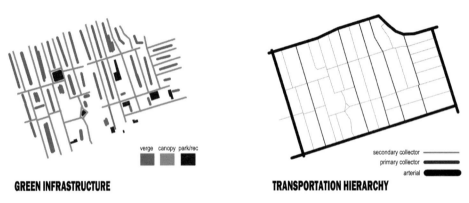

Figure 8.10: Green infrastructure and transportation hierarchy typological analysis

Courtesy of Zachary Verhulst

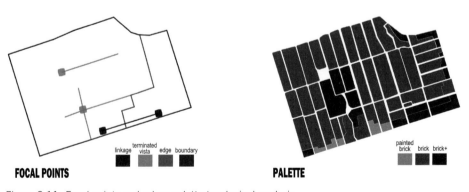

Figure 8.11: Focal points and urban palette typological analysis

Courtesy of Zachary Verhulst

relevant information to help the designer make decisions that are strongly defensible. Existing context or new conditions can be analysed for deficiencies or opportunities, then pattern-based information applied (Figure 8.12).

While the urban-level analysis is useful for providing rules to help shape the exterior of a building, it is at the building scale that patterns can be identified that can be used to organize a more detailed architectural design proposal. As in the

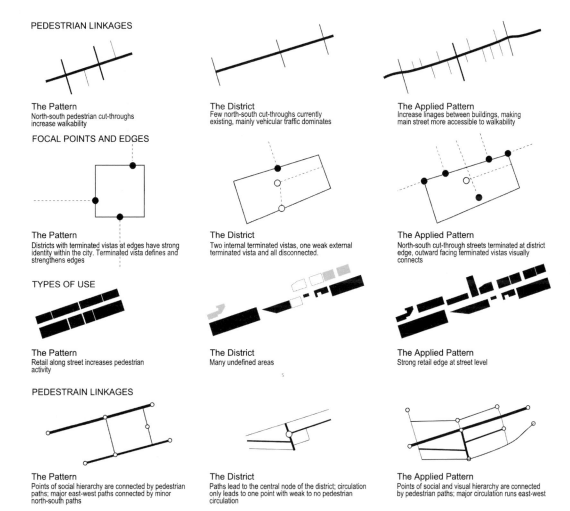

PEDESTRIAN LINKAGES

The Pattern
North-south pedestrian cut-throughs increase walkability

The District
Few north-south cut-throughs currently existing, mainly vehicular traffic dominates

The Applied Pattern
Increase linages between buildings, making main street more accessible to walkability

FOCAL POINTS AND EDGES

The Pattern
Districts with terminated vistas at edges have strong identity within the city. Terminated vista defines and strengthens edges

The District
Two internal terminated vistas, one weak external terminated vista and all disconnected.

The Applied Pattern
North-south cut-through streets terminated at district edge, outward facing terminated vistas visually connects

TYPES OF USE

The Pattern
Retail along street increases pedestrian activity

The District
Many undefined areas

The Applied Pattern
Strong retail edge at street level

PEDESTRAIN LINKAGES

The Pattern
Points of social hierarchy are connected by pedestrian paths; major east-west paths connected by minor north-south paths

The District
Paths lead to the central node of the district; circulation only leads to one point with weak to no pedestrian circulation

The Applied Pattern
Points of social and visual hierarchy are connected by pedestrian paths; major circulation runs east-west

Figure 8.12: Pattern identification and reapplication based on typological analysis

Courtesy of Rachel Kowalczyk

previous example, the elements used for analysis are based on architectural syntax and can be grouped into the categories of spatial configuration, building massing, structural organization, or surface qualities. Spatial configuration would identify patterns of circulation (entry points, points of control, volume of movement), public to private divisions (basic percentage breakdown, any recurring location and relationship to whole), and dominant plane of activity or identity for the building. Building massing and structural organizational systems would analyse for void spaces (courtyard, atrium, multi-storey opening), structural systems spanning and dimensions, and patterns in load transfer (columns, bearing walls, points and planes). Surface qualities would address patterns in how the building type mediates between inside and outside. This would include studies of dominant materiality, scale of façade (modular, panelized, tectonic, stereotomic), how light enters the building (direct, indirect, bounced, filtered, reflected), and how view operates. While these factors are a core part of any formal analysis of existing building projects, patterns can be considered typological if they can be reduced to a common denominator across several projects. This means that the identified pattern should manifest in the majority of buildings of that type, such as a school, a library, a hospital, or a theatre.

Using the example of a library, a well-known architectural type, four factors can be examined as an example of the case-study analysis. Movement through a piece of architecture is one of the major driving forces shaping its formal arrangement – how people *need* to move configures the space of architecture, or, to say it in a different way, architecture configures the space to support a characteristic of movement. Looking across exceptional examples of libraries,[29] similar patterns of movement are found in the analysis drawings. Each library presents a variation of the same pattern for public movement: a single entrance line, a control point, and a loop (Figure 8.13). While this is a very simplified version of how circulation works in a library, it does represent a reduced pattern which is typological.

In addition to circulation, patterns of massing within the building itself have a significant effect on architectural form. Massing shows the relationship of floors to each other, and includes floor to floor heights as well as significant void spaces in the building form. Comparing a representative sample of libraries, another repeated pattern of an interior void space, either courtyard or atrium, is found in a majority of them (Figure 8.14). While this space is sometimes used as an entrance volume, more often it is found deeper in the building. The void space operates in several ways, such as allowing light to enter a deep floor plate and to recognize the

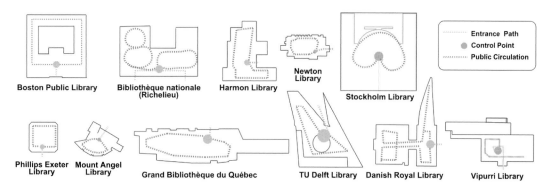

Figure 8.13: Library typological patterns of movement

Courtesy of Brendan Cagney

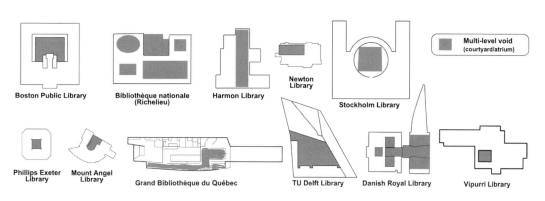

Figure 8.14: Library typological patterns of voids

Courtesy of Justine Pritchard

public forum areas of the library. At the moment, the purpose for the void can be ignored with only the need to identify its occurrence as a typological pattern.

While related to the void space, light is also a critical aspect of any building in its own right. Due to the nature of a library, and the type of content that is found within its volume, we find a regular pattern for how light is handled. There is an inherent conflict between the need to have a large amount of light enter the space for reading and study while requiring control of that light so the direct rays of the sun do not damage the books and reference material. Techniques and strategies for addressing light quality are found in case-study after case-study. In particular, the library typology shows a repeated pattern of encouraging large volumes of indirect natural light (Figure 8.15). How the light is modified varies greatly, but the basic reduction reveals that light is hardly ever allowed to enter the building without being modified by the building form in some way.

Studying the structural composition of the library type, the dominant mode of force transfer is found to be columns (Figure 8.16). The spacing of the columns is fairly consistent, being between 30 feet and 60 feet. It is significant that no structural patterns involving spans shorter than 30 feet or longer than 60 feet are present. There is an obvious relationship between span and void space: the former is necessary to allow the latter to exist. In the analysis diagrams, the voids are conspicuous as being an absence of structure.

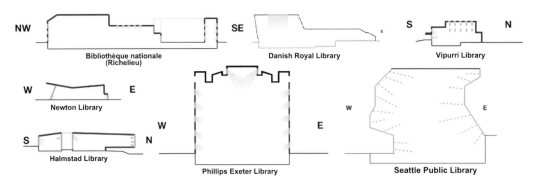

Figure 8.15: Library typological patterns of natural light

Courtesy of Lauren Hetzel

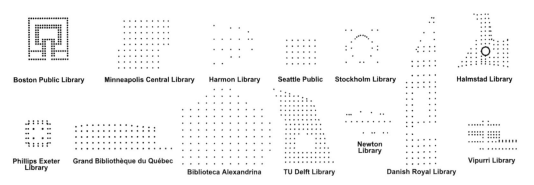

Figure 8.16: Library typological patterns of structure

Courtesy of Katherine Piasecki

So far, the building-scale patterns addressing architectural content of a library disclose typological content. There is a tendency to have large voids centred in the mass, large volumes of indirect or controlled light, and medium–span bay structure which allows for long-span moments supporting the void and light use. The layers of the analysis all have a relationship to each other, and this is the point of entry for architectural design. Structural systems reinforce lighting strategies which in turn support void spaces which then organize circulation logic. An example of how these typological patterns can be used for architectural design can be seen by looking at a classic piece of architecture, such as Louis Kahn's Phillips Exeter Library. The basis of using typology is synthesizing several patterns into a new arrangement which still meets the rules of the type.

The Exeter Library is based around a geometric square – something that comes from Kahn's framing position stressing primary geometrical shapes and proportions as priorities in architectural design. The centre core of the building is a square atrium, clear from the third floor to the roof. At the top of this atrium are two large and deep concrete beams running diagonally in the space (Figure 8.17). The beams are interesting in a couple of ways. The depth of the beams far exceeds their structural need; they produce a significant vertical surface. The orientation of the beams is also interesting as they are inefficiently arranged. The diagonal orientation makes the span much longer than necessary, as structurally it could be run across the shortest section. But the purpose of the beams is not structural. Additional roof structure can be seen above the large diagonal beams. Also visible is a separation between these beams and the roof structure – the roof span is not bearing on the diagonal beams. While the diagonal concrete beams might provide some lateral strength to building, they are really *expressing* structure rather than *being* structure. They reinforce the long span of the central void. More importantly, the deep vertical surface interrupts the direct light from the clerestory windows. This acts to address the rule for indirect light entry, as well as bouncing the light deeper into the central space. While working as a light baffle and a representation of structure, the beams address the void in two other ways. The two beams are set on perpendicular diagonals that meet at a central crossing point directly above the central point of the atrium. That crossing point also corresponds to the middle of the entire library volume, reinforcing Kahn's geometrical priorities. Illuminating the deep sides of the beams brings attention to the forms, visually reinforcing the centroid of the building through contrast. The beams are not simply beams, but meet the requirements of three of the typological rulesets based on void, light, and

Figure 8.17: Central atrium of Louis Kahn's Phillips Exeter Library

Photograph by Daderot/Wikimedia Commons

span. By doing so they present successful patterns of how libraries operate and introduce meaning of a formal nature.

Building-scale pattern synthesis (Example 1)

To this point, we have only been looking at the identification of patterns which are to be used in the pattern-based methodology. We can see that this was the first step in the generic process which identified reduction of a situation to a pattern (Figure 8.5), although the Exeter Library example gives a foreshadowing of the whole process. The first example uses the identified patterns of a building type to produce an explicit method from the generic framework. This method is based on reassembling those patterns in such a way that they produce a variation of the type group as an entire building. The focus will be on creating synthesis between the patterns, so one pattern reinforces another.

[SITUATION/TYPE] For this example, the theatre will be used as a type group. The method follows the same process as that extracted from Durand. First, if there isn't already a set of identified patterns, the rules that govern the formation of the type group will need to be generated – those things which make this particular use identifiable. A collection of as many examples of the type group as possible will be gathered to create a sample group (*exploratory thinking*). After there is a sample group, usually between sixteen and thirty case-studies, these can be analysed for their formal operation (*evaluative thinking*). Deciding on the analysis elements is important, but a standard design analysis process would follow the listed categories in the comparative case-study section above. This would explore public/private compositions in terms of circulation (Figure 8.18), occupation (Figure 8.19), floor plate articulation (Figure 8.20), massing, materiality, structure, lighting (Figure 8.21), and enclosure (Figure 8.22).

[ISOLATE PATTERNS] Just like the earlier example, the architectural designer needs to extract meaning from these diagrams. Meaning, in this case, is a recognized and legitimate pattern which represents a fundamental aspect of the building type. It is through comparing several case-study analyses which have been analysed individually that it becomes possible to begin to *isolate patterns which are typical*. As part of the analysis, one must ask how far the elements of the type need to be reduced for each criterion in order to identify their core informational values. It is this reduction which gives us the rulesets as patterns. Looking at the formal analysis in Figures 8.18 to 8.22, recurring patterns can start to be identified (Figure 8.23). The studies of public/private, light entry, and enclosure illustrate that there are two layers of building in the theatre type. The first layer is the exterior area with a thin edge condition, one that tends towards dematerialization in the public face of the building. This layer opens itself to natural light and can connect interior activity with the exterior of the city. The second layer is an internal heavy edge which controls all sound, light, and movement. A conceptual division between public and private divides the building in half and relates to how the building presents itself to the exterior surrounds (denoted by the dashed area in the outer circle). There is a strong

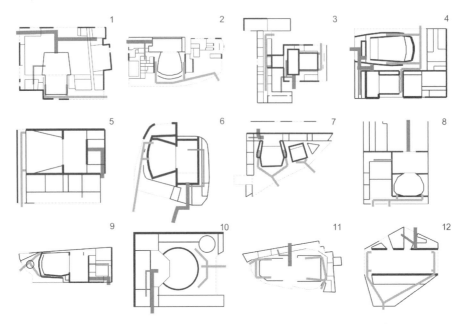

Figure 8.18: Exploration of patterns based on circulation using existing examples of the type group in the SITUATION/TYPE phase

Courtesy of Christopher Hess

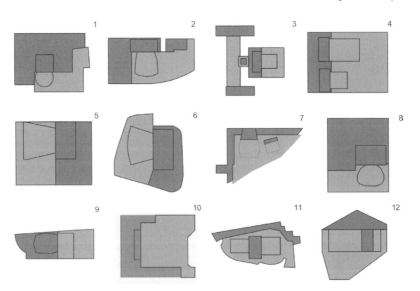

Figure 8.19: Exploration of public/private patterns based on occupancy in the SITUATION/TYPE phase

Courtesy of Christopher Hess

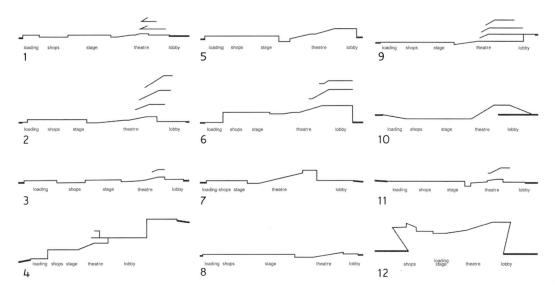

Figure 8.20: Exploration of dominant floor plate patterns in the SITUATION/TYPE phase

Courtesy of Christopher Hess

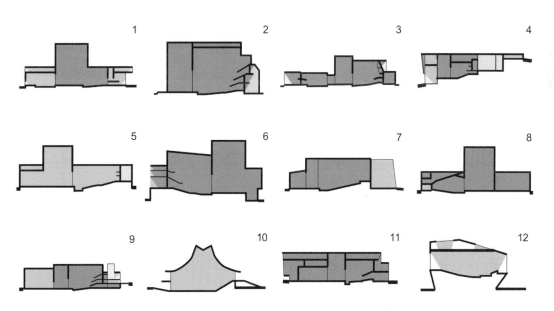

Figure 8.21: Exploration of light patterns of the type group in the SITUATION/TYPE phase

Courtesy of Christopher Hess

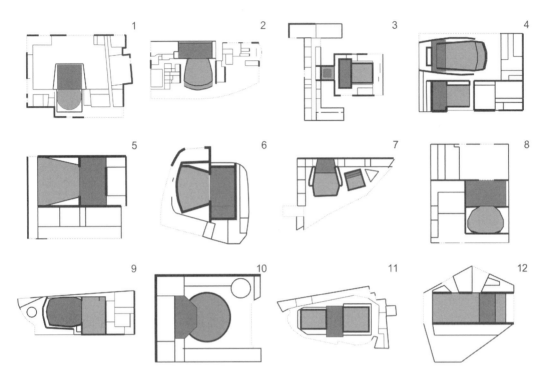

Figure 8.22: Exploration of enclosure patterns in the SITUATION/TYPE phase

Courtesy of Christopher Hess

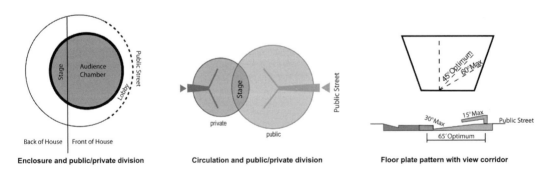

Figure 8.23: Diagrams of developed rulesets for relationships determined as ISOLATE PATTERNS

Courtesy of Joseph Adams

division between space that is public (front of house) and private (back of house) space, with the only overlap occurring at the stage location. The public/private separation is reinforced through the circulation patterns which separate the two types of movement. The stage is a critical threshold, occurring as an important point in all three of the summary diagrams. It is not only a factor in the public/private interface but the focus of view corridor. The relationship between the stage and the private areas of the building is echoed in the pattern of the floor plate section of the building. In addition to the public/private, enclosure, and major circulation patterns, there are rules for a necessary long-span structure and a column-free large volume space.

Isolating patterns by comparing case-studies does not give the designer either a building or a process, but the patterns do give *a set of relationships* among major elements. This can be used to pursue the building proposal in several ways. This example uses the patterns to arrange building-scale relationships, looking to synthesize several patterns into a stronger whole. The SITUATION/TYPE phase is not necessary if the rules of a type or a pattern are already accessible or have been identified by some other means.

[CONTEXT/ELEMENTS/PARTS] Once the process has developed a focus and extracted patterns for reapplication, it is possible to move on to the next phase of the method which compiles the elements to parts through both exploratory and evaluative processes. Exploratory thinking addresses each rule and begins to ask what variations are possible while still meeting the rule's intentions. Since all other aspects of the formal space except the focus of rulesets are suspended, this is a type of reduction. An area free of columns requiring long-span structure or a ground-to-building plane relationship which has a sectional quality might be needed. The exploratory thinking develops *clouds* of possibilities for each individual rule (Figure 8.24). Every possibility in the cloud represents one way of satisfying a rule. The possibility does not have to be expected, normative, or common *as long as the rule is addressed*. Possibilities come from the case-studies (normative) or from other applications of the principles which are not normal as a form of domain transfer. For example, while concrete and steel columns, joists, and beams might be the expected way to determine structural span in a theatre, the need for a large clear, column-free volume might lead the designer to examine the structure of other typologies, such as warehouses, aircraft hangars, or stadiums. This could introduce tensile structure, long-span arches, and other structures not considered normative for a theatre but still satisfying the rules.

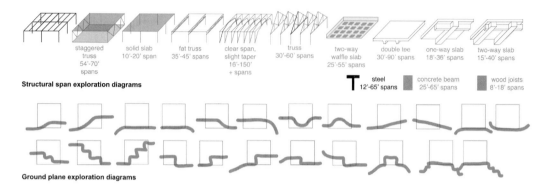

Structural span exploration diagrams

staggered truss 54'-70' spans · solid slab 10'-20' span · fat truss 35'-45' spans · clear span, slight taper 16'-150' + spans · truss 30'-60' spans · two-way waffle slab 25'-55' spans · double tee 30'-90' spans · one-way slab 18'-36' spans · two-way slab 15'-40' spans

steel 12'-65' spans · concrete beam 25'-65' spans · wood joists 8'-18' spans

Ground plane exploration diagrams

Figure 8.24: Diagrams of expansive clouds documenting patterns variations that satisfy the type rulesets in the CONTEXT/ELEMENTS/PARTS phase

Courtesy of Katherine Piasecki

The rules and expansive clouds provide the options for the designer to use as the engine of the design process. The diagrams can get more particular and detailed as long as the information stays focused on principles. The expansive cloud will start to consider compositional arrangements involving particular programme pieces and detailed configurations of space (Figure 8.25). The principles provide flexibility in the possibilities to engage other rules and context as a structure for decision-making in the evaluative process of the CONTEXT/ELEMENTS/PARTS phase. At the same time as the rules are being explored, the site and programme will also need to be analysed. Site and programme should be considered in terms of the analytical diagrams of formal patterns (Figure 8.23), which means investigating both to identify their own general priorities. This still isn't particular, but it will help to organize the design process in terms of framing and starting bias.

Once the designer has developed an expansive collection of options for each of the rules, it is time to introduce framing and starting bias. A pattern-based design method is interesting since the judgement criterion is embedded in the rules that have been identified. There is no need to test options against an external requirement, since the possibilities developed all meet the typological requirements (i.e. judgement is predetermined and contained by the patterns). It is still impossible, however, to make initial selections without introducing a bias. The bias makes it possible to choose a starting point. The earlier study of the programme, analysis of the site conditions, and identification of interesting aspects in the rules (maybe

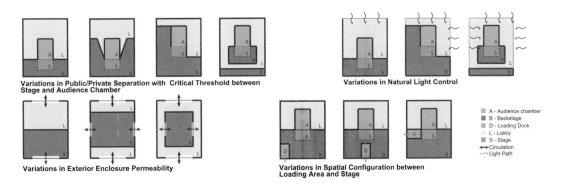

Variations in Public/Private Separation with Critical Threshold between
Stage and Audience Chamber

Variations in Natural Light Control

Variations in Exterior Enclosure Permeability

Variations in Spatial Configuration between
Loading Area and Stage

A - Audience chamber
B - Backstage
D - Loading Dock
L - Lobby
S - Stage
← Circulation
⌒ Light Path

Figure 8.25: Using evaluative thinking to combine several possibilities with strong associations from rule clouds in the CONTEXT/ELEMENTS/PARTS phase

Courtesy of Glenn Gualdoni

something was found that was surprising) can all be sources for the starting state of the design. The site might have a strong edge of public exposure, be an unusual shape, or have adjacencies that need to be considered. The programme should be understood for basic composition, public/private elements, interesting conflicts, volumes, and qualities of occupation. All of these should be examined to allow the designer to decide what interests them and what they think is important. The rules can be considered hierarchical, with one or two of the rules chosen as a starting position. The prioritization of the rules is determined by the designer – there is no natural order. Any might be chosen, be it the ground plane movements, patterns in circulation, void space, or light quality pattern – although often a situation will determine the relevance of that order. Usually it is best to select a companion to the primary focus as a way to help shape it – so circulation paths and ground planes or void spaces and public/private exposure – and then to consider them in context (site/programme). The source of these decisions might be called intuition but they really stem from the fact that the designer has spent enough time with the programme, site, and typological patterns to start to see priorities and opportunities.

The evaluative process of the CONTEXT/ELEMENTS/PARTS phase begins to arrange patterns in relation to each other. This is an iterative process which loops many times between starting priorities and the expansive clouds of patterns, selecting options from the various possibilities, looking in other clouds for support elements, and then arranging variations in context. Selection is always tentative until moving into the ASSEMBLY phase and proposing an assembled project.

Selection is based on how the various patterns satisfying the rules integrate with each other and how they respond to particular programme, site, or resident possibilities. SELECT ALTERNATIVES implies that a commitment needs to be made. Since we know that any of the alternatives will work well because they all satisfy the type rules, the commitment is a case of finding the potential *between* the various elements. We are looking for ways that one formal typological pattern reinforces another almost as a bonus or an afterthought. This is what we mean by *synthesis*.

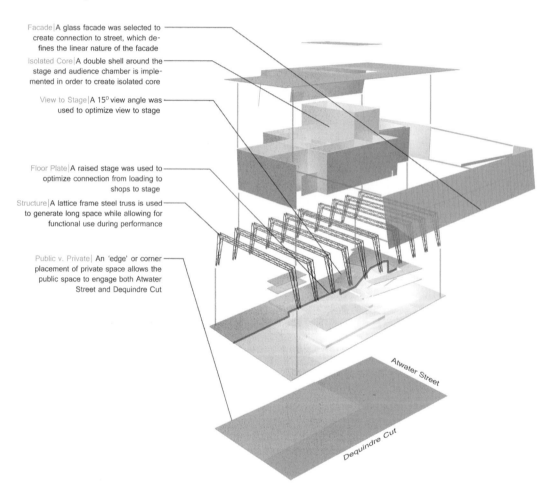

Facade|A glass facade was selected to create connection to street, which defines the linear nature of the facade

Isolated Core|A double shell around the stage and audience chamber is implemented in order to create isolated core

View to Stage|A 15⁰ view angle was used to optimize view to stage

Floor Plate|A raised stage was used to optimize connection from loading to shops to stage

Structure|A lattice frame steel truss is used to generate long space while allowing for functional use during performance

Public v. Private| An 'edge' or corner placement of private space allows the public space to engage both Atwater Street and Dequindre Cut

Atwater Street

Dequindre Cut

Figure 8.26: Final architectural assembly proposed based on typological rulesets

Courtesy of Christopher Hess

The proposal for the theatre in this example (Figure 8.26) is basic but illustrates the process. This is one of many proposals that could have been presented from the same rules, same site, same programme, and same expansive clouds. It is the framing and starting bias that affects the organization and selects one pattern over another. In this example, the bias stressed the public face and the public/private location. The tectonic structural system is visually light, reinforcing the intention of the glass façade to open the theatre up publicly. Public space is maximized on the south and east sides, as these are the major streets and expose the theatre. The private box is pushed back into the north–west corner. There is a playfulness between structure, public and private divisions, ground plane manipulation, and other rule categories as a typological response to the idea of theatre.

Module-scale pattern repetition (Example 2)

The second example uses the same underlying process, moving from reduction (SITUATION/TYPE) to deployment (CONTEXT/ELEMENTS/PARTS) and then repetition (ASSEMBLY/PROPOSAL), using exploratory and evaluative thinking styles. However, this example focuses on developing a module for repetition in order to form a building, rather than applying patterns at a full building scale. The building type is the warehouse as it allows the ability to ignore specific programme at the moment.

[CONTEXT/ELEMENTS/PARTS] There are no explicit case-study analyses or formal comparisons in this example as there was starting content accessible which fulfils the need for SITUATION/TYPE and ISOLATE PATTERNS. Due to preloading the process with starting information, the project starts at the CONTEXT/ELEMENTS/PARTS phase. If this were not the case, then another way to isolate patterns in a building type would be employed, such as using reduction through questioning. The designer can ask: what is necessary to make the building type recognizable, and how much can be removed before the typology is broken? This leads to a series of questions as a divergent process, removing parts of the building, or challenging composition until arriving at a list of principles. For the warehouse, it must be considered that it embodies the idea of horizontality, with no limits to how far the footprint might expand. The structural system is repetitive and built out of few components – reflecting the importance of cost considerations. There is a tendency towards large bays and limited columns, which creates an interior platform or stage for maximum flexibility. A modern warehouse tends to be single storey, another influence of land versus building costs. The floor plate is contiguous but a five-foot variation in section is needed to allow for shipping and unloading. The envelope, when the building does end, is based on a panellized system allowing multiple points of entry for large objects. Finally, since the primary transportation method to arrive at the building type is vehicular and the location is non-urban, the building typology exists in a field of asphalt that provides parking, storage, and delivery. If all other factors are eliminated to focus on the principles of the building type, it is these that influence the spatial configuration and formal compositions.

Starting from this point, rule-based exploratory clouds can be developed, looking at the various aspects of the building type from structure to daylighting, ground plane, and bay configuration (Figures 8.27–8.30). Context is ignored at the moment as it has little influence on the warehouse typology. The more important factor is the composition of the bay module of the warehouse. All aspects of the patterns are found within each module, from light entry to structural composition. The roof system dominates and with a single level pattern of occupation, there is an opportunity to consider natural light entry as a driving force. The exterior walls do not affect the bays directly, they are to be as flexible as possible, and they denote building termination. Since there is a pattern of repetition inherent in the bay structure of the warehouse, we can reduce the project further to look only at a bay and its variations. Once the bay is determined, the bay structure can be repeated with variations to make the whole building.

The design process is the same as in the previous example, but the rulesets and patterns are different. While there is different content, the underlying framework remains consistent. The analytical categories still focus on spatial configuration, structural systems, and surface articulation. As in the previous example, the focus is on opportunities to reassemble typological patterns in such a way that they address the compositional nature of the space while synthesizing into new variations of the type.

[ASSEMBLY/PROPOSAL] Moving to the exploratory thinking during the ASSEMBLY/PROPOSAL stage, the level of detail is different from the previous example (Figure 8.31). Instead of diagrams, there is the beginning of an architectural proposal. The proposal is still very schematic, probing possibilities as it might be necessary to abandon a line of enquiry depending on other choices that are made as part of the design process. The enclosure proposal addresses the outer surface of the warehouse. The enclosure rule dictated the need for a repeatable,

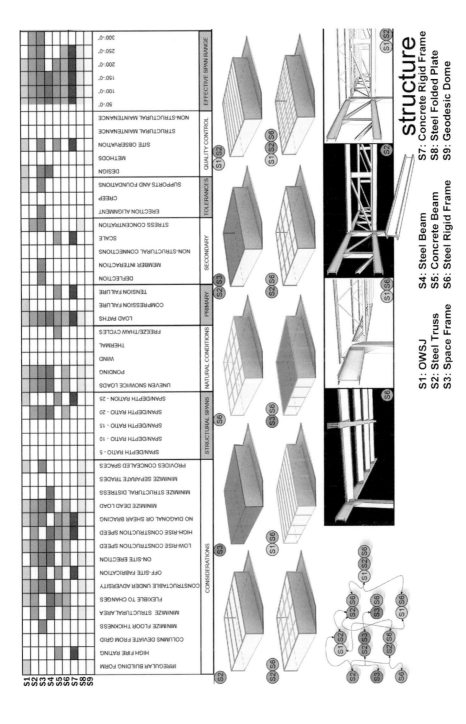

Figure 8.27: Exploratory diagrams of rule clouds looking at structural configuration in the CONTEXT/ELEMENTS/PARTS phase

Courtesy of Jason Campigotto, Jonathon Krumpe, Chris Telfer, Steve Cooper, Blake Chamberlain, Lily Diego, and Rushiraj Brahmbhatt

169

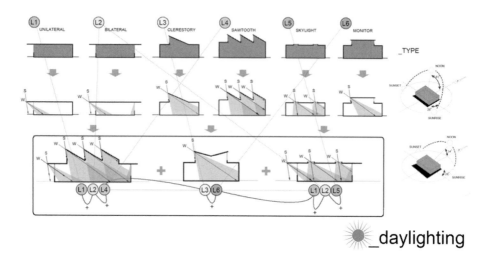

Figure 8.28: Exploratory diagrams of rule clouds looking at lighting configurations in the CONTEXT/ ELEMENTS/PARTS phase

Courtesy of Jason Campigotto *et al.*

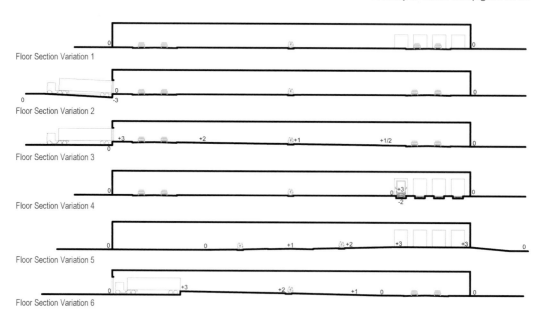

Figure 8.29: Exploratory diagrams of rule clouds looking at variations in floor slab section in the CONTEXT/ELEMENTS/PARTS phase

Courtesy of Brian Eady, Mike Gee, Kathleen Lilienthal, Ellen Rotter, Jennifer Breault, Priya Iyer, and Pierre Robertson

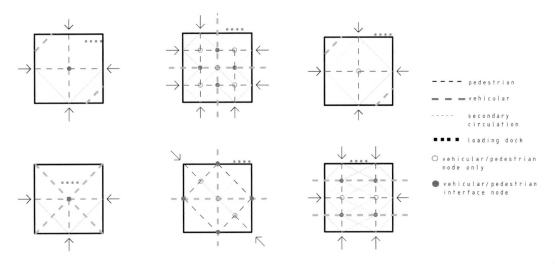

Figure 8.30: Exploratory diagrams of rule clouds looking at patterns in bay configuration in the CONTEXT/ELEMENTS/PARTS phase

Courtesy of Brian Eady *et al.*

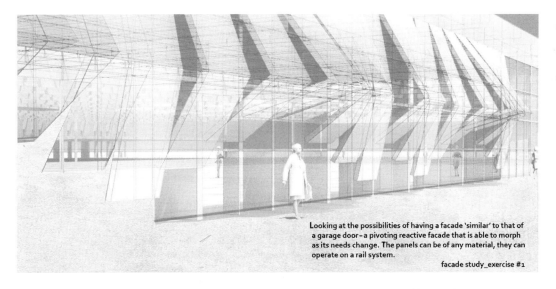

Looking at the possibilities of having a facade 'similar' to that of a garage door – a pivoting reactive facade that is able to morph as its needs change. The panels can be of any material, they can operate on a rail system.

facade study_exercise #1

Figure 8.31: Perspective rendering of an architectural study exploring enclosure possibilities while still satisfying rulesets in the ASSEMBLY/PROPOSAL phase

Courtesy of Jason Campigotto *et al.*

modular system but also a system able to provide passage apertures at various locations around the perimeter. This also addressed the flexibility of the slab rule and touched on the bay system flexibility rule. While the bi-fold garage door is not normative for a warehouse, the principle of a flexible, modular panel satisfies the rule.

In these examples, the structural system was explored in order to provide the secondary benefit of natural lighting as an integrated aspect, synthesizing these two elements. The structure and the opportunity for natural light should naturally support each other. The bay dimensions would be identified as allowing maximum flexibility for ground use, but not so large as to increase stress and cost of the structure. Parking options were explored to see if the normative sea of asphalt could become an extension of the standard bay system, while the floor slab was manipulated to integrate the loading dock and sectional change into the building. Finally, choices of enclosure supported variations that included large openings, smaller circulation paths, and climate/security protection. The decision-making process was not based on cultural values, nor was there any need to test against

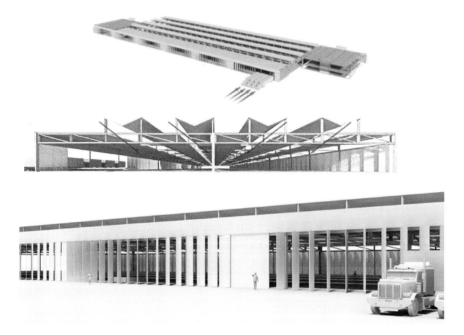

Figure 8.32: Final architectural proposal based on selected pattern variations

Courtesy of Jason Campigotto *et al.*

judgement criteria. Using patterns and rules as the organizing information for the design process assured that the result matched needs. The decision-making that did occur was driven by arranging the relationship between the various elements so that one rule would be reinforced by another and so on. This allows the design to be responsive to existing patterns of use while still addressing refinement, efficiency, and innovation. Depending on priorities and the identified opportunities in the exploratory clouds, many proposals can be found to be successful while still varying greatly.

Typological transfer (Example 3)

If we consider that typological patterns contain repeatable relationships at the level of formal principles, then it is possible to blend and scale typological patterns *if the same relationships are needed in a different situation.* This is an advanced technique which can be used to produce innovative design proposals. As in the previous examples, the success of the proposal is based on mapping and repeating found patterns back into a situation where those patterns have relevance. The underlying framework is the same as has been used for the past two examples – moving from reduction (SITUATION/TYPE) to deployment (CONTEXT/ELEMENTS/PARTS) and then repetition (ASSEMBLY/PROPOSAL). The framing, bias, and content are quite different, however. Framing, in this case, would still support a pattern-based approach but the designer would look for patterns based on qualities or principles of use rather than studying known types. They would also ignore scale if a strong example of a spatial configuration is found.

A clear example of transferring typological patterns can be found in the Villa DVDP project by the Organization and Research Group for Permanent Modernity (ORG). ORG is a European/North American architectural and urban design practice founded by Alexander D'Hooghe, Raf De Preter, Luk Peeters, and Natalie Seys. The practice and the associated MIT research centre focus on typology as a driving force in design methods. In the Villa DVDP project, typology is employed as a form of urban-to-architectural pattern transfer. Instead of mapping principles of pre-existing spatial configuration of family residence to form a variation of the same type (residence to residence), the designers used typological patterns as a way to transfer principles of use from one type to another (urban centre to residence). Since the transfer involves a shift from the urban to the architectural, there is also a mapping between scales.

[SITUATION/TYPE] This example shows that it is possible to isolate patterns from something other than case-study. In addition, it highlights that experienced designers rarely go through the exhaustive exercises of a formal comparative case-study analysis. Instead, they pull from their experience and observations of past conditions, building up a nuanced understanding of the environment. In the first phase of this example, Seys and D'Hooghe identify patterns by engaging their knowledge of urban composition combined with the desire of their client. The Villa DVDP, completed in 2006, is located in a suburb of Leuven, Belgium. For the client, the new home contained the loss of the 'pleasures of urban life',[30] a moment of being in the city that they felt they would miss in their move to the suburb. The dialogue about the city, the desires of the client, their sense of nostalgia, and the self-referentiality of the new site developed the starting bias for the project. The bias would question how the city could be part of the residence, while the framing would require the response to be typological based on qualities of use. At the end of the exploratory aspect of the SITUATION/TYPE phase, four spaces were identified (Figure 8.33). These four spaces – a square, an intersection, a public building, and a shopping street – were selected after the clients identified parts of Leuven that they liked as well as spaces 'that, together, are representative instances of Leuven's public space apparatus'.[31] The evaluative thinking aspect of the first phase needed to reduce the identified spaces into patterns.

There are several factors in this process that are different to the earlier examples. Since the spaces of the city were chosen with a degree of subjectivity, there was the need to determine what was relevant about those spaces when looking at them in the context of a typological transfer. The identification allowed the transfer and reapplication to maintain both intention and meaning in the new application. The original intention was to create a house based on the idea that a 'villa is an analogy to the city, an abstract and idealized representation of it'.[32] This meant the spaces of the city needed to be relevant to the spaces of the house. Once relevance of meaning was determined, the spaces needed to isolate formal patterns based on spatial configuration, massing, structural systems, or surface articulation. Both the factors of meaning and patterns can be determined by reduction.

[ISOLATE PATTERNS] When considering the urban spaces, the questions become: what is at the heart of their use, how do they work, and what do they address? The responses should be as simple as possible, smoothing out any nuances to give a generic answer. This is akin to the comparative case-study, but looking at the meaning of a space through its composition. In the case of the four selected

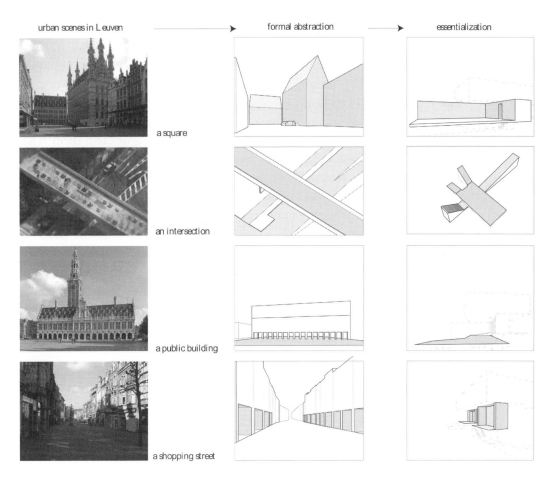

urban scenes in Leuven → formal abstraction → essentialization

a square

an intersection

a public building

a shopping street

Figure 8.33: Diagrams of developed rulesets for Villa DVDP as part of the ISOLATE PATTERNS phase

Courtesy of the ORG (Organization and Research Group for Permanent Modernity);
Alexander D'Hooghe, Luk Peeters, and Natalie Seys

urban scenes, there are clearly definable operations. The square is defined by its edges and is a void for entry into a city heart. The intersection is rich in circulation, implying a complex weave of several scales and speeds of movement. The public building sets up a forecourt, a foreshadowing of monumental façade, and a place for gathering. The shopping street operates as containers projecting outwards into the street, reinforcing issues of visibility, exposure, and display. Each of these descriptions is a reduction, through which the original urban scenes have been disconnected from their scale. Entry, circulation, gathering, and projection are all architectural issues that can be addressed at various scales. This reduction allowed Seys and D'Hooghe to map urban concerns to architectural concerns in order to address meaning in their design.

The second type of reduction is formal in nature and develops the patterns which will be applied as the typological response. This process concludes in ISOLATE PATTERNS just as in the previous two examples. In Figure 8.33, the reduction is labelled 'urban scenes → formal abstraction → essentialization'. Essentialization, in this case, refers to the underlying patterns which compose the typology. The pattern isolation is done by reduction as a process of questioning, or what D'Hooghe calls 'sawing the feet inch by inch off the table to check when it stopped being a table'.[33] The city square, the intersection, the public building, and the shopping street were all questioned: what would their minimum formal expression be before they stopped being what they were (their essence)? In the case of the square, it took a plane with two walls to create its identity. Since the corner is critical to the understanding of a square as a containment of space, one

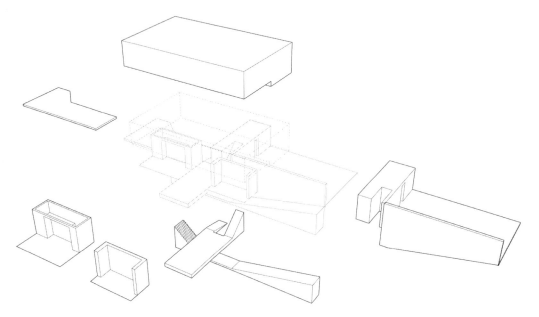

Figure 8.34: Diagram of the final selected typological objects arranged in formal relationship as conclusion to the CONTEXT/ELEMENTS/PARTS phase

Courtesy of the ORG; Alexander D'Hooghe, Luk Peeters, and Natalie Seys

wall and a plane would break the pattern. Three walls were redundant as only one corner needs to be defined. The same reductive process was performed for each of the urban scenes, identifying the typological patterns which would be used in the design phase.

[CONTEXT/ELEMENTS/PARTS] As in the previous examples, the phase assembling the elements and parts is the core of the physical arrangement of the design. The exploratory thinking aspect of the phase examined the principles of the patterns (entry, circulation, gathering, and projection) and reduced the urban patterns for possible architectural objects. Figure 8.34 presents the end

Figure 8.35: City square as residence entrance in built architectural proposal of Villa DVDP

Courtesy of the ORG; Alexander D'Hooghe, Luk Peeters, and Natalie Seys

result of this exploration, with formal compositions selected for each of the four typologies. However, while there might be a single proposal now, there were many variations of each of the final pieces explored before their final forms were chosen. The exploration would have included not only the composition of the piece itself but also the way it would relate to the rest of the context. It was a case of reassembling the reduced urban patterns into a meaningful relationship in this new residential context. The entrance to the residence used the typology patterns held by the city square as they share social relationships needing to define edge, corner, and entry (Figure 8.35). The intersection mapped to the internal circulation of the residence, and leveraged a rich multi-level flow which

Figure 8.36: Shopping street as residential office and kitchen in built architectural proposal of Villa DVDP

Courtesy of the ORG; Alexander D'Hooghe, Luk Peeters, and Natalie Seys

mimicked the richness of the city section. The patterns of the public building were applied to the exterior activity area, which defined a forecourt to the residence and supported gathering. The office and kitchen spaces took on the formal qualities of the shopping street (Figure 8.36). Both of these spaces were turned outwards, addressing the exterior and projecting beyond the enclosure of the residence as display. In each case, the typological mapping allowed a transfer between compositional patterns at the urban level to be used as the driving force of the architectural composition. This was because the patterns addressed the same principles of use and occupation.

[ASSEMBLY/PROPOSAL] The final phase of the method finalized the relationships among the building parts, refining their associations and integrating them into the site (Figure 8.37). The major variations between elements and parts had occurred in the previous phase; this point would be a final adjustment and arrangement. The judgement criterion is not active as a separate aspect of this method, as it is held in the typological patterns. For example, there is no need to test whether the square works, as the reduction provided this information and embedded it into the formal composition. As a built example of a pattern-based method, the ORG typological studies illustrate how flexible the design process can be while still adhering to a persistent underlying framework.

Bounded thinking

The pattern-based methodology can be seen not as a prescriptive process but as a bounded process. The boundaries are created by initial framing, bias, and values. The framing is the acceptance that spatial configuration and composition hold critical information which will produce relevant and significant design proposals. Bias and values allow the prioritization of rule categories and the starting point of architectural design synthesis. While Durand focused on fitness and economy as bias categories, others have focused on urban to architectural relationships, natural light, massing as cultural identity, or circulation and programme. As the examples illustrate, there is flexibility in content while the underlying framework remains consistent. If information extracted from case-studies and pre-existing use patterns is not culturally acceptable to the architectural designer as a starting point in the design process, or if there is an inability to disconnect representational values from relational values, then any methods developed from the pattern–based framework will not be considered valid by those designers.

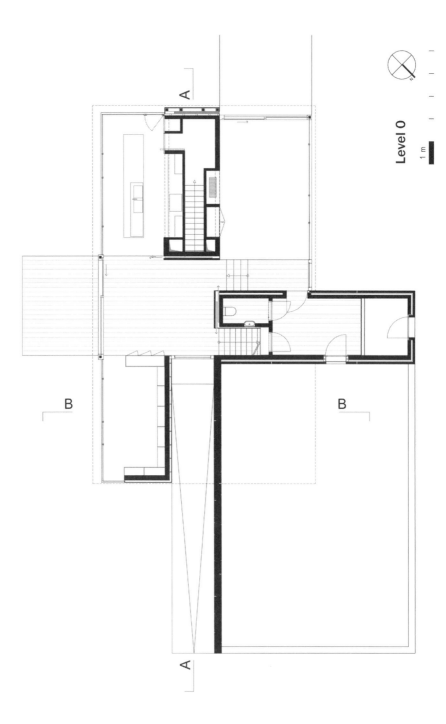

Level 0

1 m

Figure 8.37: Final ASSEMBLY/PROPOSAL plan for the architectural response using typological transfer from urban content

Courtesy of the ORG; Alexander D'Hooghe, Luk Peeters, and Natalie Seys

Typology is not used frequently today as an explicit method. Our current value system and primary biases tend to distrust repeating spatial patterns which are seen as 'historical'. The construction techniques and materiality of building have broadened and efficiency means something different today than it did in nineteenth-century France. Durand's patterns, the rulesets, are not as valid, either. Twenty-first-century Western culture rituals of spatial use have drifted away from those of 200 years ago – there are new patterns of use based on different social conventions. These include social organization, family structures, changes in understanding of privacy, and shifts in how security is considered. Some things are the same, however. Any direct engagement of space with a single human body will not have changed much, as physiologically there has arguably been little change in human hardware or software over the last 300, or even the last 3000, years.

Patterns and typology as an overarching method has been replaced as a priority by other concerns – mostly novelty and technological determinism. The content of these concerns is supported more strongly through *concept-based* or *force-based* methods rather than through *pattern-based* methods. This does not mean that patterns are not valid or not currently in use, just that they are not a dominant methodology. Many architects will recognize the process of analysing programme, laying down grids, arranging structure, and associating programme spaces. The pattern-based techniques are used in other methodologies whenever case-studies or precedences are engaged. However, what makes a pattern-based method is allowing the rulesets, containing known arrangements of space, to dominate composition and proposal resolution.

Notes

1 Quatremère de Quincy, M. Antoine-Chrysostome, *The True, the Fictive, and the Real: The Historical Dictionary of Architecture of Quatremère de Quincy*. Translated by Younés, Samir. London: Andreas Papadakis, 1999: 255.

2 Hanlon, Don, *Compositions in Architecture*. Hoboken, NJ: John Wiley & Sons, 2009: 3.

3 LaVine, Lance, *Constructing Ideas: Understanding Architecture*. Dubuque, IA: Kendall/Hunt Publishing Company, 2008: 36.

4 Eisenman, Peter, *Diagram Diaries*. New York: Universe Publishing, 1999: 27.

5 See siting of a city (1:4), patterns for healthy streets (1:6), locations for public buildings (1:7), spatial layouts for temples (3:1–2), patterns in column placement

(3:3), farm houses (4:6), and house design (4:7). Vitruvius Pollio, Marcus, M. H. Morgan, and Herbert Langford Warren, *Vitruvius, the Ten Books on Architecture*. Cambridge, MA: Harvard University Press, 1914.

6 Vitruvius Pollio, Marcus and Frank Stephen Granger, *Vitruvius, on Architecture*. The Loeb Classical Library. Cambridge, MA: Harvard University Press, 1962: Book 4, Chapter 6: 1, 183.

7 Ibid.

8 Alexander, Christopher, *The Timeless Way of Building*. New York: Oxford University Press, 1979: 417.

9 Argan, Giulio Carlo, 'On the Typology of Architecture.' In *Theorizing a New Agenda for Architecture: An Anthology of Architectural Theory 1965–1995*, edited by Nesbitt, Kate. New York: Princeton Architectural Press, 1996 [1963]: 242–246, at 243.

10 Moneo, Rafael, 'On Typology.' *Oppositions* 13 (1978): 23.

11 Etlin, Richard A., *Symbolic Space: French Enlightenment Architecture and its Legacy*. Chicago: University of Chicago Press, 1996: 129–130.

12 Durand, Jean-Nicolas-Louis, *Partie Graphique des Cours d'Architecture Faits à l'Ecole Royale Polytechnique Depuis sa Réorganisation* [*Précis of the Lectures on Architecture; with Graphic Portion of the Lectures on Architecture. Texts & Documents*]. Los Angeles, CA: Getty Research Institute, 2000: 133.

13 Ibid.: 173.

14 The basis of the analytical method is found in the understanding of the operations in the human mind. This is addressed by John Locke in *An Essay Concerning Human Understanding* and Condillac in *Essai sur l'origine des connaissances humaines* [*Essay on the Origins of Human Knowledge*] and *Cours d'études*.

15 Durand, Jean-Nicolas-Louis, *Partie Graphique des Cours d'Architecture Faits à l'Ecole Royale Polytechnique Depuis sa Réorganisation* [*Précis of the Lectures on Architecture; with Graphic Portion of the Lectures on Architecture. Texts & Documents*]. Los Angeles, CA: Getty Research Institute, 2000: 78.

16 Ibid.: 122–125.

17 Ibid.: 119–125.

18 Ibid.: 119–127.

19 Ibid.: 122.

20 Alexander, Christopher, *The Timeless Way of Building*. New York: Oxford University Press, 1979: 267.

21 Boffrand, Gabriel-Germain, 'Book of Architecture.' In *The Emergence of Modern*

Architecture: A Documentary History from 1000 to 1810, edited by Lefaivre, Liane and Alexander Tzonis. New York: Routledge, 2004 [1745]: 316–317.

22 Durand, Jean-Nicolas-Louis, *Partie Graphique des Cours d'Architecture Faits à l'Ecole Royale Polytechnique Depuis sa Réorganisation* [*Précis of the Lectures on Architecture; with Graphic Portion of the Lectures on Architecture. Texts & Documents*]. Los Angeles, CA: Getty Research Institute, 2000: 180–181.

23 Cret, Paul P., 'The Ecole des Beaux-Arts and Architectural Education.' *Journal of the American Society of Architectural Historians* 1, no. 2 (1941): 3–15, at 14.

24 For further reading on type and typology in architectural design, see the classic articles and books: Argan, Giulio Carlo, 'On the Typology of Architecture.' In *Theorizing a New Agenda for Architecture: An Anthology of Architectural Theory 1965–1995*, edited by Nesbitt, Kate. New York: Princeton Architectural Press, 1996 [1963]: 242; Colquhoun, Alan, 'Typology and Design Method.' *Perspecta* 12 (1969): 71–74; Moneo, Rafael, 'On Typology.' *Oppositions* 13 (1978): 23–45; Rossi, Aldo, *The Architecture of the City*. Translated by Ghirardo, Diane and Joan Ockman. Cambridge, MA: The MIT Press, 1984; and Vidler, Anthony, 'The Third Typology.' *Oppositions* 7 (Winter 1977): 1–4.

25 For further reading on typomorphology, see the following: Baird, George, 'Studies on Urban Morphology in North America.' *Morphologie Urbaine et Parcellaire*, edited by Merlin, Pierre. Saint-Denis: Presses Universitaires de Vincennes, 1988: 139–143; Conzen, Michael R. G., *Alnwick, Northumberland: A Study in Town-Plan Analysis*. London: Institute of British Geographers, 1960; Moudon, Anne Vernez, *Built for Change: Neighborhood Architecture in San Francisco*. Cambridge, MA: The MIT Press, 1986; Muratori, Saverio, *Studi per una Operante Storja Urbana di Venezia*. Rome: Istituto Poligraphico dello Stato, 1959.

26 Rossi, Aldo, *The Architecture of the City*. Translated by Ghirardo, Diane and Joan Ockman. Cambridge, MA: The MIT Press, 1984: 41.

27 This does not mean the books are not useful, just that composition is not approached through the repetition of typology. I would consider the following books useful for any architecture student and they should be present in the library of any architect: Unwin, Simon, *Analysing Architecture*. 3rd edn. New York: Routledge, 2009; Curtis, Nathaniel Cortland, *The Secrets of Architectural Composition*. New York: Dover Publications, 2011; Hanlon, Don, *Compositions in Architecture*. Hoboken, NJ: John Wiley & Sons, 2009; and Ching, Francis D. K., *Architecture: Form, Space, and Order*. Hoboken, NJ: John Wiley & Sons, 2007.

28 Krier, Léon, *The Architecture of Community*. Edited by Thadani, Dhiru A. and Peter J. Hetzel. Washington, DC: Island Press, 2009: 160.

29 The libraries used for the case-study analysis included: Beinecke Rare Book and Manuscript Library, by Gordon Bunshaft; Biblioteca Parque España, by Giancarlo Mazzanti; Bibliotheca Alexandrina, by Snøhetta; Bibliothèque Nationale, by Henri Labrouste; Boston Public Library, by McKim, Mead, and White; Central Library of the Atlanta-Fulton Public Library System, by Marcel Breuer; Danish Royal Library, by Schmidt Hammer Lassen; DOK Library Concept Center, by Dok architecten with Aequo BV; Exeter Library, by Louis I. Kahn; Grand Library of Québec, by Patkau Architects with Croft Pelletier and Menkès Shooner Dagenais architectes associés; Halmstad Library, by Schmidt Hammer Lassen; Harmon Library, by richärd + bauer; Hennepin County Library, by César Pelli; José Vasconcelos Library, by Alberto Kalach; Library of Picture Books, by Tadao Ando; Mount Angel Library, by Alvar Aalto; Newton Branch Library, by Patkau Architects; Salt Lake City Public Library, by Moshe Safdie and Associates; Seattle Public Library, by Rem Koolhaas; Seinajoki Library, by Alvar Aalto; Stockholm Library, by Erik Gunnar Asplund; TU Delft Library, by Mecanoo architecture bureau; UCSD Geisel Library, by William L. Pereira.

30 D'Hooghe, Alexander, Raf De Preter, Luk Peeters, and Natalie Seys, *ORG Architects and Urban Designers, Office for Permanent Modernity: Selected Work*. Boston, MA: Office for Permanent Modernity, 2009: 15.

31 Alexander D'Hooghe, personal conversation with the author, 24 September 2012.

32 D'Hooghe, Alexander, Raf De Preter, Luk Peeters, and Natalie Seys. *ORG Architects and Urban Designers, Office for Permanent Modernity: Selected Work*. Boston, MA: Office for Permanent Modernity, 2009: 12. The idea of the villa as a mapping of a city can be traced back to a famous quote by Leon Battista Alberti. In *On the Art of Building in Ten Books*, Alberti used an analogy to consider a city as a large house and a house as if it were a small city.

33 Alexander D'Hooghe, personal conversation with the author, 24 September 2012.

Chapter Nine

Forces

Does the creation of design admit constraint? Design depends largely on constraints. **What constraints?** The sum of all constraints. Here is one of the few effective keys to the design problem – the ability of the designer to recognize as many of the constraints as possible – his willingness and enthusiasm for working within these constraints – the constraints of price, of size, of strength, balance, of surface, of time, etc.; each problem has its own peculiar list. **Does design obey laws?** Aren't constraints enough?

Charles Eames[1]

What is a force? Simply stated, a force is a non-formal factor that can be used to make decisions that define form. Instead of applying patterns to drive a proposal, the architectural designer uses non-physical forces such as qualities, desires, requirements, restrictions, or principles. These are translated into constraints, assets, flows, pressures, and opportunities, then used to develop meaning and purpose (intention) in the design proposal. The architectural composition responds to the pressures of the identified forces, which shape its formal structure by matching a form to a force. Forces can operate at any scale from the geographic to the building component.

Thinking about architectural design in terms of forces introduces different priorities to methods based on patterns and types. Ultimately, though, it addresses the same concerns – how to produce an architectural design proposal that has relevance and meaning in its context. Pattern-based approaches do not directly engage spatial qualities. They allow those qualities to be embedded in composition, and by repeating the composition, the spatial and use qualities should also be repeated. In contrast to this, force approaches see architectural design as the direct resolution of formal, environmental, and social qualities. The key to force-based methods is the 'search for the qualities in all things',[2] rather than the pattern, shape, or object.

Approaching design in terms of qualities and relationships between forces can be seen as far back in architectural theory as the Renaissance architect Leon Battista Alberti (1404–1472). In his classic text, De re aedificatoria, or *On the Art of Building*, Alberti detailed the future arrangement and construction of buildings. The building was connected to the idea of a body as an analogy, and the building design process consisted of *lineamenta*, the product of thought and reason, and *materia*, the product of nature, preparation, and selection. It is the idea of lineaments which is of interest to us, as this is the point of entry for forces to affect building. *Lineamenta*, or lineaments, derive from the mind and can be translated as design, drawings, forms, or measured outlines.[3] Alberti considered the 'whole matter of building is composed of lineaments and structure',[4] independent of materiality.

The contrast of Alberti to Vitruvius can be found in the focus on arranging lineaments to shape architecture. Where Vitruvius stressed patterns, rules-of-thumb, and past arrangements as the source of decisions to be made in architectural design, Alberti looked to qualities, attributes, environmental and social factors within a context. For Alberti, 'individual parts should be well suited to the task for which they were designed'.[5] The individual parts were formed by lineaments, which then provided the mode of translation from qualities to form. While Vitruvius was also concerned with the right and healthy way to build, Alberti was supporting a type of performative design based on experiential qualities. Contemporary architectural design culture would consider this to be *function-driven* design. The term *function* should be understood in its expansive definition, rather than one limited to matching the building use (programme) to its formal composition. Louis Sullivan considered forces as an expansive and varied term when he wrote 'behind every form we see there is a vital something or other that we do not see, yet makes itself visible to us in that very form. In other words, in a state of nature the form exists *because* of the function.'[6] For Sullivan, forces were organic and function related to purpose. Ornamentation could be purposeful if it related to the occupation and expression of the building. However, through Modernism's machine framing analogy, the idea of function took on representational meaning, for example a building being stripped of anything unnecessary.[7] The question this posed was what *necessary* means; for Modernists, it is most often defined by programme and economy rather than cultural or social need. Alberti was using the idea of being *well suited to the task* in a broader way.

An example of design choices being affected by forces can be seen by examining a few of Alberti's comments about sunlight. Vitruvius recognized the importance of light, but he treated it as a general rule to be dealt with by a simple test. A comment about light is found briefly in Chapter 6 of Book 6 on the Greek house, where Vitruvius addressed light 'as a general rule, we must arrange so as to leave places for windows on all sides on which a clear view of the sky can be had, for this will make our buildings light'.[8] Vitruvius recognized that if light hit an obstruction, such as a beam, lintel, or floor, the window would need to be placed higher. However, there is little sensitivity to how light might change the location, scale, texture, and orientation of building components or how this might affect the scale of the aperture. In contrast, Alberti considered light from the point of view of a force which shapes space. Rather than introducing a general rule to create unobstructed openings on all sides, Alberti focused on the particular quality and volume of the light, treating variations of light as an aspect of architectural design. As Alberti wrote, 'It is no bad thing, then, to consider the quality and angle of the sun to which a locality is exposed, so there is no excess of sunlight or shade.'[9] Windows facing different directions would have different properties as they did *different things* in a *different context*. He went on to stress

how the sun should enter the house, and how the requirements of the apartments should govern the size of windows. Summer apartments should have windows with generous dimensions if they face north; if they face south, they should be low and narrow, so as to freely admit the breezes but avoid the glare of the sun's rays.[10]

Alberti did not provide formal rules, dictate the size of the windows, or arrange their location based on grids or layout. Instead he stressed that architectural form should adjust to meet the needs for quality of light, quality of interior space, and performance of the window opening.[11]

Alberti's thinking about architectural design in terms of lineaments allowed flexibility away from formal and typological rules. The schematic outlines of buildings arose from external forces such as site assets, light quality, occupational needs, and weather conditions, including temperature, wind, and rain. Through lineaments, Alberti described a design process rooted in cause and effect.

We can jump ahead slightly and consider some examples of the various ways that thinking about light as a force can affect architectural design. Light is one of the most straightforward but powerful forces to which architectural forms can react when addressing qualities. If we consider the urban form of our cities, much of the shape of skyscrapers and other tall buildings is dictated by zoning regulations and setbacks. The iconic shape of the tiered skyscraper grew out of zoning setbacks which required skyscrapers to move away from the property line as they increased in height. The purpose behind this requirement came not from structural issues but from concerns over the quality of light and air provided to the street below. The modern zoning code originated in the 1916 New York Zoning Code. This code was developed in response to building designs such as the massive (at that time) 538-foot (164m) Equitable Building, completed in 1915. The Equitable Building rose straight from the street in a sheer vertical façade, oppressing the street and blocking out light for seven blocks around. The new tall building designs of New York in the early 1900s caused a public outcry due to the perception of their insensitivity to others' access to light and air. Counteracting the effect of these new skyscrapers was a major purpose of the New York Zoning Code. It required tall urban buildings built after 1916 continually to set back from the property line, allowing sunlight to reach the street. The New York Code became a model for zoning codes around the world. It operates by setting up constraints through regulations that limit formal composition.

The use of regulation constraints expressing non-formal factors for buildings is highly refined in the Japanese practice of shasen seigen.[12] The term translates as slant plane restriction and sets the relationship of the building to the street and adjacent buildings. Japanese culture protects all individuals' right to access fresh air and direct sunlight for at least four hours a day. This philosophy results in a complex form of spatial regulations, including a strict direct sun law (kitagawa shasen), inhibiting larger buildings from blocking the sun for smaller buildings, and sun-shadow regulations (nichiei kisei), which ensure that surrounding buildings have access to a minimum number of sunlight hours. Architects must comply with these regulations, and on smaller sites they can be very restrictive (Figure 9.1). Often the allowable zoning envelope and the desired volume of the building are in conflict with each other, requiring careful negotiation by talented architectural designers. One example of a resolution between restrictive zoning and building

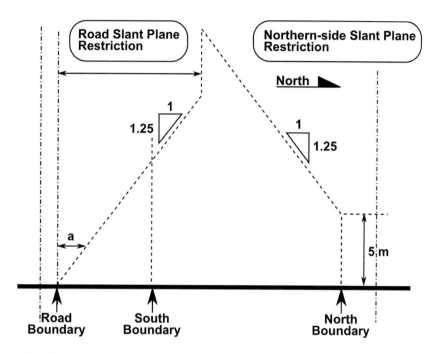

Figure 9.1: Slant plane restrictions on a small site showing allowable building envelope (adapted from Tokyo zoning floor area ratio shape control on lots)

intentions can be seen in the fourteen-sided 44m² (474-square-foot) Reflection of Mineral House by Atelier Tekuto (Figure 9.2). The exterior form of the house was developed as a dialogue between two primary sets of forces – the zoning regulations guided by sunlight access as detailed by slant plane restrictions, and the client's desire for a covered location for parking.

The design process followed by Yasuhiro Yamashita and Yoichi Tanaka of Atelier Tekuto was one of reduction focused on forces of light, occupation, and movement. The project started with constraints provided by zoning restrictions. These constraints were then overlaid with qualities of interior space, patterns of movement through the house, experiential qualities of occupation, and utilitarian needs. While the envelope set the major shape of the housing form, it was carved and punctured for architectural qualities. The covered parking became a transition plaza between the private entrance and the public street. Complexities of interior movement, view, quality of light, and usable spaces were balanced against the allowable massing. The angles created by the zoning restrictions were used to

Figure 9.2: A refined architectural response to Tokyo zoning regulations and site restrictions: the Reflection of Mineral House

Courtesy of Yasuhiro Yamashita/Atelier Tekuto; photograph by Makoto Yoshida

create a series of slippages in the interior, with the walls used to engage light and allow vertical circulation to slip between floor planes (Figure 9.3). The result is a carefully crafted form responding to forces generated by constraints and desires.

As designers, it is not necessary to wait for regulations to dictate formal response. Light quality can be seen as a force which is not based on regulations but designer bias. Instead of meeting legal requirements, a building situation might be analysed for the effect of the shadow it casts on adjacent sites (Figure 9.4: left-hand image). If one maps the locations that need direct light yet are affected by shadow, notating the times of day and the needed duration of the light, then it is possible to use this information as a set of right-of-way design constraints (Figure 9.4: centre image). This means, at a basic schematic level, that building form should not interfere with the access of light in very particular locations when the light generates the formal diagram of a perforated building envelope (Figure 9.4: right-hand image). This is not yet a completed architectural design, but it is a diagram which allows further development to be tied to judgement criteria generated by considering light as a force for shaping form.

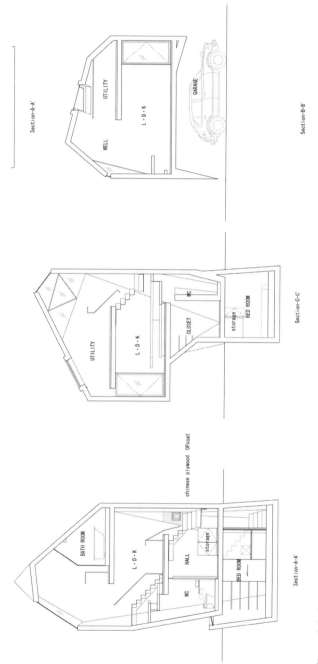

Courtesy of Yasuhiro Yamashita/Atelier Tekuto

Figure 9.3: Sections of the Reflection of Mineral House, Tokyo, Japan

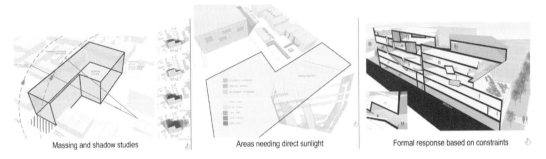

Massing and shadow studies   Areas needing direct sunlight   Formal response based on constraints

Figure 9.4: Study of building composition based on sunlight restrictive pathing

Courtesy of Joy Sportel

In the examples above, light is being used as a constraint, as described by Charles Eames at the start of this chapter. It can also be used as an asset rather than a restriction, a positive quality which brings advantage. Thinking about light as an asset allows the designer to consider it in more sensitive ways, instead of simply allowing the physical nature of sunlight regulations or shadow considerations to shape exterior massing. If we consider light as a force based on psychological perception rather than physical effect, we can use the way that light is interpreted as a source for architectural design decisions. This is a much more sophisticated approach than either Alberti's writing of 500 years ago or the geometric arrangements seen above. An example of using light as a psychological force to shape form can be found in Steven Holl's Chapel of St Ignatius (1997). In Holl's masterful composition, light is carefully introduced for experiential effect caught by architectural elements. The chapel is composed of seven distinctly different vessels, each with particular surface qualities. These vessels – what Holl called 'bottles' – shape, bend, and bounce the light entering the chapel in order significantly to affect the perception of the interior space. Daylight on the exterior of the project is consistent and mundane. It is through the light's interaction with architectural form that it becomes phenomenological – brought to a heightened level of experience based on the characteristics of the space itself. While the starting bias might have introduced light due to its cultural relationship with spirituality and ritual, a metaphorical effect, the basic principle is not based on transferring content across domains (metaphor). Instead, light is considered as a physically based force, which then determines architectural decision-making such as surface texture, form, and the colour of surfaces with which it interacts.

Light is only one of several non-formal forces. To understand these forces as an architectural design framework, we must examine the writing of Viollet-le-Duc.

Structural framework

Viollet-le-Duc worked over half a century after J-N-L Durand published his early nineteenth-century method for architectural design for students at the École Polytechnique and the École des Beaux-Arts. The major writing of Viollet-le-Duc, produced between 1854 and 1877, was in opposition to what he considered a conservative education at the École des Beaux-Arts. In this way, he differed greatly from Durand in terms of both his pedagogical alignment and the conceptual tools he chose to drive design decisions. Viollet-le-Duc did not approach architectural design as a series of rulesets, patterns, or a preconceived image. He did not *believe* these approaches would garner the best results for a project – a result relevant and sensitive to its context. This belief was part of his framing philosophy. Viollet-le-Duc did not believe in rules; he approached architecture as the resolution of system-based content. As a system, outcomes could not be predetermined by rules, as there are too many interacting variables. However, this does not mean that factors for pursuing architectural design cannot be *known*. As Viollet-le-Duc said, a 'code of morals [for architectural design] is possible, but we cannot establish absolute rules in building; experience, reasoning, and reflection must therefore always be summoned to our aid when we attempt to build'.[13] A different context, a different user, and a different requirement would produce a different response. While Viollet-le-Duc felt that the ability to determine absolute rules for design was impossible, he believed that a critical reading of programme and landscape to determine the best *fit* between form and situation was possible. Each project and site had a unique set of characteristics, but the same underlying principles were used to arrange form in space.

Viollet-le-Duc continued in the tradition of Enlightenment architects by attempting to articulate and communicate the design process clearly. His approach was a rational proposal and moved through a series of phases – all of which should be very familiar to architects practising today. The phases that Viollet-le-Duc detailed are currently the basic sequence of architectural design used in most standard, professional practices. The *framework* underlying his method is a flexible and rich way of thinking about architectural design.

Viollet-le-Duc described an explicit process for architectural design in a book he wrote for young adults entitled *Histoire d'une maison*, published in 1873. The book is also known as *Comment on Construit une Masion* in other editions, with the English titles of *The History of a House* and *How to Build a House* (British translation) and *The Story of a House* (American translation). The two English-language editions were both published in 1874. In this book, Viollet-le-Duc laid out a detailed design process for architecture using the narrative of erecting a manor house in the French countryside. While the example is particular, the method of design can be abstracted for general use. Viollet-le-Duc clearly stressed spatial qualities as assets and constraints as considered through forces rather than rules or image.

The architectural project starts by setting biases and priorities drawing from the needs of users. For Viollet-le-Duc, it was impossible to design anything if the designer didn't know the purpose of the design or how the design might be 'agreeable' to those who actively engage the results.[14] This is done through understanding the client and using this knowledge to develop a programme. The programme is understood as a series of spatial qualities and social pressures reflecting the client's requirements. The main character in *How to Build a House* is Paul, a young man who wants to be an architectural designer. His first experience with architecture is to develop a new manor house for his sister and her husband. To do this, Paul would first need to know 'what [his] sister wants – how she would like her house arranged'.[15] The programme was only one of three key starting biases that needed to be developed. The other two are the amount of time which is available for construction and the amount of money that the client is prepared to spend. These must be known so the architect doesn't take 'false steps'.[16] Both of these biases affected material choices and construction processes. If the architect didn't understand these aspects at the very beginning of the design process, then there was the danger of creating a design that would take too long to construct or cost too much. These three elements – time, cost, and programme – set the starting state in Viollet-le-Duc's design method.

After the programme had been determined, the next phase was to examine the location for the placement of the building – what is now known as site analysis. The site is examined for positive and negative qualities that include sequence of arrival, topography, view, and climatic conditions. The decision in the narrative was to

> build the house almost on the summit of the incline facing the north – sheltering it from the north-west winds under the neighbouring wood.

194

The entrance will have to front the ascending road; but we must arrange for the principal apartments to command the most favourable aspect, which is south-east; moreover, we must take advantage of the open view on the same side, and not disregard the spring of fresh water that flows on the right towards the bottom of the valley.[17]

In this particular site analysis, exposure to sun was considered as an asset while the wind was a constraint. Primary façades were to be positioned so the main rooms might have access to direct sunlight. The house, as a whole, was placed so to be sheltered from the north-west and south-west winds, using the woods and the topography to redirect air currents. View was considered as a force in two different ways, as view *from* the house and view *of* the house. It was also important to identify the direction of the best view corridor (south-east) so that it could become a factor in placing interior rooms, adding vista to natural light as a quality of interior space. However, views could also be considered as a constraint. The view of the plain to the south-west was considered to have little aesthetic effect. Gazing from the house in this direction had few positive qualities that could be brought into the architectural design. Shifting to a view *of* the house, rather than *from* the house, the entrance could be considered as a separate aspect to other programmatic elements. Entrance was controlled by creating a clear identification of access: a prominent façade and front of the house. The strongest way to do this was to connect the front façade to the sequence of arrival to the site in general. Since there was already an ascending road that provided access, in this example, the existing road controlled the placement of the entrance to the house.

Other factors in addition to wind, sun, and view could be considered as either positive or negative forces. These might be adjacencies, sound-, or odour-based qualities. In the case of Viollet-le-Duc's example, a spring of fresh water was also considered to be an asset. None of these factors by itself was strong enough to defend the choice of a location for the house. But, the synthesis of *all or most of* them could identify a strong location which was defensible by negotiating both the constraints and the assets of various forces. At the moment, the site forces exist as potentials only, acting as a series of pressures to shape the placement of various programme elements. There is not yet a detailed understanding of the relationship of the programme to the site's constraints or assets. The next phase of the design method would connect *programme to site* and *programme to programme*.

Once the site location had been determined, the rooms of the programme could be arranged, considering that the 'area of a room, its breadth and length must bear certain relations according to its purpose'.[18] Starting with the ground floor, the arrangement of interior rooms responded to site constraints and assets as well as to the adjacency of other rooms. The most important rooms were considered first, with secondary and then support programme filled in around. Rooms should be arranged for mutual advantage, considering view and light as aspects of interior space as well as circulation in terms of public, private, service, and social spaces. For example, the drawing-room, the most important room in a nineteenth-century French manor house, took the best view and light quality. Separated from the drawing-room and dining-room was the kitchen, due to the smells embodied in its use. The kitchen was placed on the north, out of sight from the entrance and public façade. Associated outlying utilities, such as the poultry-house, kitchen garden, and wash-houses, were associated with the kitchen and also hidden from view from the approach. This process continued until the programme and site considerations had negotiated the strongest composition.

On a programme to programme scale, social behaviours and conventions, as well as social forces, were constraints that shaped form. The location of an opening between rooms was not generic or standardized, but particular to the event that took place as people moved between the rooms. In the case of entering a dining-room, 'the gentlemen offer their arms to the ladies. It is therefore desirable that in going out or coming in there should be no obstacle in their way.'[19] This meant an entrance on the side of the room worked better than an entrance in the centre, given the social use of the space. The scale of openings between rooms had to be considered for the activities being performed as people moved through them. Did openings join highly social rooms, where groups of people talked and moved together? If so, a narrow opening meant for a single person would have disrupted that conversation.

While the social conventions and room definitions in effect during the time that Viollet-le-Duc practised are slightly different to those of today, the principle remains valid. The normative process for formalizing a plan is one of identifying programme hierarchy, situating rooms so they have the best access to site assets and environmental qualities, arranging adjacent spaces, and testing to see if access to qualities and response to constraints are affected, then adjusting and retesting. Viollet-le-Duc described a fragment of the process when he wrote, if we place the dining-room and the billiard-room, whose dimensions are to be nearly equal to those of the drawing-room, in juxtaposition and continuation with the latter, the drawing-room will be lighted only on one of its shorter sides, for we must put the entrance-hall in front. The drawing-room would in that case be gloomy, and would command a view of the country only in one direction.[20]

In this phase of architectural design, the formal composition is constantly shifting as all aspects of the programme adjust, affected by relationships to each other and to context. Nothing is locked into place until there is a strong fit. Decisions are based on considering the quality of spaces created by prioritized environmental and social forces (judgement criteria).

Once an idea of the ground-floor layout had been set, the plan would then be normalized for structural needs, creating an understanding of load-bearing walls and points. More focus and detail would be introduced at a smaller scale, refining the current proposal. While the first pass identified programmatic locations, room dimensions, opening locations and opening scales, the next phase would drop down to focus on elements such as alcoves, bay windows, antechambers, and recesses. These details would respond to the same forces at play in creating the larger-scale positioning of rooms. For example, recessed areas would support social forces that were addressed by the placement and aspect ratio of the room. A room that was highly social could have recesses arranged for smaller, more intimate activities, such as smoking, reading, or more intimate viewing of the garden. If the recess was to support a separation between public and service occupancies, there could be service areas providing a social buffer, such as a serving pantry between dining-room and kitchen. Vertical circulation would be considered as part of this phase.

After refining the main floor plan, the structural walls and vertical circulation from the ground floor were then projected up to form the basis of the floor above. Programme elements that had been identified to be on this floor were then arranged in the same process that had just occurred on the ground floor. Site assets were identified, primary rooms were placed in the positions that gave them the best qualities, adjacencies were set up, and secondary rooms filled in around. The floor below was used as a constraint or an asset, depending on the situation, since it had qualities of scale and occupation which affected the floor above. As part of an iterative process, the layout of the second floor might have required changes in the ground-floor plan, but only if the overall result would have been positive.[21] Once all the major floor arrangements had been determined, the plan was projected into section in order to consider roof geometry and elevations. The roof was considered to be the most important aspect of construction (since it kept out the elements) and had to be both simple and efficient. After the arrangement of the roof, the residual interstitial space between the rafters and the topmost set of joists could be programmed, infilling programme among the structural walls. This was necessary as the need for light in these areas would create dormers, affecting the elevations. Floor to ceiling heights were determined for proportion and ventilation requirements. The final elevations were a result of the projected outline of the plan, the placement of the doors, windows, and dormers as well as the floor to ceiling height requirements (Figure 9.5).

Viollet-le-Duc's description of a force-based design approach, at present, is a descriptive list of phases influenced by his own framing and starting bias. What he considered important prioritized programme and site content as the major content to drive the architectural process. It also locked his method into a rigid sequence rather than a generalized framework used to make architectural design decisions and to select relevant tools. In order to make the process more flexible, it can be reduced to a general framework by suspending the biases.

The focus on explicit categories of site, plan, section, and elevation can be explored in terms of bias, scale, and thinking style. This will allow an understanding of how decisions are being made and what information is of value. Like

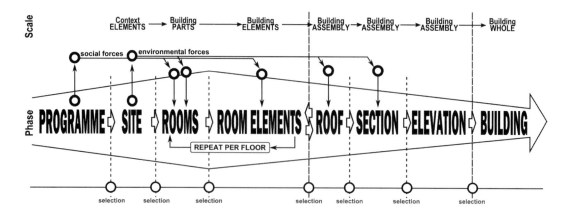

Figure 9.5: Viollet-le-Duc's architectural method for developing architecture from site and social forces

Durand's, Viollet-le-Duc's bias was towards the quality of the habitable spaces – the distribution of the plan. This bias focused the first steps of his method on programme, site, and arranging rooms. Since he was concerned with the quality of the plan arrangement, qualities such as light, view, social norms, sound, odours, and degrees of publicness were the forces which would be used for primary decision-making. These forces have a direct effect on plan quality. The architect's bias determines which forces are considered important. Using this knowledge, the first part of Viollet-le-Duc's process can be reduced to a simpler form, considering the selection of programme and site to be understood as content rather than process (Figure 9.6). The phases of rooms, room elements, roof, and elevation can be thought of in terms of scale and assembly. There are various scales at work in the process. The project starts at the site level without any intention for a building yet – there are possibilities through identified assets and constraints. Architecture, as a building, is then engaged on the scale of programme through discrete rooms, as they have the strongest relationship to the chosen forces. Environmental relationships as site assets are integrated into the project to become room assets (view, wind, quality of light). The plan is then refined by dropping to a scale of room details and focusing almost exclusively on social interactions (cooking, smell, movement, smoking, arm holding). From here, the process expands back to a larger scale to look at how the parts form a whole and plan is projected into roof, section, and elevation. Considering scale inside of discrete elements allows the phases to be reduced from eight to five.

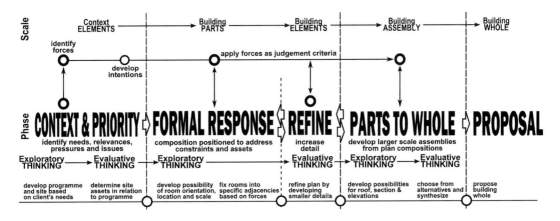

Figure 9.6: Viollet-le-Duc's architectural method thinking styles, scales, and the removal of designer bias

In addition to bias and scale, the same type of exploratory and evaluative thinking styles that were found in the pattern-based framework are present. The site and programme are examined for possibilities (exploratory), then analysed to create a programme list and establish an understanding of site priorities (evaluative). When placing principal rooms, the site assets are explored in order to develop options for programme placement and orientation (exploratory). Once the best location has been determined, rooms and room relationships are tentatively placed (evaluative). The programme elements are then synthesized so content at several scales aligns with several forces, creating the expression of a coherent relationship (exploratory). This means that all elements in the design should feel like an aspect of a greater whole rather than a set of disconnected parts jammed together (evaluative). The same process continues with secondary rooms and circulation spaces connecting them to assets while considering constraints.

We can reduce the design method even further by removing the framing and bias that led Viollet-le-Duc to prioritized programme, site, and plan (Figure 9.7). While programme and site have a high degree of relevance for an architectural response, it is not a requirement to use them. Rather, it is a starting bias. When programme and site are used, the plan tends to be the first architectural tool engaged, as it has the strongest connection with the expressed forces. However, an architectural designer could start with diagram, section, massing, or another architectural tool *depending on the type of force which is identified as most important*. The type of forces and their specific composition come from the situation to which the architecture responds. This will include context, cultural content, or recognition of need. Once forces are identified, they are then defined in terms of specific constraints, assets, and pressures. The constraints and assets are then used as the judgement criteria. Pressures can be applied as moderating factors to the proposed form. If the forces do not produce constraints and assets that are relevant to architectural syntax, then a form of domain transfer may be necessary.

The framing and starting bias determines the priority of forces to be extracted from the specific situation and translates them as constraints and assets. Once this has been completed, the initial formal response can be proposed. There must be a strong relationship between the forces and how they are translated into form. In particular, the formal response *must be at a scale which can respond directly to the forces which have been selected as the judgement criteria.* To use the example of Viollet-le-Duc, the forces which he considered most relevant to architecture were extracted from

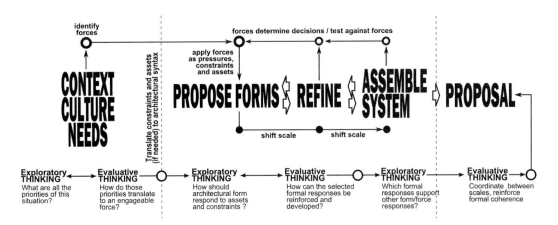

Figure 9.7: Generic framework of a force-based design process including thinking styles

conditions of site and included social conventions identified by the programme. The forces were categorized as social and environmental but translated into assets and constraints which included view, air movement, light, exposure, and public-to-private qualities. The initial scale at which Viollet-le-Duc responded to those constraints and assets was the programme element of the individual room. A programme is really an organizational structure that allows space to be subdivided into discrete units of occupancy, use, and identity. This means that a room usually has the same qualities through the space it occupies. We describe certain types of room as being well lit, private, well connected, social, having a good view, and so on. If forces which are based in quality of light are being addressed, and the room is a space which has a consistent response and need for a quality of light, then there is a strong organizational relationship between the two. Apertures, openings, and windows can be adjusted to make the room darker or brighter, the shape of the room can be configured to encourage gathering, and circulation and adjacency can be arranged to define public rather than private space. There is a strong relationship between the form and the forces.

Once initial form has been proposed as a response to assets and constraints, there is a shift in scale to examine the same forces either in more detail or for further refinement. When the scale is dropped to smaller elements, it is a point of refinement. When the scale moves to larger elements, it is about assembly, organization, and aggregation. The assets and constraints are present continuously as the judgement criteria against which decisions are tested.

While the force-based framework differs from the pattern-based framework in the generation of judgement criteria, there are some striking similarities. Both frameworks use the same pattern of exploratory and evaluative thinking. They both contain discrete phases based on outcomes directed towards a resolution. Both processes are strongly iterative, with loops and parallel lines of exploration within phases. Systems thinking and synthesis are at the core of the architectural decisions, with formal proposals tentative until reinforced by other decisions. Both the pattern-based and the force-based frameworks are emergent, parametric processes moving from pieces to form a whole. Each is a *bottom-up process*, as the whole is not determined before the assembly of the parts.

Applied methods

Any force can be used in this framework as long as the *result* of that force can be expressed in a formal response. This means there is either a natural affinity between the force and architectural syntax or there is a translation that equates the original force to possible architectural responses.[22] It is the case of knowing when something matters and when it doesn't, where 'matters' is defined as whether something can engage architectural syntax or not. The easiest forces to make relevant are environmental, physical, and social, as they directly affect formal expression. We can use the work of architects as diverse as Frank Lloyd Wright and Rem Koolhaas/OMA to clarify how forces are used in design methods. While these two particular choices are generations apart and in some ways very different, many of their projects are based on translating forces into a formal response. The difficulty in seeing that these practices share the same framework behind their methods is due to very different framing and starting biases. While Wright follows the process set down by Viollet-le-Duc, closely stressing programme, materials, and cost, OMA is much more exploratory about which forces are translated as judgement criteria.

Frank Lloyd Wright was a declared supporter of Viollet-le-Duc, considering the nineteenth-century French theorist as the only authority necessary (besides himself, of course) to understand architectural design.[23] While Wright was very careful not to detail his own design process, as that would have interfered with his self-cultivated reputation for artistic genius, the bias towards Viollet-le-Duc's method can be found in Wright's writings.

We find a glimpse into how Wright made design decisions in his descriptions of particular projects, especially in his residential work and the Usonian projects. Describing why certain of his houses were built a particular way or took on a particular form, Wright consistently referenced social issues of privacy, quality issues such as view, and environment issues such as temperature and comfort (*context/culture/need*). These are the categories Wright looked to in order to locate relevant forces to shape his projects. Wright differed from Viollet-le-Duc in framing philosophy and starting bias, which affected some of the higher-level decisions of an architectural response. The framing adjusted the overall impression or style of the architecture, while not affecting the formal relationships which the forces addressed. Wright's framing philosophy approached architecture as grounding, shelter, and extension of horizontality. He stressed the quality of plasticity as a design objective – a concept that had multiple effects on his work but did not change much of the underlying decision-making process behind many of his compositions. Plasticity biased his smaller-scale details (*refine*) towards openness and spatial continuity rather than the creation of discrete rooms.[24]

Wright's commentary regarding his projects allow insight to his method, using knowledge of Viollet-le-Duc's process as a guide. Based on Viollet-le-Duc, the first steps of any architectural project were to determine materials, cost, and programme. In the Usonian houses, as a particular case-study, we find that Wright was clear about the purpose of the houses. He stated that they were about the reduction of cost and the ability to make an inexpensive but well-constructed shelter for a family. This attitude is apparent in the decisions made about detailing and the way several programmatic elements were handled. Eliminating or reducing waste was a priority. The elimination of sloped roofs, gutters, downspouts, garages, paint, interior trim, and basements were all based on this framing position, setting up a starting state which already had bounded priorities. Materials such as wood and brick were chosen for interior finishes because they did not require plaster or paint – only their natural materiality with, perhaps, a little oil sealer. The determination of materials and formal detailing controlled time and cost.

After the bias set the foundational approach to the design, Wright considered programmatic needs against the possibilities of the site and context. The plan was considered for the 'disposition of the rooms'.[25] Wright considered the rooms in the same way as Viollet-le-Duc had done earlier – the site and social relationships of the programme were analysed for potentials and concerns. Questions were then asked. What are the assets of the context and site? Where does the sun provide exposure? In which directions are the views? And how do adjacencies, such as gardens, provide benefits for living spaces? These questions, and their responses, then allowed programme elements to be placed in a context which supported their need for particular qualities. Constraints created by adjacent buildings and events would also affect formal composition. The attitude introduced so clearly by Viollet-le-Duc was echoed in Wright when he described one of his houses as wrapping 'around the northwest corner of a lot sloping to the south – a fine vista in that direction. The plan protects the Willeys from the neighbors, sequesters a small garden and realizes the view to the utmost under good substantial shelter.'[26] The vista was connected to the type of room, a choice of façade detail and glazing pattern, while the overall building is located for maximum privacy in the areas that require it, following Viollet-le-Duc's example of a house design. There are many other parallels between the two architects. Discussions of kitchen placement, airflow, odour venting, and oversight of playing areas for children are other examples of how spatial qualities affected by forces develop the final design proposal. At the heart of Wright's process was the activity of applying forces as constraints and assets which would then determine the proposal of an architectural form in space. For Wright, a wall was a response to forces in context. The wall became solid if privacy was needed, included clerestories if both privacy and light were required, and dissolved into plate glass without a frame if it was desirable to bring the exterior qualities into the interior and privacy was not an issue. Primary forces were concerned with views and degrees of privacy as well as quality of light and air movement.

There are glimpses of Wright's method in his writings, a method based on the relationship of forces to formal proposal shaped by larger philosophical framing and biases. It correlates closely with the documented method of Viollet-le-Duc, although Wright's design method has never been publicly detailed. In contrast, through the writings and presentations of Rem Koolhaas and other principals, the Office for Metropolitan Architecture (OMA) is explicit about its methods and decision-making.[27] These include how forces are used to develop innovative proposals that are also highly relevant to context and use. OMA has a tendency to approach their architectural design work through the bias of programme combined with issues of scale (or *bigness*) to align relationships among associations, occupancy, use, and culture. The office's framing philosophy and bias allow it to suspend expected outcomes by developing strong research that identifies significant forces and relationships not at first apparent. Even though the result seems to be non-traditional, many of the design proposals emerging from the office are based on the underlying framework using forces to provide the content in which to make decisions pertaining to form – the same framework operating behind the work of Viollet-le-Duc and Frank Lloyd Wright. A highly visible example of this is the Seattle Public Library project (2004).

The design for the Seattle Public Library didn't follow a standard method of identifying forces of programmatic elements and site to create a formal proposal. Instead, the CONTEXT/CULTURE/NEEDS analysis looked into the nature of libraries as both traditional and future assets to society. The analysis, moving through exploratory and evaluative phases, identified forces based in indeterminacy and fixity organized around categories of social responsibility and media holding. The cultural importance of a library was determined to be not only access to media but also the social engagement with the community and provision of public space (social role). In addition, there is a conflict between the social and media roles which positioned the growth of one to be detrimental to the other (constraints). When media holdings grow they displace the social space of the library. The interplay between these constraints and assets highlighted the need for an approach that would accommodate forces based both in fixity and in indeterminacy.

[IDENTIFY FORCES] The fact that libraries have a social role might not be apparent at first. However, for the Seattle Public Library, it became clear that this role was important when the programme was analysed in an exploratory process which challenged expected associations (Figure 9.8). The initial client programme (left-hand column) was the starting point for the design process. The first step looked at the programme through the two categories of book holding and public role. The process analysed the client's programme and identified whether a programmatic element was in one category or the other. The result was surprising as it turned out that only 32 per cent of the original programme was based on housing books (second column from the left). This is a much smaller percentage than would be expected from the *image* of the library, whose identity rests on being a building *full of books*. Realizing two-thirds of the library is not about books but about the library's social role introduced the forces of fixity and indeterminacy. These forces are relevant to the context of designing a library because, as the research highlighted, changes in the volume of media holding occurred at the expense of the social role.[28]

Next, through first principles reduction and convergence, the client programme was rearranged to associate like-with-like occupations based on programme

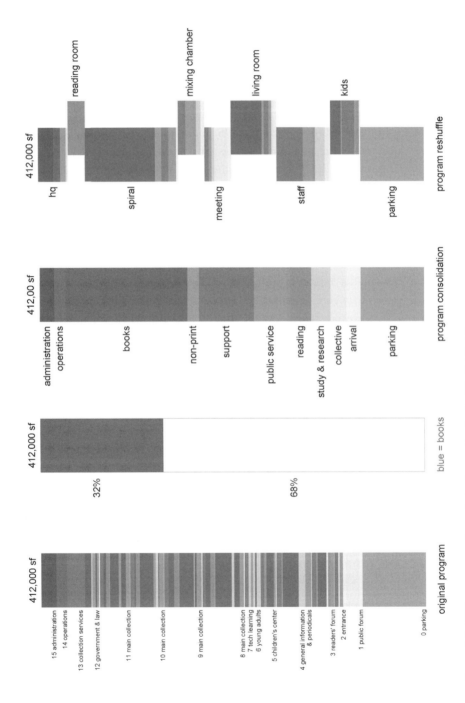

Figure 9.8: OMA's programmatic analysis diagram for the Seattle Public Library

Courtesy of OMA

qualities.[29] Instead of room names defining the programme, categories based on social responsibility and media holding clustered the library into spatial volumes. These clusters took on labels based on general use, such as books, support, public service, reading, administration, and so on (third column from the left). The forces of fixity and indeterminacy were then applied to the use categories, remixing those programme occupancies into new clusters (right-hand column). The new organization of programme, still based on qualities and forces, created flexibility in the volume but through emergence produced a compartmentalized structure. The library can expand aspects of its role and its holdings based on changes in societal needs, but the results are constrained to a small region, preserving the operational qualities of the library.[30] The clusters on the left of this column (HQ, spiral, meeting, staff, parking) represent fixed spaces, while the clusters on the right of the column (reading room, mixing chamber, living room, kids) can be considered less defined and indeterminate in terms of use and predicted future.

[PROPOSE FORM] The programmatic categories arranged by the identified forces produced a first pass at the proposal of a form in terms of section (see Figure 9.9). The clusters based on fixity and stability were translated into platforms, or large masses. Each platform was designed for a particular type of occupancy which then affected its size, structure, and circulation. Next, the scale of the architectural design would move to smaller details regarding more traditional forces affecting rooms to determine the area, volume, and aspect ratio of each platform.

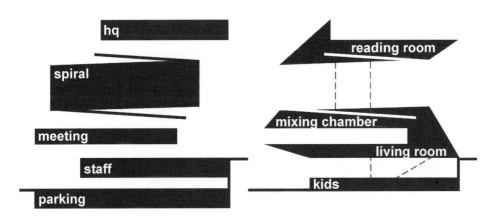

Figure 9.9: Diagrams for floor plate occupancies for the Seattle Public Library showing the platforms (left) and the in-between spaces (right)

Courtesy of OMA

The platform clusters would have flexibility in their programmatic content but any change within any of the platforms would not affect any other platform. In this way, book collections could be expanded, and new media could be introduced, but the effect would be contained, thus meeting the judgement criteria for project success. The fixed platforms were stacked based on hierarchy, adjacencies, and larger-scale programmatic needs such as publicness, accessibility, and connectedness. The second set of programmatic clusters based on indeterminacy simply occupied the interstitial space between the platforms. These became spaces of interaction, engagement, and social roles.

[REFINE AND ASSEMBLE SYSTEM] Once the major schematic intentions were clear, the proposal was refined for its massing and relationship qualities (Figure 9.10). These phases would have blurred with the form proposal phase in a series of iterative passes. When the platforms were being developed for massing, details such as the book spiral, as a way of not interrupting the sequence of the Dewey Decimal system, would have been proposed and developed. This then would have affected the volume of that cluster, which would also have affected adjacent massing. New forces came into play during this sequence, as fixity and indeterminacy have done what they needed to do in the schematic organization. Now the platforms were shaped and located based on more normative architectural forces, such as the desire for shade or light, as well as relationships to desirable views.[31] It was only at this point that site and context influenced composition.

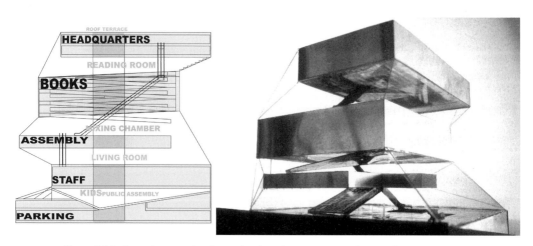

Figure 9.10: Formal proposal and massing based on programmatic groupings

Courtesy of OMA

The platforms, from headquarters to parking, were arranged for maximizing positives, the essence of a force-based method. The process moved from the detail to the whole, allowing the design response to emerge from the associations and relationships of the elements.

Figure 9.11: The Seattle Public Library as a built proposal

Courtesy of Pragnesh Parikh photography OMA/LMN Architects

OMA's design narrative for the Seattle Public Library clearly identifies itself as a variation of the same process detailed by Viollet-le-Duc and followed by Frank Lloyd Wright. It used the principles of identifying forces to act as constraints and assets to allow decisions to be made about formal composition. However, OMA has a particular framing which gravitates towards non-standard forces as being priorities for starting bias. They are concerned with issues of relevance and significance in the identification of these forces and apply exploratory research and strong abilities in analysis as critical factors early in the method.

Many architects use those forces detailed by Viollet-le-Duc, yet we can see with OMA's work that it is not necessary to do this. Non-standard forces can be discerned through analysis, exploration, and research. In the end, identifying constraints, assets, and pressure from forces gives the architectural designer a framework to explore early schematic work, but also a way to structure decisions throughout the project since those decisions need to support intentions for design coherence. Changing the force will change the decision, which changes the form. While forces can be found as content in other methods, methods based on the force-based framework approach the design as emergence where the forces imply the form rather than the form being applied independently at the will of the architectural designer.

Programmatic forces (Example 1)

The first example adapts the explicit method of Viollet-le-Duc to a generic process which can allow some flexibility of focus. The framework uses programme in relation to site as the generator of design decisions. Many force-based approaches use some variation of site and programmatic content as they are so relevant to architectural syntax and expression. However, this particular method engages programme and site directly through the idea of *qualities*. A programme is simply a collection of bounded spaces identified as containing particular events. When we talk of a bedroom or an office, we are speaking of the activity that occurs in that space – the event of sleeping, working, writing, cooking, sitting, learning, etc. Each event is supported by particular environmental and social characteristics which allow that activity to be performed as successfully as possible. These characteristics – qualities – include type and intensity of light, degree of publicness, amount of connectivity, types of adjacencies, volume of space, and relationship to view. Each of these elements can be understood as a degree or characteristic, as in the quality of light, the quality of view, the quality of connection, etc. In turn, qualities can be shared between spaces, or set up in opposition. The qualities and their relationships are forces to which architectural form and composition can respond.

[CONTEXT/CULTURE/NEEDS] Every design project starts with research and this method is no different. Using qualities of programme as a formal generator engages first principles reduction along with the expansive thinking techniques of questioning and challenge. In order to make that reduction, there must be a clearly identified list of programmatic spaces. Programmatic spaces are determined from discussions with clients, research on trends in the use type, case-study analysis of previous projects of the same use type, and interviews with users – to name a few sources. Once a programme has been determined, the next step is to reduce each space to its component characteristics. This can start with simple metrics, such as possible ranges of area, aspect ratio, and volume for each space. A database or spreadsheet can be generated as a way of keeping track of the characteristics of each programmatic space. The database can be left in a numeric format or translated into graphic representation for easier visualization (Figure 9.12). These initial parameters will form the base to which other qualities will be added to build the data cloud from which all the other phases of the method will proceed.

While the programme is being reduced, the site is also analysed for its essential assets and constraints. The process of site analysis for this method is very similar to the typological study, except instead of reducing the plan to persistent patterns, the conclusion identifies constraints, assets, pressures, and flows. At a minimum

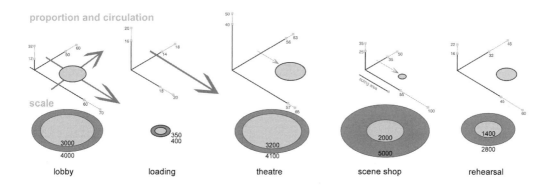

Figure 9.12: Diagrammatic visualization of programmatic characteristics for a theatre type

Courtesy of Christopher Hess

this should include the public-to-private exposure, public sightlines that need to be preserved, access to significant views, location, volume, and types of circulation (vehicular, pedestrian, public transit), zoning restrictions, sun–paths, vertical sun angles, shadow patterns, wind patterns, and existing urban density patterns.

Once there is a basic understanding of the programmatic elements to be used in the design project and the site characteristics, one must *identify the forces* which will direct the composition. Questions can be asked concerning what makes a programme element work, which qualities and needs are required for that programme element to thrive, or which other spaces the element likes or dislikes. Each individual programme element is expanded into as many individual qualities as the architectural designer wishes. Addressing the core of architectural syntax, the minimum should include category of use, intimacy gradient, need for commonality, degree of connectedness, importance of visual presence, need for view, degree of visual isolation, degree of auditory isolation, type and quality of light, and relationship to ground.

Category of use is a way to associate programme elements into larger groups. These might be general categories, such as meeting, office, utility, and gathering, or identities, such as fixity or indeterminacy. The category of use should not replicate the programme item title, but rather should be one classification level below it. Along with category of use, a series of qualities relates to adjacency and circulation in social terms. *Intimacy gradient* describes the degree of publicness or privacy of a space, while *need for commonality* addresses space as social function. A space does not need to have same degree of publicness as commonality, but often the two are related. One way of determining the difference between publicness and commonality is to ask whether the space encourages or requires gathering to be successful. Spaces with high values of commonality can be either public or private, but they must support social interaction as a primary requirement. *Degree of connectedness* relates the space to the structure of circulation and the accessibility of the programmatic element. Basic questions to determine connectedness concern how many other spaces physically connect directly to the programmatic element. A lobby or a lounge has a high degree of connectedness, while an office with a single entrance has a low degree.[32] It is also worth noting whether a programme element needs some association with the exterior or the ground plane, as this will have particular spatial ramifications when placing elements on a site.

In addition to the circulatory qualities, there are some qualities that relate programme spaces to human senses, such as sight and sound. The *importance of visual presence* relates to a space's need for visual status or its requirement to broadcast into (be seen in) adjacent spaces. Questions about this quality centre on how identifiable a particular space is from either other parts of the building or from adjacent areas beyond the site. The *need for view* is the opposite, asking whether a space needs a vista outwards as a spatial quality in order for the space to be successful. If so, the next question is the nature of that view. In addition to visibility, programmatic elements can be described in terms of the *need for isolation*. Spaces that need quiet to perform are isolated for sound while other spaces may require visual privacy or, conversely, perform best when viewed. Light, being a very important force in architectural design, can be broken down into several subdivisions. *Type* and *quality* of light can be identified under the categories of direct or indirect, natural or artificial, soft or hard, and can have a range of intensity from dim to bright.

There are many ways to notate the type or intensity of the programmatic qualities. One of the easiest ways is to equate each with a scale, although it might go against the nature of a designer to use a quantitative device to describe something considered qualitative. It is useful to introduce a matrix, however, because, if the qualities can be expressed numerically, then it is possible to diagram them, relate them, and determine patterns of interaction. A diagram allows immediate access to situations which might be used for interesting design opportunities. An example is comparing the need for visual isolation with connectedness (Figure 9.13a), or commonality with visual presence (Figure 9.13b), for a library project. These are useful comparisons since a space that needs to be highly connected in terms of circulation will be problematic if it also needs to be isolated from view. Or a space that requires both qualities of gathering and high visibility can become a focus point in the design proposal. For visual isolation and connectedness, points where both lines meet either at the outer perimeter (highly visually isolated but highly connected) or the inner perimeter (highly visually present but not connected) become sites of opportunity. Likewise for commonality with visual presence, those spaces which need to be highly visible and designed for social gathering (outer perimeter) can be quickly identified.

The same studies can be done with any other combination of qualities that the designer might be interested in examining. Intimacy gradient can be mapped with degree of connectedness to examine the relationship between circulation flow and private space (Figure 9.14a). If qualities such as need for natural light and access to the exterior perimeter are diagrammed (Figure 9.14b), then the architectural

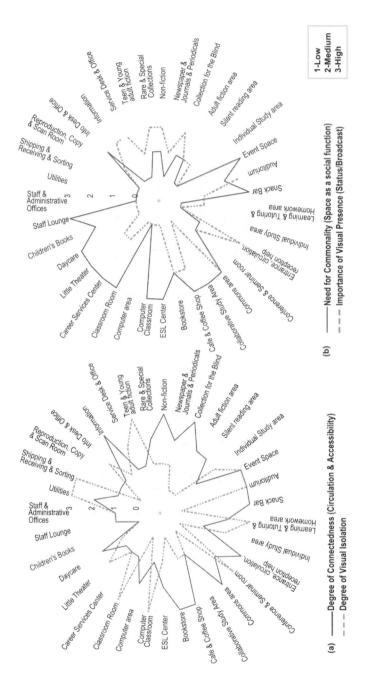

Figure 9.13: Comparison analysis using weights based on spatial qualities for a library as analysis of exploratory content

214

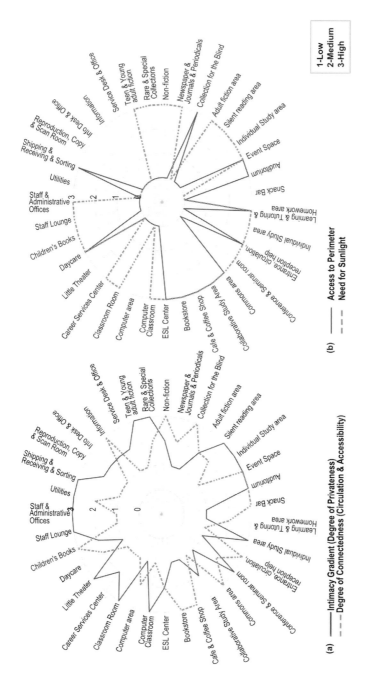

Courtesy of Malwina Dzienniak

Figure 9.14: Comparison analysis using weights based on spatial qualities for a library as analysis of exploratory content

215

designer can look for spaces which are sited back from the outer façade of the form but will require light, implying the introduction of courtyards, atria, and other internal voids.

[IDENTIFY FORCES] While the analysis provides the content for making decisions in the design process, it is also used to organize a bias. This is possible as some forces will take precedence over others for reasons of decision-making. Choosing to focus on light-based forces, or social visibility factors, or public-to-private pressures, will produce a different project based on the same programme list even if done by the same designer. This does not mean that other forces and spatial qualities are ignored or abandoned, only that there must be a starting point, and that starting point will predetermine the possibilities and arrangements for the proposal. In the case of the library project diagrams, public-to-private factors (connectedness, visual access, physical access) were prioritized, along with light quality. The programmatic elements can be organized into possible patterns or clusters using convergent techniques. The clusters will be based on ordering principles developed from the architectural designer's bias.

[PROPOSE FORMS] Once the initial analysis has been completed, a series of questions can be asked to drive the proposal forward. The primary questions are based on how the programmatic elements interact with the site, where the individual programmatic spaces need to be located in order to thrive, and if there is a need or an ability to compress, overlap, interlace, or repulse programmatic elements with each other. The constraints and assets of the site become pressures for distributing the programmatic elements or clusters. There is little regard for structure, floor plates, or even the idea of building at this point. The purpose is to get the programmatic elements in the location that matches the required qualities and needs. If there is a fantastic view forty feet in the air on the west side of the site, and there is a programmatic element which requires a fantastic view, then this is where that element is placed. It doesn't matter that there isn't anything below that element at the moment. On the first pass, there is no attempt at refinement; it is just a matter of locating all aspects of the programme in the places that best fit their qualities (Figure 9.15).

There are several variations that can occur at this point. The introduction of bias might allow the designer to filter the programme list to identify those programmatic elements that have a high degree of relevance to the proposal's intentions. From a programme with sixty or seventy items, there will be program-matic anchors which will act as attractors for other spaces – an auditorium has

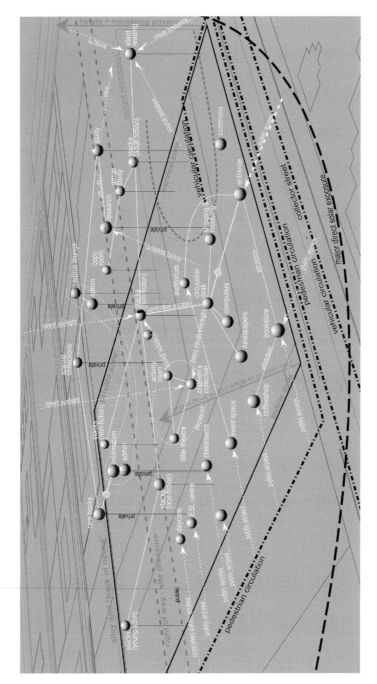

Figure 9.15: Spatial diagram of formal relationships based on forces as divergent–convergent process in PROPOSE FORMS

Courtesy of Malwina Dzienniak

support and service spaces; a children's library has office space, activity rooms, and service washrooms. The bias might provide a larger organizational structure, such as accepting the public-to-private gradient as the core of a theatre, an idea that would cluster the entire programme into two or three major groups. However, these do not need to be normative associations like the front-of-house/back-of-house division. Larger programmatic clustering could occur by identifying all spaces which had the same need for rich sunlight, were highly social spaces, or required high visibility. This is the choice of the designer, based on the situation in which they are working. Reducing and filtering are necessary skills in architectural design, but they must be done in consideration of the larger context to ensure relevance of proposal.

Several iterations are needed to develop even a very early schematic idea of the proposal's form. The first pass might be focused on the relationship of elements to site; the second pass would pull together programmatic elements; while the third pass would need to negotiate between the clustered programme and larger pressures of circulation and adjacencies. Throughout the entire process, the same consideration of meeting qualities would continue, as these set the judgement criteria.

[REFINE and ASSEMBLE SYSTEM] Once there is a schematic under-standing of where all the pieces want to be, the scale of focus can be shifted from programmatic elements to their larger organization. At this point in the design process, there is a gesture for a project that will need to be analysed again for potential and refinement. The configuration that has emerged, based on program-matic qualities and site pressures, is reviewed for large massing logic that can drive the next stage of the design process. In the example of the library, the site assets and constraints, combined with the programme qualities and designer bias stressing public-to-private factors and light quality, produced an initial composition. Looking at the spatial logic that developed through letting the forces organize the programme distribution, the ground floor became dedicated to unrestricted public access with second and third floors becoming the controlled library core. This was based on setting up visual access to the children's library while controlling accessibility to that space (Figure 9.16). Once the control point for entering the library (circulation desk) was located (set back from the main entrance and immediately before vertical circulation), the rest of the main floor opened up for public use and pass-through circulation (Figure 9.17). Moving through the circulation desk is considered 'entering the library', so the rest of the main floor could be populated by programmatic elements that are non-collection based, such as community functions, training, and lecture/performance. The controlled/non-controlled organization of the programme, the need for natural light in both the children's library and the deep floor plate of the stacks opened up a void in the centre of the building.

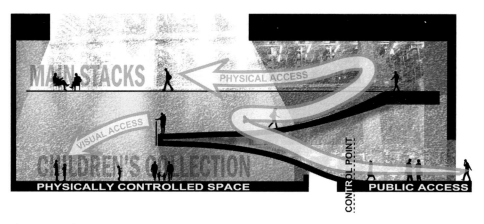

Figure 9.16: Schematic section detailing intentions for physical versus visual access and light entry for a library type as selection in REFINE and ASSEMBLE SYSTEM

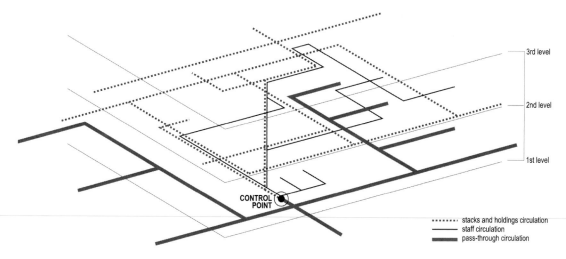

Figure 9.17: Circulation diagram identifying control point and open public nature of ground floor as selection in ASSEMBLE SYSTEM

Courtesy of Malwina Dzienniak

Organizational logics will produce a set of formal intentions which can be applied back to the programme for refinement. This might include shifting, distorting or moving programmatic elements so they have stronger associations. The ranges of spatial area, aspect ratio, and height information for each programmatic element can be applied, which begins to lock spaces into shapes and locations. Individual rooms can be massed and connected, while floor plates are considered as another larger-scale organizational device. This is the action seen in OMA's Seattle Public Library where fixity and indeterminacy were used as clustering logic which then had smaller-scale programme forces applied. The mass of programme can be normalized and skinned as the elevations are composed (Figure 9.18). Again, all of these decisions will be based on required qualities, especially those of visual prominence, need for view, and lighting needs. Circulation will be developed based on intimacy gradient, connectedness, and commonality. There is a constant reference back to the listed qualities of each space to make sure that they are being met in the design proposal. All decision-making and formal selection is checked against these qualities as judgement criteria.

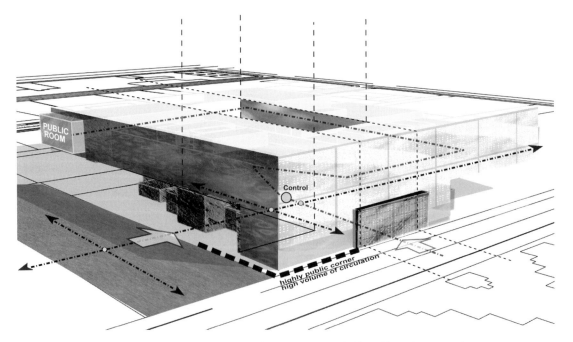

Figure 9.18: Schematic axonometric proposing normalized and skinned intentions stressing penetration of public space into the ground floor, light core, and eroded base as schematic PROPOSAL

[PROPOSAL] As part of the process of refinement which includes normalizing the programme elements, skinning the mass, and developing strong relationships in occupations, the architectural designer will constantly move back and forth in scale. The schematic phase presents a proposal at the level of a refined (or articulated) massing showing programmatic intentions. The same content can be used to develop the project through to construction. The difficulty in architectural design is knowing what to do (intentions). The strength of a force-based proposal is that intentions are constructed by identifying forces relevant to the project.

Time- and memory-based site forces (Example 2)

While programme is a powerful and relevant tool to use when developing an architectural proposal, it is not the only way in which forces can operate in design. Programme is simply a formalization of how spaces are occupied and what events occur within them. Occupation and events can be addressed directly without the framework of programme. Also, forces based in site, memory, environment, or human activities can be allowed to dominate over programmatic content, affecting all or part of the design proposal. The second example looks at the proposal for Bowtie House, designed by LOOM Studio, the architectural practice of Ralph K. Nelson. In this project, landscape forces based in cyclical and long-period natural events are used to generate a design proposal. The identified forces used as a formal generator are topographical composition through glacial action, tree growth, and fire activity as a cyclical event. While programme is involved in arranging the relationships of interior space, it is not a primary influence.

[IDENTIFY FORCES] The location of the project, a house on the edge of a lake in north-western Wisconsin, led the architectural designer to examine the geological and human history of the context. The landscape of this region of the United States still bears the marks from forces of a millennium ago. Retreating glaciers raked the landscape and sculpted the highlands, rivers, swales, outwashes, and lakes. The organic deposits left by the glaciers became fertile locations for foliage growth. Forests grew in the glacier's wake. As the forests densified, intermittent natural fires swept through the trees, removing overgrown vegetation and priming the landscape for the next generation of growth. With the trees' stabilizing effect removed, erosion and sediment movement shifted the topography slightly. As the forests regrew, traces of the past generations of trees were still present as charred marks in the landscape. The cycle of topological form (swale) to vegetation (trees) to disturbance (fire) was repeated over and again. While it might seem that this all happened so long ago or in such lengthy cycles that it would have little relevance for architectural design, these forces have left marks which can be used to generate a formal response. Though the forces might be non-traditional site pressures, LOOM identified outwash in the lake's watershed, fire as a temporal event, and the pattern of tree regrowth as the primary forces to be used in the design proposal (Figure 9.19). The designer was interested, as a starting bias, in the way one force revealed another. The glacier defined topography, water and sediment allowed trees to grow, fire removed the trees and nurtured the land, the absence of vegetation revealed the topography and allowed water to erode it, then the trees grew again, repeating the cycle.

The interaction of human forces with natural forces began to shape the possibilities for the architectural proposal (Figure 9.20). Human forces act both as constraints and as possibilities of event. The legal site boundaries and setbacks became limiting factors, as did the need for adjacency to (view of) the lake. The client's desire for flatness – a building on a single level with no changes of section – was also a constraint. In addition to property line and single plane of occupation, there was a high water setback which acted as another constraint to the formal proposal. An old access road created a human-made outwash, now claimed back by the landscape and filled with ferns and sedge. This outwash became an asset for movement into the site and was mapped to a possible entry circulation as it created a natural path. The human factors were balanced with the natural forces of the site. The geological forces of glacier and natural outwash marked possibilities through

watershed   outwash formed   tree growth   fire strips land

Figure 9.19: Research into geological and human history of the site in IDENTIFY FORCES

Courtesy of Ralph K. Nelson/LOOM Studio

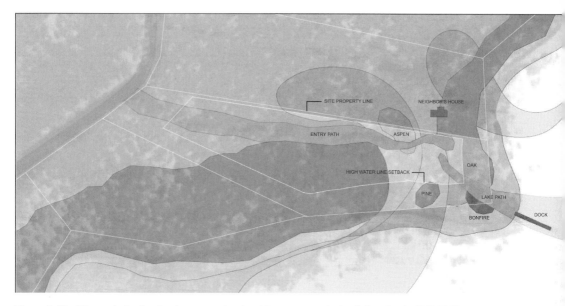

Figure 9.20: Site analysis showing human and natural forces as analysis of situation in IDENTIFY
FORCES

Courtesy of Ralph K. Nelson/LOOM Studio

landscape topography, while tree stand identities set up boundary pressures. An outwash ran down the eastern highland to the lake, populated with blueberry plants. Three stands of pioneer trees – an aspen stand, a scrim of sand oak, and a grove of red pine – were set in relationship to each other but not touching.

[PROPOSE FORMS] As part of exploratory research on the refined situation, what became interesting to the designer was the point where all these forces almost met. The architectural proposal of a domestic residence became positioned at the gap between the major site forces of outwash, highland, tree clusters, and burn evidence (Figure 9.21). Rather than being seen as an addition of the natural landscape, the response to forces allowed the house to be considered as a way of joining elements of the landscape, including its human and geological history.

[REFINE and ASSEMBLE SYSTEM] Now that an initial formal massing proposal with a clear formal intention had been generated from the application of forces, those same forces could be used to refine the form. The first consideration of the human and natural forces was based on massing and siting location. They could also be used to develop smaller details by moving scales and content. The

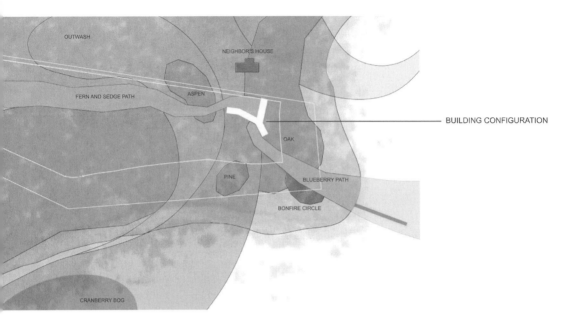

Figure 9.21: Research into geological and human history of the site as exploration and evaluation

Courtesy of Ralph K. Nelson/LOOM Studio

outwash, tree, and fire forces define different types of space (Figure 9.22). Outwash forces were understood as pressures of movement and circulation, tree forces as constraints of boundary and edges, and fire forces as patterns and structure. These began to address a building rather than a landscape scale. Outwash forces operated in plan with actions of movement and procession as well as in sectional ideas of view and water movement. The tree-based forces mapped to issues of elevation, including materiality and patterning, while the memory of fire became moments of rhythm and tracings in the ground plane and building construction.

The final proposal integrated all the various scales, but remained focused on the content provided by the geological, natural, and historical forces (Figure 9.23). The initial research located a threshold between landscape forces as the placement for the building's occupation. The identified forces suggested the thin, long shapes of the architectural proposal. To refine this form, forces of water in the context of outwash were engaged as they had the most relevance to the idea of roof. The roof composition then became a combination of the need to shed water and the particular shape of outwashes in performing this function. The water moving from

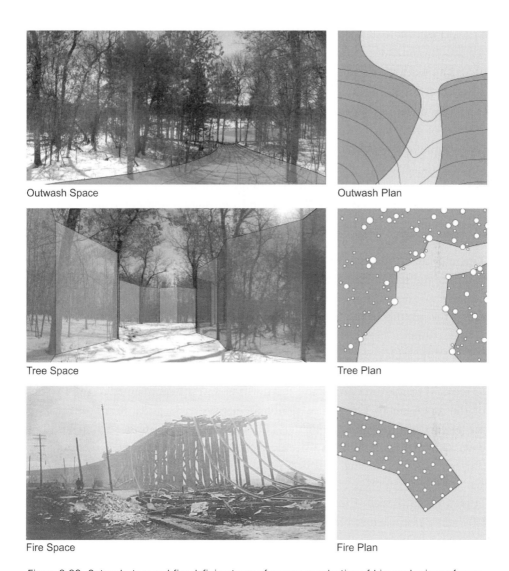

Outwash Space

Outwash Plan

Tree Space

Tree Plan

Fire Space

Fire Plan

Figure 9.22: Outwash, tree and fire defining types of spaces as selection of bias and primary forces in REFINE and ASSEMBLE SYSTEM

Courtesy of Ralph K. Nelson/LOOM Studio

the roof to the ground then shaped topography of entrance as the flow of the human construction was connected to the natural patterns of water movement. The entrance sequence was also refined with other identities of natural integration.

The need to support the movement of heavy vehicles is generally addressed with the normative asphalt or concrete driveway. This surface material eliminates the wear vehicles have on plant life and the rutting of soft earth (by eliminating the plant life and soft ground). But it also creates a water-impermeable surface as well as a harsh, unnatural appearance. If the forces at work in washout were mapped to the idea of driveway, with particular concern for the absorption and movement of water, a different conclusion could be reached. Mapping the movement of vehicles in the space, structure was provided only where needed to support the weight of tyres. This allowed the driveway to be composed of sedge and other natural grasses instead of asphalt or concrete. The ground remained absorbent while the tracks of structural paving bricks marked a history of movement through the space – the flow of vehicles. These bricks were cast as integrally coloured, charcoal-grey concrete slabs at the scale of fallen tree logs echoing a memory of the situation. To complete the refinement of the entrance space, and in other courts throughout the proposal, patterns from the forces of fire in the form of charcoal stumps demarcating the ground were placed as further markers of landscape memory.

The elevation details were pulled from the patterning of the trees with relief and texture arranged based on immediate adjacencies (Figure 9.24). The east elevation was patterned from the oak scrim while the south elevation was made to respond to the pine grove, and the north elevation was mapped to the rhythm of the aspen stand. The forces identified as priorities at the initial research of the project were carried through and connected to decisions at various scales of development, beginning with placement of the building footprint, and continuing through primary massing, elevation detailing, roof composition, and materiality.

Infrastructural forces (Example 3)

It is also possible to use forces at various scales to inform architectural design. The third example looks at the Nature-City proposal of WORKac, a New York-based architectural, urban, and interior design practice led by Amale Andraos and Dan Wood. Nature-City shows how larger-scale infrastructural forces can become the catalyst for the organization of architectural form.

WORKac approach their design work with a particular philosophical framing and bias that influences which forces they select to drive their design process. They are interested in the contemporary crisis of energy, natural resources, and density, and are focused in particular on sustainable practices around food and

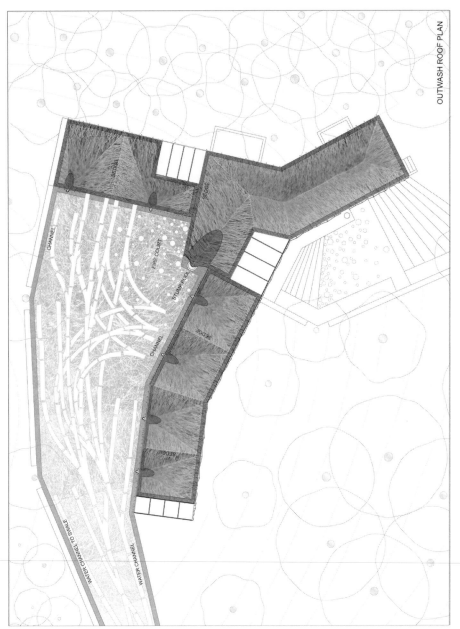

Figure 9.23: Final proposed roof plan of the architectural proposal as part of PROPOSAL

Courtesy of Ralph K. Nelson/LOOM Studio

FROM PINE GROVE

Figure 9.24: Integration of building façade to context as part of PROPOSAL

Courtesy of Ralph K. Nelson/LOOM Studio

energy production as well as a critique of traditional urban/suburban development. In addition, WORKac intentionally engage their architectural design through a visionary, utopian point-of-view in order to challenge our current practices of development. The framing position creates a bias which focuses their design decisions towards information held in the relationships among ecology, sustainability, and urbanism. The focus on these larger-scale systems, rather than discrete objects or smaller elements of programme or site, generates an architectural proposal driven by related infrastructural forces. This bias introduces the idea of hybridity into their work, a form of synthesis that focuses their priorities on creating new programmatic spaces and typologies through intentionally mixing types of occupation. In turn, the synthesis will 'exploit interconnectedness and [...] create situations where 1 + 1 = 3 – where new conditions are [created] simply through combination and sharing'.[33] It is this framing and bias that informs the starting state of many of their projects.

There are a few collateral effects of WORKac's framing and bias. While they use force-based methods, the practice often attempts to define a new typology. This might seem to make their work lean towards a pattern-based approach, but this is not the case. WORKac are interested in *new* typologies, and new types cannot be reduced from existing patterns because the patterns do not yet exist. Instead, their framing sets the focus on prototypes – the first in a new series, which will then be repeated. In addition, their utopian tendencies affect how they analyse and engage forces. While many designers use forces to engage and reduce constraints, WORKac focus on assets and opportunities. They approach their work looking for advantages and synergies rather than decreasing or removing conflicts.

One project which illustrates both the use of infrastructural forces and how framing and bias affect choices is Nature-City. The project was commissioned by the Museum of Modern Art in New York for its 2012 exhibition 'Foreclosed: Rehousing the American Dream', in response to the foreclosure crisis affecting the American population.[34] The premise of the exhibition was to reconsider the idea of the American Dream and ownership of a single family home after the recent burst of the housing bubble. WORKac responded to this challenge by using their framing based in synthesizing infrastructural forces. Their framing generated starting biases that positioned nature and city as not artificially separated and that challenged suburban sprawl. The belief in a utopian realism grounded the project in existing political and economic theories, making the proposal possible, rather than an exercise in fantasy imagination. The starting state then selected infrastructural forces which would address these positions.

The project is located on a 225-acre site, formerly owned by the City of Keizer, Oregon. The situation of the project was to provide housing for 13,000 people on this site, eliminating the need for Keizer to expand its 'urban growth boundary' (Figure 9.25). While attempting an increase of density – without an increase of urban area – the further challenge that the architectural designers took on was how to increase population while providing more choices of housing, less area of development, more resource availability, less impact on non-human factors, and a decreased cost. The judgement criterion would be one of economy and hybridity with a project proposal interlacing current infrastructures with new ecological infrastructures.

[IDENTIFY FORCES] Rather than using general cultural or context-based research to examine the situation for design priorities, it was designer bias through framing philosophy which predetermined the selection of forces. Since WORKac prioritize sustainable infrastructures, the identification of forces was based in these infrastructural systems – transportation, water, renewable energy, recreation, landscape types, non-human inhabitants, and food production. Basic environmental forces, such as the ones used in the last several examples, were ignored, except where they had a direct impact on the infrastructure. Sunlight was not considered as a primary force for human activities and biological needs, at this point. Instead, it was considered as an asset for the renewable energy infrastructure

Courtesy of WORKac

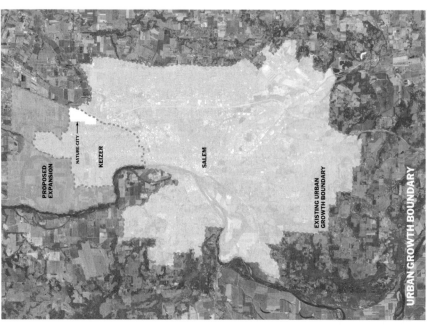

Figure 9.25: Left: Urban growth boundary. Right: Large-scale circulation mapping as review of situation

and became a factor in locations concerned with producing solar energy. Unlike previous examples, the forces are not directly defined in terms of human experience as the scale of information is much larger than normative architectural content. Thus circulation was defined as the movement of masses and products, rather than individuals; green spaces were about the productive field, orchard, and wetland, not human biofilia.

[PROPOSE FORM] Since the basis of the formal proposal was the synthesis of infrastructural forces, the architectural possibilities needed to be delayed until the infrastructures were designed. The scale at which this would occur would be the masterplan – large enough to address regional concerns but focused enough to imply architectural responses. At this point, the priority for the design process was to explore infrastructural possibilities which supported the designers' bias and intentions at multiple scales. Once the infrastructures were expanded, evaluated, and then related to each other, particular architectural responses could be connected to this greater structure. As in all other architectural design methods, a pattern that moved between exploratory and evaluative thinking styles was the major way in which content was developed. Since this was a force-based method, the exploratory and evaluative thinking was focused on responding to constraints and assets in the situation. Of course, the positive utopian framing of WORKac also redefined constraints *as* assets, so we end with assets and opportunities driving the design decisions.

The exploratory phase after the initial identification of forces developed in two concurrent studies. The first exploration analysed the context for natural infrastructures. As in a normative site analysis, the purpose was a more refined identification of forces which could be located spatially. The conclusions reached from exploring the context identified a series of animal habitats and movement patterns. These would be introduced as new forces as a way to organize and shape the architectural proposal (Figure 9.26). WORKac's framing position located human development as part of a larger closed ecosystem that accorded wildlife landscapes as much priority as human environments. Mapping the territories of non-human inhabitants suggested preserving as much of the current terrain as possible. It also identified wildlife-critical environments such as the Douglas fir forest, the oak savannah, and the wetlands. The wildlife–flora habitats then acted as pressures to exclude areas of development, pushing architectural form into the smallest footprint possible. Since the designers were focused on architectural massing with high density and a small footprint as a starting premise, this was a

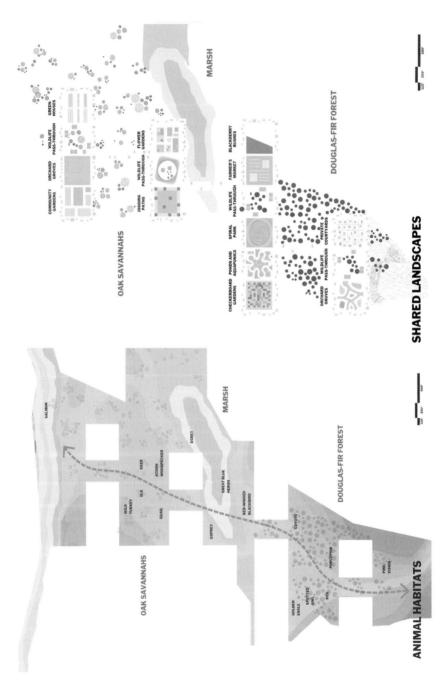

Figure 9.26: Left: Analysis of animal habitats and landscape resources. Right: How those elements might be shared between human and non-human occupation as PROPOSE FORM

Courtesy of WORKac

positive outcome and supported the overall intentions. In addition, rather than just preserving non-human occupations, the goal was to minimize the negative effect of human intervention in the overall situation. This would include such things as barriers, sprawl, heat islands, and an impermeable ground plane.

One of the major conflicts between human and non-human inhabitants comes from the disruption of wildlife movement patterns. Human constructions and transportation infrastructures, such as roads and highways, tend to be continuous. There is no provision for the passage of anything other than the mechanized human courier – which is why so many conflicts occur between automobiles and animals. To support priorities of both humans and non-humans, a pressure was introduced based on the wildlife movement force. This pressure would prohibit interruption or blockage of movement from the south end of the site to the north, supporting a pattern of wildlife travel. Considering the landscape in this way was a choice made by the designers to support coherence in the design intentions. It also became an opportunity when developing typologies later in the project.

The second study explored infrastructures that were artificial or human-based. The focus for this study was to move into an exploratory thinking phase using the identified forces of transportation, water use, renewable energy, and food production. Each type of infrastructure was expanded to examine its infrastructural chains as well as ways those chains might connect together. For example, rather than just thinking about electrical infrastructure as a series of power lines from the production centre to the individual residence, the full life-cycle of electrical production was considered as a reduction. The process would start by looking at as many alternative sources for electrical production as possible, the raw materials needed, and their life-cycles, assets that those alternatives might bring to other aspects of the project, adjacencies that could be set up based on those assets, different ways of distributing the power, and offshoots or side-benefits to various modes of production and delivery. Since the project was built around the framing of sustainable infrastructure, the desire would be to make choices based on a closed cycle – some element that is produced in the overall situation as waste should be identified and integrated back into the production loop, thus supporting a sustainable position.

The same process was repeated for each of the human-based infrastructures as well as the natural systems. Then the two studies were brought together. All of the chains that had been developed, along with several options for each infrastructural category, would be evaluated for their advantages. Questioning would explore

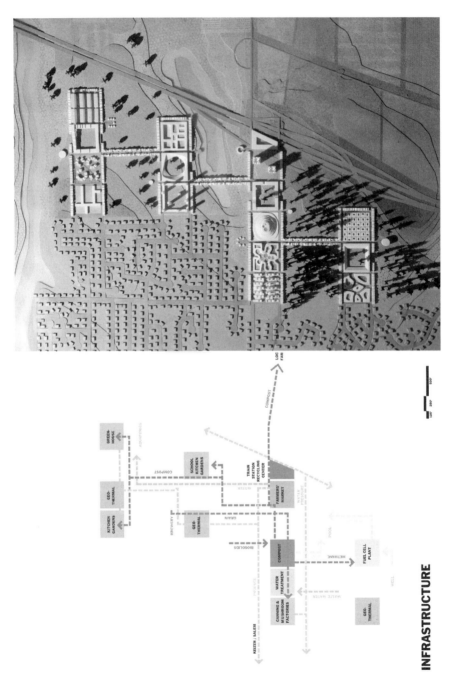

INFRASTRUCTURE

Figure 9.27: Left: Infrastructural chains and spatial relationships. Right: Model of final proposed masterplan form as PROPOSE FORM

Courtesy of WORKac

connections, such as the secondary benefits each type of renewable energy would bring, the by-products that would be created, and how these might be incorporated into other infrastructural systems. Final selections were based on linking assets to opportunities (Figure 9.27). The explored infrastructures included those that were spatially located, such as existing transportation routes and wildlife habitats, as well as those not yet fixed in space, such as food and energy production. Fixed locations would start to inform the placement of non-fixed elements by considering the advantages those locations could bring.

What makes design complex can be seen in this example – while each of the chains might be easily defined, the process of design worked by creating interactions between multiple chains. The overall proposal, like all architectural proposals, was system-based. Any change in one part of the system changed the overall composition and many of the secondary choices. This meant that a small decison could have a non-linear effect.

[REFINE and ASSEMBLE SYSTEM] The final project was built around selected and refined infrastructural chains developed from the initial categories identified by the designers (Figure 9.28). Food production infrastructure included produce grown in local farms, gardens, orchards, and greenhouses. As a chain, the produce was connected to local distribution locations (farmers' market) and transportation infrastructure for off-site commerce. Questioning the needs of food production as a cycle identified compost and water as critical inputs. Compost could be developed through the decomposition of organic waste as a by-product of food production and household garbage. However, compost production gave other benefits since its by-products were methane and heat – a way of connecting food infrastructures to energy infrastructures. It also produced a unique form as the action of composting organic solids for methane has a particular formal response: it requires a dome in order to capture the gas. While methane could provide electricity through a fuel cell power plant, other energy sources were also identified, including geothermal and solar power.

Water infrastructures were also considered as a closed-loop system. All waste water would be treated on site through natural water filtration, while the increase of permeable ground surfaces would keep natural aquifers strongly connected to run-off and precipitation. Some of the treated water could be stored as part of an aquaponic system for producing fish as part of food production and distribution (farmers' market). The rest of the treated water would need to be pressurized in order to be delivered to residences and businesses through plumbing systems. The

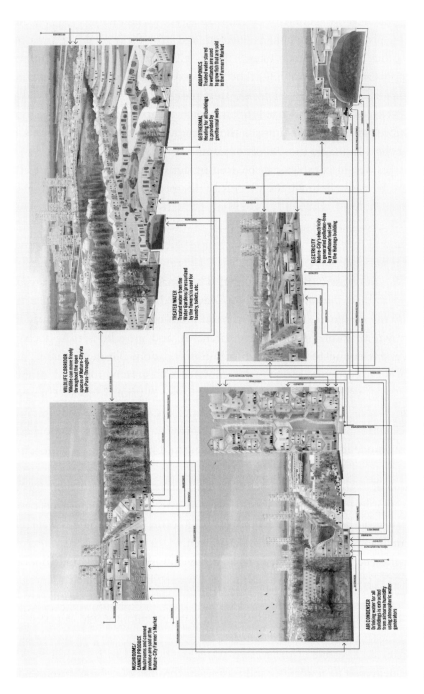

Figure 9.28: Infrastructural connections between architectural elements as REFINE and ASSEMBLE SYSTEM

Courtesy of WORKac

normative solution for pressurization is the large, dedicated water tower which can be found on the skyline of most towns and villages. Since design projects benefit from synthesis, the question of how else to engage the need to lift and store water arises – how to make one form do two things? This created an opportunity to engage the use of water towers with other aspects of the project which also needed or generated height.

Once the infrastructures were explored, scaled, and connected, the designers used the systems this had generated to develop the architectural scale. The mechanism was to ask the question: what opportunities for residential development were present due to the infrastructural assets? Since the desire was to develop new typologies, what was important was not just the individual proposal, but understanding the *system* of development it implied. Typology requires the ability to reproduce the formal relationships in other contexts.

As a judgement criterion, the landscape pressures were used to identify discrete plots of land in four rows connected to existing suburban road and rail routes, while preserving critical landscape areas. The development typologies were created by assigning an infrastructural use and a social responsibility, public amenity, or landscape opportunity to each of the squares. The final proposal for each type emerged from engaging the idea of housing with the first two factors, looking for how a residential opportunity might arise. Fifteen different typological patterns were developed, with each square unique due to the particular forces it engaged and the residential opportunities it implied (Figure 9.29). So, while geothermal heat was addressed by both Field Houses and Thru-de-Sac, the fact that the former required clearly ordered and plotted community gardens while the latter permitted less structured foraging gardens created different architectural responses.

[PROPOSAL] Once the major relationships had been developed, the proposal moved into more detailed exploration of the individual differences between living units and developing organization within the typologies (Figure 9.30). Environmental and circulation forces were applied to the architectural forms, including light access, privacy, view, and adjacencies. An infrastructural opportunity generated a new landscape for housing, such as the bio-gas digester which produced a landscape for terraced housing (Figure 9.31), or the need to pressurize water which produced a vertical structure of live-work stacked housing (Figure 9.32). The exploration of maintaining qualities of living, based in environmental and circulation forces, dictated formal composition, such as depth of rooms, access to exterior, and paths between private and public areas. In Compost Hill,

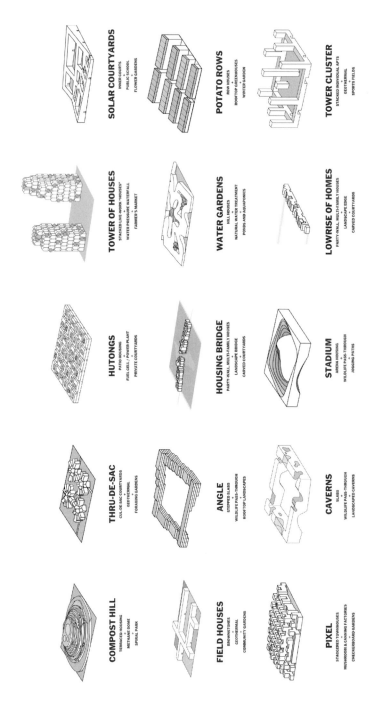

Courtesy of WORKac

Figure 9.29: Housing typologies as REFINE and ASSEMBLE SYSTEM

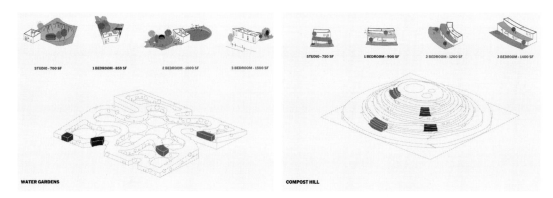

Figure 9.30: Housing typologies of Water Gardens and Compost Hill as part of PROPOSAL

Courtesy of WORKac

Figure 9.31: Compost Hill typology with methane extraction, waste heat and terraced housing in PROPOSAL

Courtesy of WORKac

the inclusion of a public park, consisting of swimming pools warmed by waste heat, introduced public-to-private pressures that would need to be resolved in successive passes.

The final proposal is coherent in its intentions. There is a clear line of development from the designers' framing philosophy through the selections they made to direct the design decisions to the formal responses. While not commissioned as a built project, the proposal could easily move through a few more phases of

Figure 9.32: Tower of Houses typology includes pressurization of water and ground area dedicated to a farmers' market. The sports field and geothermal-based Tower Cluster can be seen in the distance (PROPOSAL phase)

Courtesy of WORKac

development to become one. The next iterations of design would begin to refine structural systems, tighten spatial qualities, develop façade systems, and propose materiality.

Emergent thinking

Force-based methods are premised on developing parameters and identifying content to drive decision-making and selection as part of the process. They create limitations which makes it possible for a designer to engage in the design process, and negotiate the layers of content and choices that are available in any situation. A method generated by the force-based framework can also be considered an analogue to a parametric process. Technically, parametrics comes from mathematics, and refers to a measurable factor that interacts with others to define a system. In an architectural sense, parametrics has come to mean a process that uses factors to determine a formal resolution. The term used for those factors in design methodology is *forces*. Forces set parameters which are then used to set limits and boundaries. The process of design through forces allows emergence to occur, the generation of a design response through revealing those forces in form without a preconsidered idea of the final resolution. Emergence means making visible that which was hidden.

Notes

1 Eames, Charles, 'What is Design? An Interview with Charles Eames.' In *Eames Design: The Work of the Office of Charles and Ray Eames*, edited by Neuhart, John, Charles Eames, Ray Eames, and Marilyn Neuhart. New York: H. N. Abrams, 1989: 14–15.

2 Wright, Frank Lloyd, *The Natural House*. New York: Horizon Press, 1954: 16.

3 Alberti draws a distinction between design and construction which is represented in his terminology of *lineamenta* and *structura*. This could be considered as mapping to the contemporary separation of theory and practice as the thinking of a thing versus the doing of a thing. See Alberti, Leon Battista, *On the Art of Building in Ten Books*. Cambridge, MA: The MIT Press, 1988: 423.

4 Ibid.: 7.

5 Ibid.: 9.

6 Sullivan, Louis, *Kindergarten Chats and Other Writings (Documents of Modern Art)*. New York: Dover Publications, 2012 [1918]: 46.

7 De Zurko, Edward Robert, *Origins of Functionalist Theory*. New York: Columbia University Press, 1957.

8 Vitruvius Pollio, Marcus, M. H. Morgan, and Herbert Langford Warren, *Vitruvius, the Ten Books on Architecture*. Cambridge, MA: Harvard University Press, 1914: Book 6, Chapter 6: 185.

9 Alberti, Leon Battista, *On the Art of Building in Ten Books*. Cambridge, MA: The MIT Press, 1988: 11.

10 Ibid.: 29.

11 Ibid.

12 I am indebted to Tom Daniell for bringing this practice in Japanese architecture to my attention. See Daniell, Thomas, 'Fitting in: Small Sites in Urban Japan.' In *After the Crash: Architecture in Post-Bubble Japan*. New York: Princeton Architectural Press, 2008: 163–169.

13 Viollet-le-Duc, Eugène-Emmanuel, *The Architectural Theory of Viollet-Le-Duc: Readings and Commentary*. Edited by Hearn, M. Fillmore. Cambridge, MA: The MIT Press, 1990: 141.

14 Viollet-le-Duc, Eugène-Emmanuel, *How to Build a House: An Architectural Novelette*. Translated by Bucknall, Benjamin. 2nd edn. London: Sampson, Low, Marston, Searle, and Rivington, 1876: 8.

15 Ibid.: 10.

16 Ibid.: 11.

17 Ibid.: 14.

18 Ibid.: 15.

19 Ibid.: 19.

20 Ibid.: 18.

21 Ibid.: 22.

22 Forces can be translated between domains using domain-to-domain mapping through first principles reduction. It is probably more exact to say that forces can be *identified* through first principles, and through identification can be made relevant to architectural syntax. See Chapter 6 on first principles and Chapter 7 on domain-to-domain transfer for more information.

23 References to F. L. Wright's admiration for Viollet-le-Duc can be found throughout his published writing and letters. A good summary is found in Cronon, William, 'Inconstant Unity: The Passion of Frank Lloyd Wright.' In *Frank Lloyd Wright: Architect*, edited by Riley, Terance and Peter Reed. New York: Museum of Modern Art, 1994: 8–31. Original source material can be found in Wright, Frank Lloyd, *An Autobiography*. New York: Duell, Sloan, and Pearce, 1943.

24 Wright, Frank Lloyd, *The Natural House*. New York: Horizon Press, 1954: 40.

25 Ibid.: 88.

26 Ibid.: 69.

27 The methods and approaches by OMA have been detailed in many writings published by the practice. While not comprehensive, see Koolhaas, Rem, *et al.*, *S, M, L, XL*. New York: Monacelli Press, 1998; Koolhaas, Rem and Nobuyuki Yoshida, *Oma@work*. Tokyo: A+U Publishing, 2000; Koolhaas, Rem and Office

for Metropolitan Architecture, *Content*. Edited by McGetrick, Brendan, Simon Brown, and Jon Link. Köln: Taschen, 2004.

28 Prince-Ramus, Joshua, *Joshua Prince-Ramus on Seattle's Library*. Long Beach, CA: TED, 2006. http://www.ted.com/talks/joshua_prince_ramus_on_seattle_s_ library.html.

29 While not addressing a brainstorming session, a convergent clustering technique was applied to the programme as a way to bring clarity to the organization.

30 Koolhaas, Rem and Office for Metropolitan Architecture, *Content*. Edited by McGetrick, Brendan, Simon Brown, and Jon Link. Köln: Taschen, 2004: 140.

31 Ibid.: 143.

32 Space syntax has a series of tools to analyse the built environment for latent social content especially in the area of circulation and connectivity using visual accessibility through point isovists or grid of isovists. More information can be found at the UCL Barlett (http://www.bartlett.ucl.ac.uk/graduate/ research/space/space-syntax) and Space Syntax (http://www.spacesyntax.net/ software/) websites.

33 This information was presented to a graduate-level architectural design studio at Lawrence Technological University, Southfield, MI, in 2008. The studio was led by Dan Wood and Amale Andraos of WORKac and coordinated by the author. Intensive conversations ranged over a ten-week charette project focusing on urban farming and framing the primary philosophical position and approach of WORKac.

34 'Foreclosed: Rehousing the American Dream' took place between 15 February and 13 August 2012 in the Architecture and Design Galleries, Museum of Modern Art, New York. The show also included work by teams led by MOS, Visible Weather, Studio Gang, and Zago Architecture.

Chapter 10

Concepts

In order to execute, it is first necessary to conceive. Our earliest ancestors built their huts only when they had a picture of them in their minds. It is this product of the mind, this process of creation, that constitutes architecture and which can consequently be defined as the art of designing and bringing to perfection any building whatsoever.

Étienne-Louis Boullée[1]

A concept is an abstract idea used to order the elements of an architectural design project. There are other words that are sometimes used instead of *concept*, such as *big idea*, *position*, and *strategy*. While each of these terms has its own nuances, they all pertain to the same methodological approach. In a concept-based framework, the architectural proposal is generated by selecting and organizing architectural elements based on aligning them with a larger idea. The process identifies large priorities from the central idea and then uses those priorities to drive the design process. Anything that does not align with the overall concept is ignored or limited in influence. Hence, the concept-based framework moves in the opposite direction to pattern and force frameworks. Patterns and forces are emergent processes, allowing the proposal to be determined by small-scale decisions. They produce a whole by the aggregation of the parts, using a bottom-up approach that does not predetermine the final form. Concept-based methods set out the major organization of the proposal first, and then determine how to make the elements fit. While the central idea may be developed from many sources, it will always be a top-down process.

The contemporary use of concept as an architectural design method developed over several centuries and owes much to the idea that architecture, like art, must express something beyond its own materiality. Methodologically, the issue is not whether a concept can be used to generate a design proposal, it is how that idea operates to produce a legitimate and repeatable framework which addresses quality, meaning, and purpose. For architecture, it was literature and poetry which provided the structure and theoretical basis to understand concept as a process. Influence can be traced to several foundational events in the literary and architectural theory of the eighteenth and nineteenth centuries. The philosophical structure was developed by Alexander Gottlieb Baumgarten (1714–1762) in his project to consider the judgement of poetry under the terms of rational philosophy. Baumgarten's work followed the foundations set by René Descartes (1596–1650) and Christian Wolff (1679–1754). After Baumgarten, the architectural theory of character was introduced by Gabriel-Germain Boffrand. This theory, based on emotive effect in poetry and theatre, addressed the issue of meaning through expression in architecture. The expression of a building, its character, became synonymous with the mood or ambience found in a play, story, or poem. Thus, the methods and judgement for literature crossed to architectural design.

There were many attempts to address rational thought structures in art and design during the Enlightenment period. However, the judgement of quality in poetry by means of 'extensive clarity'[2] by Baumgarten in his 1735 thesis *Meditationes philosophicae de nonnullis ad poema pertinentibus (Meditations)* stands as a critical moment for both literature and architecture. In the *Meditations*, Baumgarten attempted to translate the philosophical principles of rational philosophy into practice. In fact, he intended to 'demonstrate that many consequences can be derived from a single concept of a poem which has long ago been impressed on the mind, and long since declared hundreds of times to be acceptable, but not once proved'.[3] In his demonstration, Baumgarten redefined the term *aesthetic* to mean the science of sensible cognition or, to say it another way, the ability to judge based on the senses rather than the intellect. Baumgarten's philosophy set the foundation of our modern philosophical discipline of aesthetics. While Baumgarten's work was based in the consumption rather than the creation of poetry, the effect that he had on architectural design methodology was important, as it evolved into judgement qualities and compositional strategies in the nineteenth century.

Baumgarten addressed certainty in poetry by the idea of *extensive clarity*. Extensive clarity addressed a *way of knowing* which was at the heart of judging poetry for its perfection. Clarity was important because it would allow access to truth and certainty – goals of rational philosophy. In Descartes's philosophical system, upon which modern Western philosophy and intellectual culture are built, both clarity and distinctness were needed to produce certainty. However, distinct representations were not considered to be poetic as they did not address information accessible to the senses.[4] Distinctness was achieved through reason and by sharply isolating the object of enquiry from all others around it. Poetry and the arts cannot work in this way as their impressions are blurred, jumbled, and packed tightly. As such, distinctness is not just impossible but undesirable. This meant that the classic rational structure to assess certainty – using both clarity and distinctness – could not be used to judge poetry in terms of its perfection. Only clarity could be used. Baumgarten developed a philosophical Rational approach that built upon clarity to provide certainty.

Working from Horace[5] (65 BCE–8 BCE) as a classic source, Baumgarten used the idea of *lucid order* to develop a structure for extensive clarity by which a poem could be judged.[6] He defined poetry as a sensate discourse, terminology that means written or spoken communication based on knowledge provided by the senses.[7] There are three parts to sensate discourse: the representations (what we might call imagery) created by the poem; the relationships between the representations; and the words with which the poem is constructed.[8] While the subject of a poem is not considered to be distinct as it is based in sensory information, it can be presented with clarity if all parts of the poem – the representation, the relationships, and the words – support the same overall idea. There is no confusion between the parts as they all reinforce the meaning of each other and the overall subject, including its presentation (the sensate discourse). To say it a different way, even though the subject is indistinct, it can be organized in such a way that all parts build towards certainty by the selection and alignment of the imagery supported by the choice of words. When all aspects align on the same purpose, creating coherence among the parts, a poem judged to be in good taste is achieved and is able to be proved so. The stronger the agreement among parts supporting the overall imagery, the more perfect the poem was considered.[9]

The same idea of coherence as judgement of quality is found in the French architectural theory of character. The theory was developed by the French architect and theorist Gabriel-Germain Boffrand (1667–1754) in his 1745 treatise *Livre d'architecture contenant les principes generaux de cet art* (*Book of Architecture*). Like Baumgarten, Boffrand worked with Horace's *Art of Poetry* to develop his ideas. He believed that there was a great affinity between poetry and architecture and that it was possible to take principles from one and apply them to the other.[10] In this case, it was the overall effect of poetry in terms of its genres in which Boffrand was interested. Each poem had a characteristic of language and expression which would render it tragic or comic, epic or romantic. As Baumgarten considered the effect of the poem to be created by the relationship between the representations and the words chosen, directed towards a point of convergence as an impression, Boffrand applied those principles directly to architecture. He focused on the idea of expression and style through the association of the parts to reinforce a greater whole of effect.

Boffrand applied to architecture what Horace, when paraphrased, called *artistic unity*,[11] and Baumgarten termed *lucid order*. The composition of the whole should be consistent with the intention of the purpose and all of the parts should support the whole. In the case of the theory of character, purpose came from the building's fitness through use or occupation. Character allowed fitness, not usually associated directly with ideas of beauty or pleasure, to be integrated into the growing stress on appearance and emotional effect. The character of a building, then, was a psychological effect centred on the observer and became the medium of expression for subject matter that no longer belongs to architecture but is only *expressed* by architecture.

In poetry, the structure and choice of words create character. In architecture, Boffrand identified the selection and arrangement of building elements as generating character, from massing and proportions to decoration and ornamentation. He gave the example of designing a grave, serious, and solid doorway as the entrance threshold to a palace and then adorning it with floral festoons or elaborate ornamentation which conflicted with the design's solemnity.[12] The concept of gravity, the intention of the palace supported by the design of the doorway, is contradicted by ornamentation that is not of the same character. There is a conflict of intention with a misalignment of parts, just as if a poem about death used words to elicit images of joyful spring mornings.

The source material for character in architecture was borrowed from the genres of poetry and included effects such as bold, serious, naive, graceful, mysterious, grand, and awe-inspiring. An architectural designer was not free to choose just anything as a source of expression, because the theory of character was originally tied to ideas of truth. Character was a way to connect the inside of the building with the exterior – the inner life would communicate through the exterior composition to create a truthful expression of use. As Boffrand wrote, it was by 'their planning, their structure and their decoration, [that] all such buildings must proclaim their purpose to the beholder'.[13] Sources for character would include not only the type of occupation, an early form of typology, but also the personality of the master of the building. The 'sound judgement of the master for whom it is built'[14] set the possible choices of character, for it must match with that person's rank and dignity. Boffrand went on to write,

> But if the master has petty notions, he will build to suit them; his house will be composed and ornamented with gewgaws. If the master's character is modest and sublime, his house will be distinguished more by elegant proportions than by rich materials. If the master's character is wayward and eccentric, his house will be full of disparities and parts out of agreement. In short, judge the character of the master for whom the house was built by the way in which it is planned, decorated and furnished.[15]

The theory of character did not maintain its requirement to express use as it developed over the next couple of hundred years. However, the theory did reinforce the idea that an overarching conceptual idea, a point of convergence, could be used to organize the elements of the architecture.

Character was central to architectural design during the next generations. It was Jacques-François Blondel (1705–1774) who developed the theory of character for the generation after Boffrand. Blondel felt character was so important to architectural design that it was impossible for a building to please any intelligent person if the relationship between the interior and the exterior was ignored. The source for character, as a conceptual position, was still the building's usage which then helped to select and organized the parts into a cohesive whole. It is in Blondel's work that the first modern use of the term *style* is found, as a representation seen to be generated by character.[16] Character produced style in the sense that while character is the expression of usage, style is the effect. The source for style did not originate from typology or any internal syntax of composition, but emotions and expression.[17] Blondel positioned that true style (*vrai style*) would lead to true architecture, and that style was found in the expression of each building, driven by ideas of taste and character.

Blondel's students, Étienne-Louis Boullée (1728–1799) and Claude-Nicolas Ledoux (1736–1806), took character as the expression of usage to an extreme.

The architectural proposal became a representation of usage through analogy and pictorial effect. Character was more closely tied to emotiveness, and function began to take on a symbolic expression rather than a more nuanced actual use. As always, it is the engagement of architecture as an art that supports the use of a concept-based approach such as character and the fundamental belief that architecture should express meaning. Ledoux extended character using the content from the activities performed within the building as a concept for its formal proposal. Rather than rich associations of packed imagery reinforcing a central idea, as advocated by Baumgarten, Ledoux's architectural designs were shallow, image-based physical symbols. The project of the Oikema, a Temple of Love and otherwise known as 'a brothel with an educational function',[18] was in the shape of a phallus (Figure 10.1); the House for a Hoopmaker was shaped using intersecting cylinders to create the impression of rings used in the work of hoopmaking for salt casks (Figure 10.2); while the House for the Inspector of the River Loue ran the river through the centre of the house as an expression of the job of its occupier. Ledoux's proposals acted as an educational tool using expression driven by social content, broadcasting the role of the building's owner as a symbol.

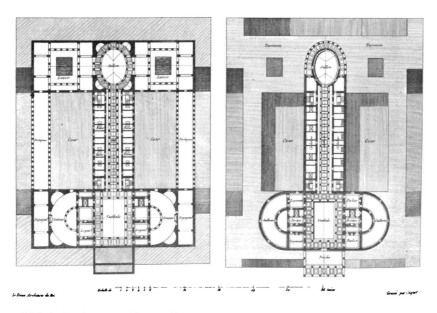

Figure 10.1: Ledoux's proposal for the Oikema, or the Temple of Love (1773–1779)

Source: Ledoux (1804): Plate 104

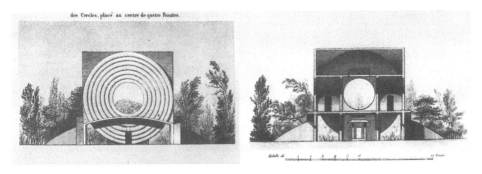

Figure 10.2: Ledoux's concept-driven design for the unbuilt House for a Hoopmaker at Saline De Chaux (1775–1779)

Source: Ledoux (1804): Plate 88

While Ledoux was developing buildings as symbolic representations, Boullée approached architecture *as* art. He was concerned with only poetic expression and pictorial effect. Boullée expressed his priorities in his 'Architecture: Essai sur l'art' ('Architecture: An Essay on Art') when he wrote,

> It is impossible to create architectural imagery without a profound knowledge of nature: the Poetry of architecture lies in natural effects. That is what makes architecture an art and that art sublime. Architectural imagery is created when a project has a specific character which generates the required impact.[19]

Character in Boullée, as an approach based on concept, became geometrically driven, with no concern for constructability, occupation, or materiality. Boullée reinforced the belief that architecture was a medium of visual communication based on a central idea, theme, or expression.

Concept, as a large-scale gesture of how architecture should be composed and how it expresses itself, is persistent as an aspect of architectural theory and method from the eighteenth century to the present day. While mostly associated with the poetic and visual metaphors, support for this idea can be found even in users of other architectural design frameworks, such as the Rationalist Durand. Durand focused on the application of patterns as the process of architectural design, but a formal concept developed through the building's character would influence the arrangement of those patterns. The building's use and occupation would set the *parti* of the building, then analysis of the composition, programme, and axis would set a *croquis* or quick sketch. The croquis would then be used as a guide for the application of patterns. Modern architects, such as Le Corbusier, responded to architecture mostly with force-based methods. Le Corbusier's *five points of architecture* – the raised structure, open plan, roof garden, continuous horizontal strip windows, and free façade – was an attempt to create a prototypical response to forces based in light, view, comfort, and movement, in order to address health and quality of life.[20] As a prototype, the response of *five points* was codified into patterns to be applied in new situations. However, in later work, such as Le Corbusier's Chapelle Notre-Dame-du-Haut in Ronchamp (1951–1954), there are clear references to character and concept (Figure 10.3). The starting state of the design set out to develop a proposal with the overall intentions of meditation and reflectivity while expressing the Catholic commissioning body's wish to move away from ornamentation and the appearance of decadence.[21] Formally, the design operates by the curving of the inner walls, which created acoustic parabolas, the use of massing to separate visual domains of difference, and a shaping of light to create transcendent experiences. There is also a sense of surrealism as the massive roof seems to float over the thick walls without support, creating a small crack of light intended to be a moment of contemplation.[22] The small building dominates the

Figure 10.3: Chapelle Notre-Dame-du-Haut in Ronchamp by Le Corbusier

Photographs courtesy of James Stevens

landscape. While Ronchamp continued to play on the primary concerns that Le Corbusier developed over his life, it operated as a design process in the realm of expression and emotion.

The usefulness of concept as a design method is its ability to address non-architectural knowledge as core content in early phases of the process. Openness to non-architectural influences to address meaning and purpose became more important during the development of Postmodern culture.[23] In addition, an overall conceptual position can make it easier to engage in synthesis during the refinement stages of the design process as there is a clear set of judgement criteria, fixed by the conceptual position to guide the formation of the whole. All parts of the design proposal can be checked against the judgement criteria to identify if they are in alignment or not. Of course, the danger of concept as a design method is the risk of mishandling non-architectural content, creating irrelevancy at the very least. As information is brought from external sources, the acts of translation occurring within concept-based framework are difficult to do well, as they need to be mapped to moments of significance and relevance in architectural syntax.

Structural framework

While there are many examples of concept-based proposals, there is no clear source of concept as a documented method in architecture. Instead, it is literature that provides the framework, in an essay titled 'The Philosophy of Composition' (1846) by the American poet, author, and critic Edgar Allan Poe.[24]

In this essay, Poe reinforced the philosophical position Baumgarten had developed over a century before. Picking up on *artistic unity or lucid order*, the rationalistic yet romantic Poe called for the development of a *unity of impression*. In order to have unity, there would need to be a focus. For Poe – as for Boffrand, Blondel, Boullée, and Ledoux – that focus or central idea would be first and foremost on *effect*. This was his starting bias as Poe did not believe in constructing a narrative around a character, event, or location. He was careful to say that this was his preference, not a requirement. Effect would be supported by two things, originality and vividness – what might be called novelty and evocativeness in architectural design.[25] From this start, the final outcome of the plot would be developed through to its conclusion before any writing was attempted – a sketch of the writing was created, which then guided the development of the work. Such a sketch would be called a *parti* or *esquisse* in architecture.

As an example to how composition worked using effect and unity, Poe reconstructed the development of his classic poem, 'The Raven' (1845). In doing this, he provided a clear and accessible illustration of the framework behind a concept-based approach to design. While the description of the poem's creation is overly simplified and the cognitive explorations are compressed to what was selected, its structure is clearly evident. As in Baumgarten, the priorities are to produce a series of elements and parts which reinforce the impression of the greater whole. The entire structure of the proposal is developed from the central effect, and each choice should more and more clearly represent that conceptual position.[26]

For Poe, the first step in considering the design of the poem was to consider its 'extent'[27] or length. Poe *believed* that writing should be short, so the entire composition could be considered within a single sitting – part of his starting bias. In order to achieve quality, brevity was critical to convey the effect of the composition. Hence, the extent would act as a limitation but not a judgement criterion – meaning that it would help to structure the poem but not to select the elements that supported the concept. Once length was determined, it was joined by effect and tone to set the starting state of the proposal. Along with length, Poe *believed* that effect and the tone of that effect were the most important characteristics from which to develop the proposal. It would be these final two items which would guide the development of a central concept to formulate the work. For 'The Raven', Poe selected beauty as the effect and sadness as its tone.[28] He did this after exploring many options and the final selections grew out of an evaluative thinking process, selected over other choices due to their greater effect and vividness.

From this point, the design process could start to engage the selection of elements and their relationships (Figure 10.4). There was no need for domain translation, as the proposal was to be constructed in language whose syntax could directly engage the ideas. Knowing the starting state as melancholy beauty, Poe explored that idea by looking for a *keynote* around which to build the proposal. He sought something that was novel, provocative, charming, interesting, or attractive. In this case, he concluded his search by focusing on the idea of the *refrain* as an underexplored but well-understood device. A refrain is a phrase or verse which is repeated throughout a poem or a song, like a chorus. Playing with the idea of the refrain became his conceptual structure for the poem. The use of the refrain was 'to produce continuously novel effects, by the variation of *the application* of the *refrain*. The *refrain* itself remaining, for the most part, unvaried.'[29] The refrain, as a conceptual device, also needed to be related to the central idea of melancholy

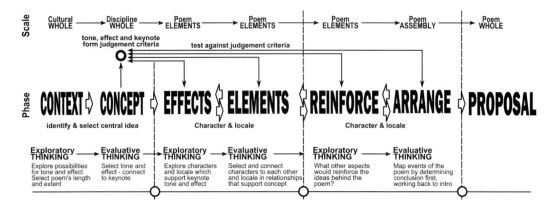

Figure 10.4: Diagram of Edgar Allan Poe's method of constructing a poem

beauty. In Poe's opinion, it would have to be brief, possibly as short as a single word, and evocative within the theme of the concept. Again, Poe employed exploratory and then evaluative thinking, which isolated and selected the word *nevermore* for its powerful impact both as a single word relating to his chosen effect and because of its tone.

The difficulty then became how to refine the structure of the poem with the chosen major element of refrain. Repetition was required when building a refrain, but Poe was looking to support novelty as well as the effect and tone. There did not seem much purpose in having a human repeat the word, as it was difficult to conceive of a context in which this would occur, not to mention its monotony. Instead, Poe connected the word *nevermore* with a non-human animal that was capable of speech. Choices were limited but there were at least two birds that would work – the parrot and the raven. However, to keep in coherence with the tone of the proposal, only the raven would align with the intentions. The parrot would operate in a grave poem in the same way as Boffrand's example of the floral festoons next to a sombre doorway.

The rest of the selections found in the poem followed the same structure, with elements chosen to support the concept and reinforce earlier elements. The choices would be tested against the judgement criterion of *melancholy beauty* and the structure of *refrain*, focusing on effect and tone while producing both novelty and accessibility for the reader. Death was selected as an extreme of the melancholic situation, reinforced in mournfulness by the subject of that death being a beautiful woman. The dead woman became the counterpoint to the raven. A relationship between the two was developed by the association with a third element, the lover of that woman who was set up as the narrator of the poem. These decisions did not just occur; they were parts of explorations around the theme to select the major elements and their relationships. The strongest effects were put in place first, and locale (or site, in architectural terms) developed to support the main elements. The first piece of writing was the conclusion, which provided a sketch for a path of development by anchoring the poem in its ending. Then, secondary elements were arranged to support the conclusion while still engaging the central effect.

Poe's stress on accessibility of experience is an echo of Boullée's statement that the 'arrangement should be such that we can absorb at a glance the multiplicity of the separate elements that constitute the whole'.[30] The important part of that sentence is *absorb at a glance*. To succeed, concept-based approaches need both simplicity of legibility and richness of layered associations. Reading 'The Raven', there is no mistaking that this is a highly sophisticated structure and composition, yet the ideas present themselves with extreme clarity. The design work of the poem became the construction of the words and their relationships to create representations, rhythm, metre, stanza length, and arrangement. Poe's starting bias selected for originality and vividness.[31]

While the method that Poe illustrated was clearly orientated towards the writing of a poem, the description is valid for any design process focused on cohesion around a central concept. What matters is how the elements and their relationships engage each other to support a larger, predetermined whole. The poetic process can be transferred to a more generic structure to be used in architecture (Figure 10.5). One of the major differences between how Poe described his thinking process in designing a poem and the possible use in an architectural design process is the closeness of poetic syntax to its source material. Since words can easily represent effects and emotions, the poet did not need to make an explicit transfer between intentions of thought and response in poetry. However, in architectural design, a conceptual position can be built from almost any starting domain of knowledge, as long as the content can be mapped successfully. Thus, there must be some point in the design process that accommodates a point of domain-to-domain transfer of principles using a technique such as first principles or structure-mapping.

As in the other frameworks, a process focused on concept moves through exploratory and evaluative thinking constantly and in multiple parallel threads. Possibilities are generated, then analysed for their potential to engage the central

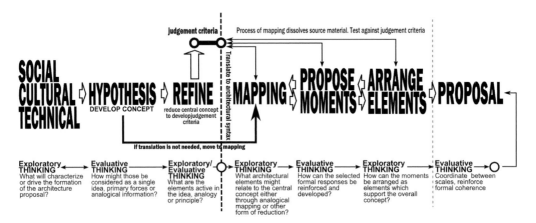

Figure 10.5: Generic framework of a concept-based design process including domain transfer and thinking styles

concept, strengthen other elements, and reinforce overall coherence. The process is not strictly linear but iterative, with all decisions tentative until reinforced by other elements. Elements of vividness or evocativeness will take precedence over supporting elements and, ultimately, all results will be expressed in architectural syntax, such as circulation, occupation, massing, and formal articulation.

Sources of concepts: internal and external content

The large variety of source material that might be used to guide the design is both a strength and a weakness of concept–based methods. A concept can be developed from any domain of knowledge; the source material may come from a physical, psychological, social, biological, cultural, literary, technical, historical, or philosophical knowledge domain. However, much of that source material will not be directly accessible by architectural syntax or tools. This does not mean that architecture *doesn't* respond to external content, just that the response is not directly represented in the materials and syntax of the discipline; rather, it is inferred. This is what is meant by using the terms *outside* and *inside* when discussing knowledge used in architectural design. Outside knowledge needs to be mapped to inside knowledge in order to be used. Inside knowledge, for architecture, involves the relationship between physical elements which will be interpreted through the visual field and human senses. Formal characteristics, spatially based social activities, human movement, and environmental effects are internal content – architectural form can respond directly to these factors. When an architect draws a series of lines on a plan to represent how people will move, there is no need to interpret those lines. We naturally place the human body conceptually between the lines and understand how it shapes circulation. In the built space, structural logic, spatial configuration, massing elements, and surface characteristics all engage directly with the human body without the need to know anything that is not actually present. This produces intrinsic meaning.

However, it is possible to take ideas from outside of architectural syntax and use them to organize a proposal *if* those ideas have a degree of relevance to the situation. *Relevance* means there is a correlation between the design response and what is actually happening in the situation to which that response is applied, rather than something made up. The correlation might be cultural, social, mythological, or physical; it just needs to matter. Successful design projects *require* relevance between the conceptual idea and the situation of the proposal. The designer is responsible for determining whether the outside source, and its conceptual position, has this relevance. This is usually best achieved by researching the context, situation, operation, or aspirations of the proposal through exploratory techniques of questioning. When a designer has accepted a conceptual position and acts to move information from outside architecture in order to use it as part of a design process, this is called domain translation, cross-domain transfer, or domain-to-domain transfer.[32] The source material, called an *analogy* or a *metaphor*, is used to guide the design proposal.

The transfer of knowledge between domains can be an incredible source of innovation and richness for an architectural designer. However, the transfer also brings risks. Transferring content between domains and maintaining relevance of that information is very difficult as there is not a one-to-one relationship between the outside and inside knowledge sets. A designer concerned with social equity might develop a conceptual position based on ideas of justice, but these are not naturally found *in* the language of architecture. There is not a direct, literal relationship between ideas of justice and the formal distribution and refinement of space. However, justice can be used as an *analogy*, and the design process would seek out and map relationship structures in aspects of justice to correlated struc- tures in architectural syntax as an inference.

While external content and domain-to-domain transfer can bring richness and innovation, they can also be a major source of irrelevance and shallowness when the transfer is done badly. The key to successful transfer is the ability to reduce the conceptual position to a series of principles that are domain independent *and* have relevance to the situation. The reduction can be done using either first principles transfer or, if the conceptualization is complex, an analogical transfer using structure-mapping. The result of the reductive process then becomes a guide to relationships between architectural objects. Being a reduction, the content is independent of specific domain knowledge and can easily move information across domains maintaining relevance. Not all concept-based positions require the transfer of principles across domains. If this is the case, then the process would move directly from a hypothesis to mapping a response in architectural syntax. Ultimately, regardless of the source of the idea, the designer is looking for organizational principles that can work on multiple scales, since the design proposal will be in architectural syntax.

Concept-based methods of architectural design are still focused on making decisions driven by relationships between elements rather than overlaying images and symbols. Since architectural designers have a tendency to stress visual relationships over all others, care must be taken to assure that the transfer and mapping do not produce a project based on symbolism, where the shape of the building *represents* something else. The conceptual position needs to be resolved in architectural syntax or it will remain as an external overlay that is artificial and non-enriching to architecture. While the shallowness of symbolism in architecture might be considered a failure of significance, it is really a failure of method.

Variations of conceptual sources

There are many examples of concept-based design that use both internal and external content to develop and organize built architectural responses. Often an analogy, question, or categorical approach is developed as a way of reducing the complexities of the variables involved in the situation, or to help arrange those variables. This is a way of limiting priorities and organizing the thinking approach when developing a response to a situation. Regardless of the starting position, all final architecture proposals are housed in architectural syntax – addressing formal relationships, spatial composition, and human occupation.

The range of source material and approaches to using a top-down, concept-based design framework is extensive. One way to develop a design concept is through questioning. This can be very strong as it can uncover significant ideas which are not apparent at first. It is also a way to ensure a degree of relevance between the concept and the proposal, provided the questioning addresses the situation in which the architectural design is engaged. The OMA/REX project for the Wyly Theater used questioning based on client needs, setting up a 'what happens if [...]?' scenario. The client, the Dallas Theater Company, had been working in a temporary building for the past thirty years and needed a new structure. However, a discussion between the client and the designers led to an understanding that the old building provided benefits that would not be met by a new structure based on standard theatre typology. In particular, there was a flexibility and lack of preciousness to the original location which allowed for dramatic renovation of the space to occur for particular performances.[33] The question which OMA/REX developed as the central concept of the project was how a new performance chamber could be freed from the obstacles presented by standard theatre typology, so that it might enjoy the flexibility offered by the old building.

The question became *refined* to the conceptual position of arranging the theatre. As OMA has a bias towards programmatic distribution in their architectural responses, and REX focuses on assets and constraints as design generators, the exploration of the concept centred on these particular areas. Joshua Prince-Ramus, the principal-in-charge of the project, illustrated the point when he said, 'So our thought was to literally put the theatre on its head: to take those things that were previously defined as front-of-house and back-of-house and stack them – above house and below house – and to create sort of what we started to call a theatre machine.'[34] The massing and programmatic response centred on freeing the performance space of its traditional position as an isolated core surrounded by service, administrative, and utility spaces (Figure 10.6).

The concept of rotating the theatre to stack vertically was then mapped to possible relationships in architectural space through programme distribution. The Wyly design process used nested typological information – patterns and relationships between programmatic spaces – because in most buildings those patterns are part of the spatial organization needed to make the building successful for occupancy. It also used social and environmental forces in adapting the location of many of the programmatic pieces to put them in positions to succeed as moments of occupation and circulation. However, the need for a flat, open performance space that blended with the ground plane drove the arrangement of the traditional patterns and forces, creating an innovative response. It has to be stressed that

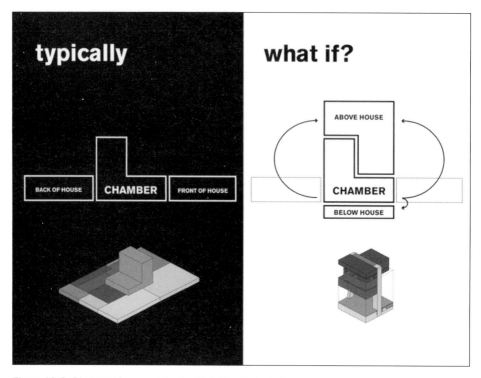

Figure 10.6: Diagram of concept for the Wyly Theater's design process

Courtesy of OMA/REX

this was not an arbitrary idea but a key response to the situation of the design. The resulting architectural design proposal arranged the backstage area and lobby directly below the main floor, extended a vertical flytower above the performance space, situated a lounge at mid-building, and placed the offices, rehearsal, and shop spaces at the top of the building (Figure 10.7). All of the programme spaces are arranged to satisfy their occupational requirements, yet the overall arrangement becomes something more.

As a point of process, if the concept refined from the initial question did not result in strong benefits for the design proposal, then the architectural designer would return to the questioning and select another position from which to develop the project. It might not be until the development of spatial moments or even arranging a relationship between moments that the strength of the conceptual position could be determined. The design process would be iterative, with many

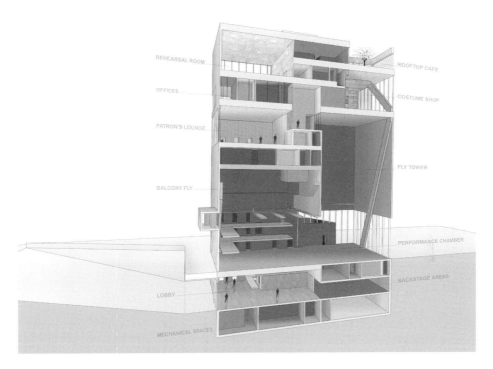

Figure 10.7: Rendered model of room distribution based on conceptual position of liberating the ground floor

Courtesy of OMA/REX

variations of programme composition investigated before the final proposal was confirmed and, ultimately, the concept assessed as strong. In the case of the Wyly Theater project, the concept of a vertical theatre with a free ground floor brought many benefits *to this particular situation*. As Prince-Ramus stated, 'it allowed us to go back to first principles, and redefine flytower, acoustic enclosure, light enclosure, and so forth'.[35] The arrangement of internal spaces, such as the extended vertical flytower, introduced speed and flexibility not normally achievable in a standard arrangement. The theatre company as a performance practice utilized varying arrangements of stage and audience space that the new performance chamber permitted. The unusual flat floor of the main performance space, combined with the ability to open that space completely to the exterior, created new revenue opportunities for the theatre, as off-season renting was possible for non-theatre uses. The resulting twelve-storey building brought a compact footprint but created a visual presence in the larger AT&T Performing Arts Center complex (Figure 10.8) which a short, large footprint building would not have achieved, thus addressing the social value and presence of the building.

While questioning a design situation can set up a process challenging normative internal knowledge, it can also access external knowledge by an analogy. Using an analogy supported by environmental and social events can be seen in the project Aqua (2010) by Studio Gang, a Chicago-based architectural office led by Jeannie Gang. Aqua is a 1.9-million-square-foot tower, significantly larger than the Wyly Theater and having a completely different set of priorities and situation. However, the same thinking framework was involved in both projects. Differences occurred due to the priorities and interests of the designers along with the particular situations that contained the design proposal. The analogies used also came from

Figure 10.8: Completed built proposal for the Dee and Charles Wyly Theater, Dallas, TX

Courtesy of OMA/REX, photographed by Iwan Baan

different source domains. While OMA is concerned with programmatic information affecting architectural design, Studio Gang often approaches an architectural situation by exploring natural science and landscape patterns, including geology and topography. The different interests bring different biases into the projects, which then change the starting points for the architectural investigations.

Aqua is a residential tower located in the heart of a cluster of large mixed-use high-rises in downtown Chicago (Figure 10.9). The surrounding context created a dilemma for the designers – namely, how to introduce positive spatial quality to the residences when the proposal is a tall tower in the middle of a series of tall towers. Since the floor dimensions, structural system, and interior organization were all set by the development company, the priority for quality in architectural terms became focused on views. It is often the case in new tower design, as Jeannie Gang notes, that 'new towers must negotiate views between many existing buildings'.[36] Views are an important component that not only engage basic human

Figure 10.9: Perspectives of the completed Aqua project in urban context

Courtesy of Steve Hall © Hedrich Blessing

needs but also create pleasure, identity, feelings of safety, and relaxation. The upper third of the Aqua tower could achieve positive views to the surrounding city, but the lower floors would be buried among the other towers. The design process was then driven by questioning the idea of views and how to achieve them.

For this project, views were not defined as a single large vista of a clear horizon. Instead, they were identified as a series of smaller moments in Chicago that might possibly be seen from Aqua's site through gaps between existing buildings. The moments included the North Shoreline, Millennium and Grant parks, the Chicago River Loop laced by bridges, Navy Pier, Lake Michigan, and significant architectural projects in the city such as the Carbide & Carbon Building. Each possibility was explored, with selected views mapped onto the site of the tower (Figure 10.10).

Rather than simply allowing the mapping to create a one-to-one relationship between the view and the point of observation, as would occur in a force-based method, Studio Gang looked to external content to help them organize the project approach. The addition of a concept would make creating a cohesive project somewhat easier to achieve, as it would be used as a single point of testing. The designers considered other domains that addressed variable views and returned to an area of their interest – topography. Unencumbered views, for the designers, were considered as a property of landscape in which the variation of topography allows for alternative angles of vision, changing perspectives, and assorted view corridors. Thinking about the vertical façade in terms of a horizontally focused source domain, such as topography or geology, introduced the idea of 'hills' into the project. Depending on where a person was standing on a hill, their view and relationship to the surrounding context would change. It also meant that the façade could be considered not as a single element but as a series of discrete events which could be *tuned* to a particular view (Figure 10.11).

The idea of hills was just a starting point, which needed to be considered and translated. The idea became reduced to considering the façade by way of analogies of landscape. This created a complex interplay between the vertical and horizontal as well as the introduction of water, topographical, and cliff analogies. The landscape analogies allowed the designers to consider contour lines as a way of describing building elevation, a very non-normative but innovative way of developing a façade. In this case, it was also *relevant*, as the variation of surface was a positive outcome that reinforced the concept of variable moments of view. As a tool, contour lines maintained coherence for the designers because their

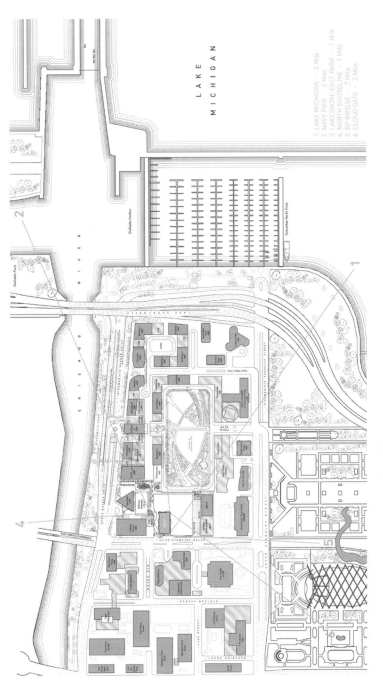

1. LAKE MICHIGAN - .3 Mile
2. NAVY PIER - .5 Mile
3. LAKESHORE EAST PARK - .1 Mile
4. NORTH SHORELINE - 1 Mile
5. BP BRIDGE - .2 Mile
6. CLOUD GATE - .2 Mile

Figure 10.10: Aqua site plan and context identifying important views

Courtesy of Studio Gang Architects

265

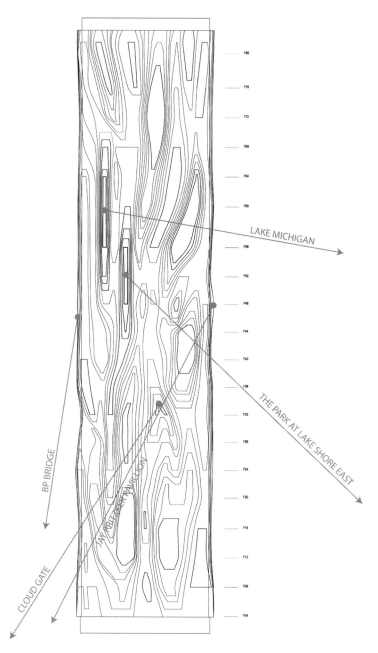

Figure 10.11: Aqua elevation diagrams with views identified

Courtesy of Studio Gang Architects

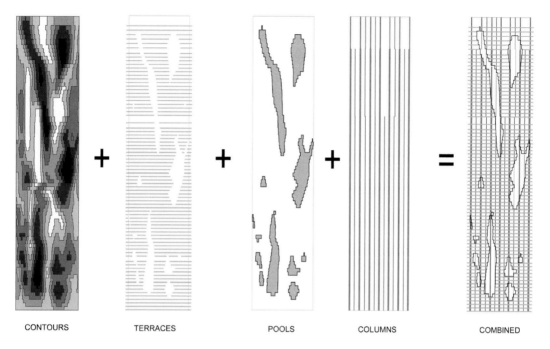

CONTOURS   TERRACES   POOLS   COLUMNS   COMBINED

Figure 10.12: Aqua elevations with analogical content mapped to architectural responses

Courtesy of Studio Gang Architects

use would not allow the elevations to be brought back into flat plane. Contour lines *required* variation of surface to be maintained, otherwise the lines could not describe anything. The contours, conceptually horizontal, were then rotated back into a vertical position and sliced into floorplates in order to create terraces based on standard floor-to-floor heights (Figure 10.12). What were originally contours on the façade now became understood as the strata of stacked plates. The term *terrace* was used in place of *balcony* to reinforce the idea that the elevation was a landscape. The extruded pieces were to be considered as a series of habitable flat areas carved from the building's face rather than as appendages stuck onto the surface.

While the analogies gave the conceptual understanding of how to think about the formal design, each perimeter on the terraces needed to be shaped and refined by the best fit to the asset of view (the judgement criterion). But at the same time, the individual terraces had to be considered with respect to how they aggregated into larger patterns on the façade, weighing both the experience of the person occupying the terrace and how the terrace presented as part of a larger system of building relating to the city. This meant sculpting the areas through a series of iterative studies. New terminology based on lake and cliff references – such as flare, swell, wave, cleft, and pool – was introduced into the project as a way of describing the effects on the building surface. If this exercise was not complex enough, the terraces were also considered in terms of 'solar-shading, apartment size, form and structure, accessibility, cost, and construction methods'.[37] These factors guided the formal decisions by acting as parts of the judgement criteria. A terrace shape would be adjusted and then checked against these criteria to assess if the adjustment would be positive overall.

Relevance for the concept was reinforced by the positive aspects it brought into the proposal.[38] The idea of façade as topography created a series of assets with social and environmental effects. The variation in the plan at the terraces allowed for diagonal views between exterior spaces and the ability to engage with other housing units through the exterior spaces – something not normally possible in high-rises. The variation of the overhangs, which ranged from two to twenty feet, also created large variations in solar shading (Figure 10.13). Areas not needing shading, or where the solar gain could be dealt with through glass choice, were smoothed out, which created 'pools' on the elevations. These brought visual relief from the striated bands, reinforced the sense of fluidity of the façade (an aesthetic benefit), and projected implied occupation onto the exterior. On the more technical side, the topography of the balconies produced a surface which disrupted wind patterns, reducing wind loading on the building. The decreased wind pressure allowed large balconies on every floor to the very top. This meant that a damping system, which is usually required for a tall building, was not needed – a design side-effect supporting the choice of concept.

The OMA and Studio Gang projects used a single focus for their concept-base designs, but it is also possible to combine several concepts. The Oslo Opera House (2008) by Snøhetta is an example of three conceptual positions being used to organize a single project (Figure 10.14). None of the concepts was dominant, yet as the concepts related to different aspects of the project, they engaged each other to produce a unified whole.

The design of the Oslo Opera House was selected through a competition initiated by Den Norske Opera & Ballett (Norwegian National Opera and Ballet). The Snøhetta proposal won the competition because it significantly addressed the two mandates with which the client had challenged the competitors – the

Figure 10.13: Terrace space with views into the city and variable perimeter

Courtesy of Steve Hall © Hedrich Blessing

Figure 10.14: Oslo Opera House at night by Snøhetta

Photograph by Rafał Konieczny/Wikimedia Commons

creation of monumentality and the encouragement of regional development. The use of a clear conceptual position to respond to these mandates was important because, as Snøhetta notes, 'In architectural competitions, the task is primarily to find a concept – a fundamental concept – that binds together the functional and architectural aspects [...] [and it] can be a verbal formulation, a simple model, a chart or a sketch.'[39] They go on to note that a concept is not the final architectural response but a way to organize and develop further work. The ability to combine particularity with flexibility is important, as a 'good concept is robust; meaning that there is clarity and generality at the same time and that [the concept] may be used for contemplation, elaboration, and addressing the real friction that always occurs in complex planning processes'.[40] As shown in the framework, and noted by Snøhetta, the concept cannot produce the architecture by itself, but it can generate judgement criteria to test decisions and reveal relationships that can, in turn, be mapped into architectural syntax.

The first steps of the design process for the Oslo Opera House consisted of Snøhetta reviewing the 'place, geography, climate and building program [as well as] ideological background, organizational and political factors, socio-economic framework, relevant references in art and literature, and free association'[41] of the building location. The environmental, social, cultural, and technical contexts were investigated to find a relevant and significant response to the idea of an opera house in Oslo. Based on this exploratory phase of the process, three conceptual positions were selected and used to drive the final design proposal. The concepts were based on the analogies of *wave wall*, *factory*, and *carpet*, and then translated into architectural gestures (Figure 10.15). The three analogies were used to help organize different aspects of the building. The wave wall addressed the threshold between public and art; the factory was used to consider the production of an opera; while the carpet became a mechanism to address the role of the Opera House as a catalyst in the public life of the city. Since they focused on different aspects of the building, the concepts worked together to form a whole rather than conflicted with each other. However, their refinement and integration would be a significant part of the design process in later phases, such as propose moments and arrange elements. Differences in material choices would also reinforce the three elements.

The concept of the wave wall was generated by both location and cultural context. The site for the Opera House was at the edge of the water in Oslo harbour. The wave wall became a mapping of that threshold between land and

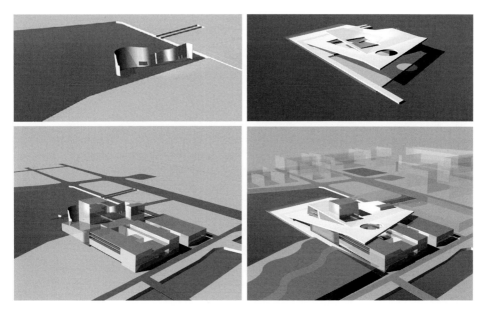

Figure 10.15: Conceptual organization of the Oslo Opera House based on the concepts of wave wall (upper left), carpet (upper right), factory (lower left), and the composite of all three (lower right) from original competition proposal

Courtesy of Snøhetta

water, pulling from some of the attributes of water touching land to inform its composition. However, more than this physical mapping, the wave wall was a conceptual threshold between the public and art, an idea that has architectural ramifications. The wall is designed in its final form as a multi-storey undulating timber surface and marks the separation of the public foyer from the activities of the opera (Figure 10.16). At higher levels, the wall becomes a buffer between public and performance as it takes on the task of hosting public galleries which allow entry to the heart of the building yet engage the public spaces and harbour below.

While the wave wall would address the idea of threshold, the actual operation of the building was organized by the analogy of factory (Figure 10.17). Rather than attempting to be innovative with the programme arrangement through expressive forms, Snøhetta used the ideas of efficiency and flexibility found in a factory model as a way of conceiving of the activities contained by the Opera House building. The Norwegian National Opera and Ballet engages 600 people in

Figure 10.16: The wave wall marks the boundary of conceptual interior and exterior

Photograph by Bjørn Erik Pedersen/Wikimedia Commons

more than 50 professions in its productions. Each of these requires unique spaces and particular climatic and acoustic conditions. In addition, there is a complex set of relationships among the activities – from costume shops to rehearsal space to set builders to stage performance. Some distances need to be short and some adjacencies are more critical than others. Using programmatic qualities to arrange relationships, as a nested force-based method, the concept of factory suggested a back-of-house based on a clean, flexible, rational organization.

The final concept, the carpet, was used as a way to tie the other two concepts together as well as relating the overall composition to the city, residents, and visitors (Figure 10.18). The carpet was Snøhetta's response to monumentality in the competition brief. Rather than considering the monumental as an object, monumentality was considered by the designers as a *destination*. The analogy of the carpet, which can also be translated as 'blanket', was mapped to a plane of activity draped over the activities of the opera. The monumental destination became driven by a 'concept of community, common property, easy and free access for everyone'.[42] As a conceptual position, it is possible to conceive of the sloped, white marble surfaces as overlaid on the programme of the opera. This meant that while the opera physically filled the harbour site, there was still public space

Figure 10.17: View of the south side of the Opera House showing the factory

Photograph by Helge Høifødt/Wikimedia Commons

maintained for open and free access. The opera occupied physical volume yet at the same time returned the site where it was situated back to public use, aided by the application of the analogy. The slopes of the carpet also work visually to merge the Opera House with the harbour and act as a visual transition between landscape and city.

All three of the analogies that Snøhetta used to develop the design proposal for the Opera House were mapped to types of occupancy and event in architectural terms. The analogies were chosen for this reason. Although there is some cultural and social symbolism, such as the wave wall representing the meeting of Norway and the world or the carpet representing freedom, the major use of the analogies was to structure architectural relationships and maintain coherence. The source domains – industrial engineering (factory), product design (carpet), and nature (wave wall) – were close to the architectural domain in terms of form and use. The mapping involved moving relationships of physical organization in the source domains to physical organization in the architectural domain. In addition, the analogies were the major point of testing used to maintain cohesion in the design proposal. The testing determined success or failure when judging options and making choices in the process. The factory analogy maintained the priorities

Figure 10.18: The carpet showing relationship between building and water

Photograph by Bjørn Erik Pedersen/Wikimedia Commons

of efficiency, adjacency, and production flow (material and human). Programme distribution prioritized these factors over social hierarchy, social status, privacy, isolation, and view due to the mapping of the analogy. The wave wall acted as a mediator of change as programme shifted from public exterior to artistic interior. Rather than proposing a vertical plane in which a person is simply on one side or the other, mapping a concept based in threshold introduced depth. Relationships which included transitory occupation could be developed in three dimensions. Design decisions were made to reinforce the exploration of a territory of difference that negotiated the transition between major categories of use. The final analogy, the carpet, mapped the idea of a plane of free activity while supporting the development of the site for a major cultural centre. By using the analogy of carpet to organize the design approach of the building to the site assets (fjord, hill, city, and harbour), the characteristics of draping and cover could be brought into the design intentions of monumentality. The concept of carpet could be reduced to the idea of a soft plane of thick covering, an idea that is possible to map directly into architectural relations as part of formal syntax. Now, rather than an exclusive massing of a building, there is a shared space of opera building combined with the public activity plane developed through the analogy. The testing criterion would maintain the priority of the monumental plane as a public resource rather than an internal asset to the opera programme. Conceptually, the carpet covered the factory, which, in practice, meant that the mapping reinforced a fully functional opera but did not exclude anyone from the best resources of the site – view, water, and public events.

Source domains do not need to be as immediately usable in a physical way, but they do need to be mappable to aspects of the design situation in such a way that they add quality to the relationships. While the examples of product design, industrial engineering, and natural systems have an affinity to architectural relationships, there are also examples of content from more distant source domains of literature, narrative, and history. As previously noted, Steven Holl used a source domain from literature in the House at Martha's Vineyard. Jean Nouvel's Cartier Foundation (1994) in Paris used the analogy of a *phantom in the park*. The source, a narrative involving a complex set of relationships, was mapped to issues of transparency, opacity, threshold, and visibility. The mapping transferred the narrative to a set of architectural ideas that engaged the dissolution of the building into nature. The Alésia Museum (2012) by Bernard Tschumi Architects consists of two buildings set in relationship to existing context and historical events. The design response took on the major concept of *non-obtrusiveness*, but also developed mappings based on history. Building location, materiality, and relationship to the surrounding landscape are all informed by mappings from historical content.

In these examples, the concept does not make a project through a one-dimensional representation. It is a high-level structure which sets up a measure to prioritize certain aspects of the organization and materiality of the architectural proposal, in order to create coherence in the overall proposal and to help structure the design response. The easiest concepts to use are those internal to architectural syntax, while the hardest, especially in terms of relevance of association, are those requiring mapping from other domains of knowledge. The more distant the source domain to architecture, the more tenuous the connections and the more necessary it is to have a strong mapping of relevance explored through reduction. The ultimate goal is to have the source domain dissolve into the architectural response, transferring only those aspects that enrich the proposal.

Applied methods

While the examples above present a general understanding of conceptual ideas as the basis of coherence in design proposals, they do not explicitly detail the design process. Since the projects are being seen from a point of completion, the central concept and the architectural response seem fairly straightforward. Yet they would have involved a fair amount of research, exploration, analysis, and discussion in their development. It is possible, however, to get to a greater level of clarity on the thinking process through a concept-based method. In order to do this, the next three examples will present the use of various source domains: landscape and natural environments; commerce and business; and politics and activism. The underlying framework will be the same for all the examples: moving from exploration of situation to a hypothesis (HYPOTHESIS/REFINE), to mapping possibilities as an architectural response using judgement criteria (MAPPING/PROPOSE MOMENTS), and then to deployment, which usually involves forces and patterns (ARRANGE ELEMENTS/PROPOSAL). The variables that will change the results dramatically are the designer's framing and bias as well as the source domain and particular relationships of the chosen concept.

The core sequence of concept-based methods is as follows:

- HYPOTHESIS/REFINE
  1. Explore the situation of the architectural proposal. Ask, 'What might matter here?'
  2. From the exploration, develop a question, position, or idea which has a high degree of relevance to the project intentions, then translate the central position into an hypothesis (concept).
  3. Identify the source domain for the hypothesis. This can be done through a *first principles reduction*.
  4. From the reduction of the hypothesis, develop a set of judgement criteria in order to maintain focus and coherence in the design process. The judgement criteria should be general and foundational so as to be flexible in terms of scale and application.

- MAPPING/PROPOSE MOMENTS
  5. If the hypothesis can be expressed directly in architectural syntax:

a. Begin to map potential relationships, moments, and anchors among the priorities found in the hypothesis and the content of the architectural proposal. The focus is on large-scale organizations and major objects/forms that can be used to align smaller-scale details.

6. If the hypothesis cannot be expressed directly in architectural syntax:

a. Then it is an analogy. Develop a list of attributes and relationships among objects in the source frame of the analogy. If the content in the source frame has attributes but no relationships, then it needs to be abandoned. Successful domain transfer stresses structural relationships.

b. Create a transfer frame by examining the attributes and relationships in the source frames. Select those frames which have a high degree of relational connection between source and target domains. Pull those aspects of the source frame forward while reducing the relationships, objects, and attributes to principles.

c. Use the transfer frame content to map the principles of the relationships and attributes to architectural equivalents in order to create a series of moments and priorities.

- ARRANGE ELEMENTS/PROPOSAL

7. Using the moments developed by the hypothesis and testing against the judgement criteria, reinforce the priorities of the conceptual position. This phase often engages force- and pattern-based information. However, if forces and pattern are used, they are filtered by the priorities of the concept.

8. Constantly check proposal arrangements and selections against the judgement criteria developed from the hypothesis. Abandon anything that does not meet the principles found in the judgement criteria. Align all aspects of the proposal towards the same goal (coherence).

9. Loop between developing moments and arranging elements that support the larger-scale intentions. All decisions are temporary until they are reinforced by other decisions and elements. Everything must align with the priorities of the conceptual position.

Methods using concept depend on a valid starting hypothesis, since it drives the arrangement of the parts. If either the hypothesis or the mapping is weak, the architectural proposal will have a tendency to fail in its significance, its richness, or its associations. The hypothesis is developed through an exploratory investigation of the situation. The situation can be defined in architectural terms as the building occupation, the performance, or the client intentions. It can also be as expansive as cultural, social, or mythological desires that are connected to this context. A concept-based project might take on current attitudes around a society's perception of the project type, the project's relative importance in a culture, nuances of client vision, or trends affecting potential changes of programme or operation in the near future. Concept-based methods are not confined to architectural syntax so the hypothesis might also be defined in socio–cultural or technical terms. Accordingly, the context can be very broad; current issues, fashions, trends in ethics, societal myths, desires, or concerns are often used to develop a concept.

Architecture addressing nature's serenity (Example 1)

The first explicit example explored the idea of a library in socio-cultural and phenomenological terms. The initial phase of any concept-based method is to develop an idea which has enough depth, breadth, and relevance to drive the design process. This project, developed by Lauren Hetzel, looked at a library in its role of user experience (starting bias) and kept returning to the idea of the library as a place for accessing knowledge through reading and study. It was the designer's bias towards how she thought about libraries that influenced the selection. All other aspects of the situation, such as new forms of information storage and the introduction of digital media, were suppressed for a reading of *library* as *vessel for relating humans to printed text*. Exploring the idea of reading and studying reduced the original interests to the concept of *serenity*. This was arrived at by considering the quality of the environment for acquiring knowledge in terms of a cultural idea of personal growth. This connected reflection and meditation as important qualities to encourage in the creation of place. Reflection and meditation, in turn, were supported by the environmental quality of serenity. While the library performs many other social and cultural roles, the designer decided to prioritize this particular aspect over all others.

The first phase of this concept-based design engaged the same thinking pattern as the other frameworks. There had been exploratory thinking through exploration that started with questioning the role of the library, focusing through evaluation which chose to focus on study and contemplation as a function of library, and the selection of a starting state to explore (serenity as a quality of place).

[HYPOTHESIS] At this stage, serenity was not yet a hypothesis; it was only a broad conceptual interest. Serenity was still too generic to have a source domain or identify specific relationships or applications for architectural use. Another exploratory and evaluative process was therefore generated, based on questioning what could be a strong analogy or other mechanism to use as part of the design. Exploring the idea, the designer started to list things that made spaces serene. After brainstorming as many aspects of serene space as possible, she selected moments of nature which supported human acquisition of knowledge through reflection. As a hypothesis, the concept became rephrased as the association of architectural spaces with natural spaces focused on making moments of serenity. The mapping in this case became a hybrid. Rather than dissolving the source into the target domain, the domains were so close (landscape/building) that desired qualities from one could be left untranslated and instead be *negotiated*. The individual identities of both 'architecture' and 'nature' would be maintained. This last part was critical for nature as a concept needed to be considered as its own entity and not as an extension of the architectural space (Figure 10.19a). There was now an hypothesis that could engage architectural syntax.

[REFINE] The developed hypothesis could then be considered directly in architectural syntax using environmental and experiential factors. There was no attempt to consider architecture *as* nature, so there was no application of an analogy. Instead, moments found in nature would be associated with moments in architecture. Since there was no analogy, the process could move straight to MAPPING and did not need to consider domain transfer. It still needed to locate relationships that might be mapped using an exploratory and evaluative phase. This phase would explore, and then select, the content that the proposal would use. When considering the concept of serenity in the natural world, the architectural designer considered events such as the sun setting over the horizon, the sound of water, the sight of ripples in water, light shining through a canopy of trees, leaves falling, fish swimming, birds calling, crickets chirping, and herbal aromas wafting.

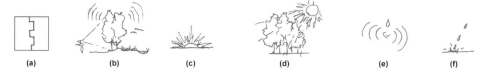

(a)   (b)   (c)   (d)   (e)   (f)

Figure 10.19: Icons to help identify priorities in the conceptual position during HYPOTHESIS

Courtesy of Lauren Hetzel

Each of these was examined for its strengths and weaknesses in the context of the project. Four events were then selected to move forward into the mapping phase. These were the view of the sunset (Figure 10.19c), light shining through trees (Figure 10.19d), the sight of ripples in water (Figure 10.19e), and the sound of flowing water (Figure 10.19f). Again, *there was no attempt to transfer any of these events through principles as an analogy.* The domain content of nature was being used directly as an asset in the architecture. Rather than an analogy, the concept that the designer accepted to guide design decisions required juxtaposition of architectural moments and natural moments. The qualities of the natural would be interlaced into events of architectural space.

[MAPPING/PROPOSE MOMENTS] Each of the selected natural events was considered as a reduction in order to determine the principal relationships' tolerances and variations. This created the possibility of flexibility in how the natural events might be applied in context to the architectural proposal. The reduction was explored through a series of questions and answers, such as: what made the sunset a sunset? What type of tree, and what scale, developed the best quality of light? Where was the effect of the shadow pattern from the leaves best viewed? What speed, angle, and volume of water produced the best effect to aid contemplation? The answers to these questions were used directly to map to locations adjacent to moments in the architectural programme, looking for positive adjacencies or sympathetic relationships. Architecturally, the priority was to create moments of blurred threshold that were points of interaction between the architectural space of the library and spaces representing nature. These could be reading nooks pushed into a natural surrounding and brought level with a grass field (Figure 10.20), internal circulation brushing against the foliage of full-grown trees, the acoustic element of falling water creating a quality of space, or an architectural water element activating visuals and reflecting light. Proposals of interlaced natural and architectural spaces were developed using the framework's same internal process that we have seen in other projects – exploratory thinking, evaluation of choices, and then selection.

The site, context, and programme of the architectural proposal were analysed using the same techniques as in pattern- and force-based methods. These included understanding the needs of the spaces, their qualities, circulation movements, environmental requirements, and privacy patterns. This information was loosely integrated with the architectural–natural moments based on the synthesis of their qualities. Vignettes were developed before working out a plan or programme

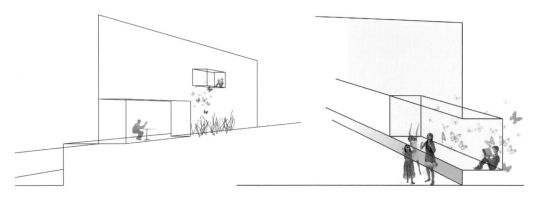

Figure 10.20: Interlacing architectural and natural spaces – merging landscapes as part of
MAPPING/PROPOSE MOMENTS

Courtesy of Lauren Hetzel

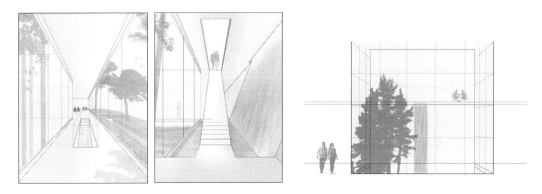

Figure 10.21: Vignette sketches developing the interlaced moments that encouraged serenity as part
of MAPPING/PROPOSE MOMENTS

Courtesy of Lauren Hetzel

arrangement as they held content which prioritized the concept and would
help guide the composition of the building proposal. These vignettes were of
greater detail than the previous sketches and contained more specific information
(Figure 10.21). Water was considered as both a horizontal and a vertical element
as well as something to view, to touch, and to hear. The event of sunset was related
to the programmatic element of café, which would act as a place for viewing.
Primary circulation slipping through two planes of natural vista started to develop
as an important idea to support the concept. Movement through the library

would conceptually be pushed 'outside' as a scenic path of travel. As the process continued, all aspects of the design were checked back against the judgement criteria to maintain coherence to the overall intentions.

[ARRANGE ELEMENTS] To this point, the conceptual position had developed discrete moments with only tentative relationship to the site context and the architectural programme. Moving back and forth between the mappings, the moments, and their arrangement would develop a proposal for the building. The section was addressed first since many of the relationships between architectural space and natural events were three-dimensionally specific (Figure 10.22). The view of the sunset required height and a west-facing orientation. The scenic circulation was determined to be best supported by a large central courtyard whose dimensions would be large enough to simulate a natural identity. The reading nooks varied from engaging the ground to being pushed into tree foliage. Trees required direct sunlight but the nooks required some controlled shade, resolving into a building with a long north–south axis orientation. As the library would be occupied from the late morning to early evening, the west façade was developed as the protected side to avoid direct solar issues, while the east side was left exposed. The building location was then moved to the west side of the site, creating a sheltered courtyard to the east. The courtyard became one of the main resources for access to natural events.

Water was addressed in several ways. It required a drop in elevation in order to create the desired amount of ambient noise, implying a sectional shift. Water was also used for its ability to reflect light and create moments of human contemplation when still. Through the project's development, the designer was increasingly interested in situating people at unexpected views into natural moments. In practice, these concerns meant sinking the central courtyard down two storeys to produce a quiet forest glade in the heart of the library which benefited from the cascade of water from ground level. A second advantage was the association of the lobby with this interior courtyard so patrons would be face-to-face with the tree canopy as they entered.

[PROPOSAL] As the moments became associated with particular locations in the context and relevant programmatic pieces, the final proposal began to take shape. No part of an architectural design process is truly linear, although it has directionality – there is a sense of movement from a beginning to an end. However, the designer always needs to be willing to abandon an aspect that does not work and loop back to pull other choices forward. Nonetheless, it is necessary

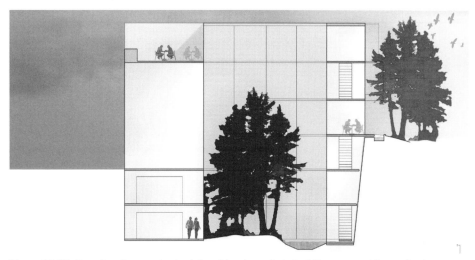

Figure 10.22: Transfer of conceptual relationship of events to building proposal in section in ARRANGE ELEMENTS

Courtesy of Lauren Hetzel

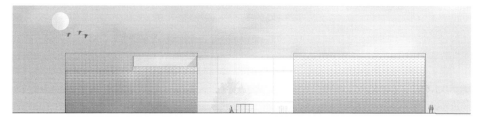

Figure 10.23: Schematic design elevation with implied façade treatment in PROPOSAL

Courtesy of Lauren Hetzel

to consider some selections as fixed so they can be used to develop secondary aspects of the project – otherwise, no decision could be made. If it proves difficult to reinforce those primary parts or if aspects of the design interfere with other strong parts of the project, then the designer needs to be willing to return to MAPPING and even REFINE to pull new material forward. At all times, synthesis of the pieces is the goal, and the concept remains the primary mechanism to test for valid selections. In this case, the dematerialization of the core of the building, extruded seating areas, rooftop gathering area, and social areas pushed to the east wall were accepted as the major aspects. Schematic elevations were developed alongside plans which reinforced these aspects of the project (Figure 10.23).

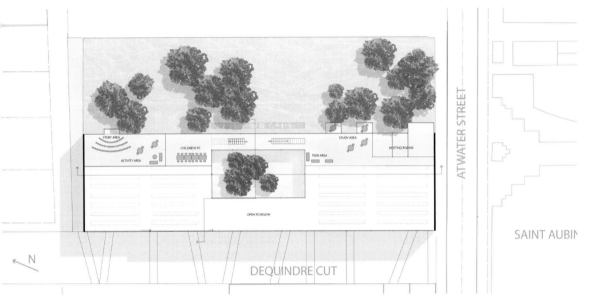

Figure 10.24: The proposed schematic plan (level 3) for a library based on serenity using the interlacing of natural events and architectural moments

Courtesy of Lauren Hetzel

Any part of the programme that implied a moment of pause, reflection, or thought was used as a point to engage nature as a catalyst for serenity. As parts of the section were locked into place and the elevations developed, the plan came to be more precise (Figure 10.24). The final proposal smoothed out the relationships between the parts and dealt with issues of proportion and efficiency.

Architecture, landscape, and shopping (Example 2)

The second explicit example approached the design process through exploring the situation of a landscape and how architecture might interact with it. The project, Consumption Landscape by Shuang Wu, responded to a challenge that asked for architectural spaces to be developed as an act of interpretation of nature. Shuang identified the location for the project as the Changbaishan National Nature Reserve in Jilin Province, China. The location was considered interesting, introducing designer bias, as it meant negotiating a landscape with significant cultural and aesthetic value. Changbaishan covers 2000 square kilometres and includes

Tianchi (Heaven Lake). The lake is a volcanic crater lake of deep blue at the summit of Mount Baekdu on the Sino–North Korean border. Baekdu is one of the five holy mountains of Korea and is located 16 kilometres from the reserve's entrance. The lake, a popular tourist destination, may be reached either on foot or in an off-road vehicle after a long climb. The initial response of the architectural designer to the chosen situation was to provide a viewing centre at the ridge of the crater, balancing the extremity of the landscape's aesthetics with architectural form (Figure 10.25).

This formal proposal quickly became unsupportable, as it had little depth or inter-action with the situation. The priorities of the proposal needed to be 'committed to a strategy of implementing architecture in a protected natural environment' and based on 'a deep understanding and assimilation of nature'.[43] The viewing centre did not meet these goals, so it was abandoned. However, initial investigations also included considering the landscape as a series of natural occupations – the relationships between elevation, soil, and vegetation (Figure 10.26). Returning to investigate the situation using the landscape relationships as a hook, the designer explored possible ways to engage architecture in such an environment. The search expanded beyond just the natural, as the region was heavily trafficked by tourists. Human occupation of natural landscapes became another line of enquiry. Each

Figure 10.25: Initial conceptual position considering architectural significance in a landscape of contrast and sublimity

Courtesy of Shuang Wu

Location

Changbai Mountain Protection District is located on the border of China and North Korea. In the district. altitude of peaks ranges from 750m to 2189m. More than 140 million people come here each year. In summer. the maximum occupation is nearly 2.3 million people.

Content

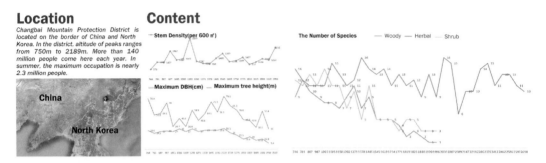

Figure 10.26: Early research into context – location, sequence, and vegetation characteristics as part of exploring SOCIAL/CULTURAL/TECHNICAL

Courtesy of Shuang Wu

ELEVATION (m)	Vegetation/Soil
2279	Alpine grass - Mountain original tundra soil
2106	Alpine tundra - Mountain peaty tundra soil
1725	Betula ermanii forest - tussock forest soil
1690	Meadow- tussock forest soil/low vegetation
1474	Mixed Shrub
1441	Changbai larch forest - brown coniferous
1410	Spruce fir forest
1113	Broad leaf forest
978	Mixed broad leaf and Korean pine forests

Figure 10.27: Early research into context – developing knowledge of the relationship between elevation and vegetation type

Courtesy of Shuang Wu

line of enquiry was expanded through a series of questions and responses, which purposely maintained their naivety while conducting basic sociological research into human activity, passage, and desires.

[HYPOTHESIS] The evaluative phase during the early stages of the design proposal created a series of interesting connections through highlighting. The information on the relationship between elevations and vegetation illustrated the rapidly changing nature of the environment in a relatively short distance. There were easily nine altitudinal zones in 16 kilometres creating a natural layering of ecosystems (Figure 10.27). Cataloguing the regional attractions identified 80 different tree species, over 300 medicinal plant species, canyons, pools, waterfalls, and several lakes in addition to Heaven Lake. Combining this information with the behaviour of visitors led the designer to develop a concept for the project. The resulting convergence of information and selection through designer bias produced a design concept that positioned *nature as a form of shopping* (Figure 10.28).

[MAPPING/PROPOSE MOMENTS] Shopping became a major aspect of the project through the evaluative part of the hypothesis phase. While landscape is not normally considered in this way, the concept was evocative in its possibilities. Shopping was not immediately relatable to architectural syntax, so it was an analogy. As an analogy for interpreting landscape, it required exploration and mapping between the knowledge domains. Shopping was relevant as a concept as there are strong parallels between how tourists interact with a destination and the general behaviour of individuals in terms of commercialism, consumption, and retail. The designer considered the events that took place as part of shopping experience, including moving, wandering, browsing, listening, talking, resting, and scanning. These events were then linked to objects as possible points of interaction. Using shopping as a concept also allowed the designer to narrow the site of her intervention. Instead of the entirety of the Changbaishan National Nature Reserve, a linear sequence of space orientated between entrance and volcano rim was selected to bound the proposal. The sequence would allow the content of the

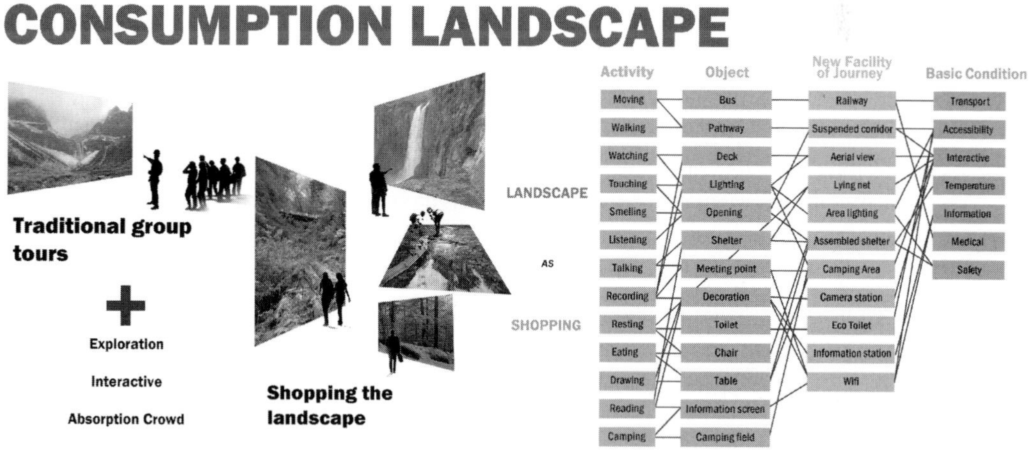

Figure 10.28: Selection of concept after research – landscape as an act of shopping as a HYPOTHESIS

Courtesy of Shuang Wu

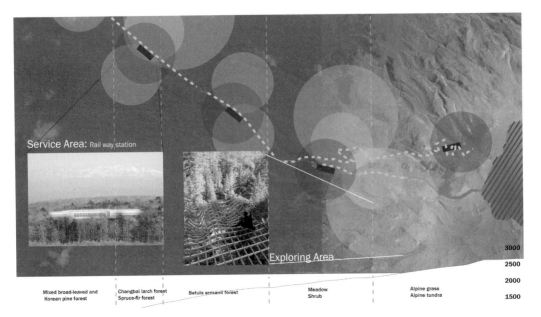

Figure 10.29: Early mapping of design concept allowing the architecture to be considered as expanded moments in the landscape

Courtesy of Shuang Wu

shopping analogy to be mapped into specific locations. An early study began to identify possible points of relevance (Figure 10.29).

Parallel to considering shopping as a series of relationships between objects and humans which create events, the particulars of the context were developed in greater detail. Altitudinal zones of layered ecosystems became the entry point for creating different experiences of retail branding if the landscape were considered a consumable. The quantity of plant species, maximum tree diameter at breast height (DBH), tree height, and stem density were mapped and correlated with each other, looking for points of interest as part of exploratory thinking (Figure 10.30). Several locations were tagged for further review and detailing. As sequence and variation of landscape became priorities in the design content, it was decided that the architectural intervention would be a series of interpretative pavilions (reduction and selection). The flora information would be used to help shape the pavilions, along with the mapped content from the shopping analogy.

As part of the evaluative phase identifying the parameters of the design proposal, the shopping analogy mapping was used to prioritize vista, browsing, and rest

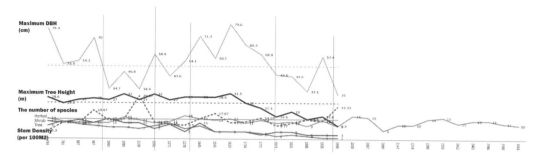

Figure 10.30: Early mapping of design concept looking for opportunities in the landscape through found objects in MAPPING/PROPOSE MOMENTS

Courtesy of Shuang Wu

as key events. More than this, the relationship between the architecture and the landscape was arranged according to the principles of a retail display. Product, placement, props, displays, and promotion (terminology of the retail domain) suggested a structure for the designer to think about the architectural interventions. The pavilions were to be discreet, using no more than 20 per cent of the area allotted, as props and displays should highlight the product, not themselves. They should support the theme of the landscape to create a unified experience, integrating rather than contrasting. The pavilions should be placed to create points of feature, and each should have a clear purpose. In addition, no pavilion should interfere with adjacent locations, the sequential experience, or points of interest.

[ARRANGE ELEMENTS] The judgement criteria developed from the concept were combined with the site research and identification of landscape principles. This suggested that, for the experiences required, a proposed form and structural system should be repeatable but flexible, adjustable and installable, based on context. At this point, that form was not yet designed; only its principles had been identified. The locations of points of interest in the landscape had been determined, however. Each identified location, as an event, was catalogued for its quality and became the major siting mechanism for the pavilions. The resultant travel sequence linked the pavilion locations in four loops off the main access road (Figure 10.31). While not meandering, the movement sequence is sufficiently offset from a purely efficient 'point A to point B' route to allow for an enriched experience supporting the goals of tourism. Vehicular traffic was also now separable from hiking and walking traffic, improving the experience for all visitors.

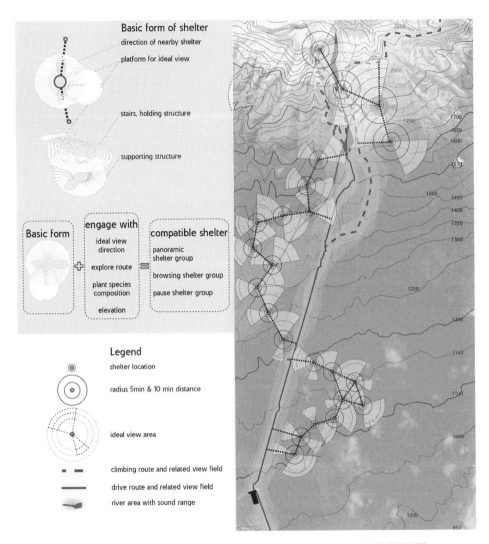

Figure 10.31: Refined site plan and formal response to concept in ARRANGE ELEMENTS

Courtesy of Shuang Wu

Once the locations of the pavilions had been identified, the formal design proceeded. A series of investigations, as an exploratory thinking sequence, examined possibilities for a form based on the structural particulars of each location and the priorities of the shopping analogy (Figure 10.32). The size of trunk diameter, canopy coverage, points of interest, access to vista, average hiking distance segments, and scale of the 'consumable event' all acted as parameters. This information, along with any nuance particular to each location, became the context for a repeated but adjustable assembly. As a force, it would set the requirements of the form. After researching this requirement, the architectural designer selected a light waffled platform to be the major surface of occupation. It could be assembled in pieces and could be carried to the erection site. The members could also be adjusted in relation to each other to create a wide degree of variation as each platform would be distorted by its particular role and context.

[PROPOSAL] The final proposal produced three types of pavilions, each tuned to the nuance of a location and the activity of the tourist, supporting a deeper understanding of the surrounding context than would normally be available. The pavilions would be repeated at intervals throughout the sequence of movement from the entrance to the rim of Heaven Lake.

The Pause Shelters were located at regular distances from each other to allow for contemplation, rest, and recovery (Figure 10.33). The surface of the pavilion stressed isolated spaces in various capacities to allow some privacy and multi-group use. The pavilion was inwards focused and protective in character with some opportunities for surveying the immediate area.

The Browsing Shelter engaged the landscape at points of close-to-medium viewing relationship (Figure 10.34). The form allowed ascendance into the tree canopies for closer investigation without harming any vegetation. The form of the shelter varied in slope, becoming a climbing wall and pockets of seating for study.

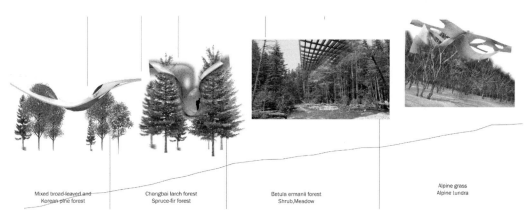

Mixed broad-leaved and Korean pine forest   Changbai larch forest Spruce-fir forest   Betula ermanii forest Shrub, Meadow   Alpine grass Alpine tundra

Figure 10.32: Three-dimensional investigations of consumption pavilions supported by nuances of context in ARRANGE ELEMENTS

Courtesy of Shuang Wu

Figure 10.33: Architectural resolution for the Pause Shelter prioritizing rest as part of PROPOSAL

Courtesy of Shuang Wu

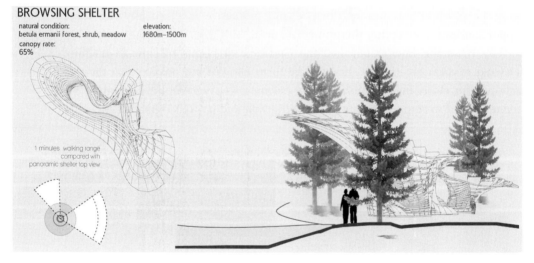

Figure 10.34: Architectural resolution for the Browsing Shelter prioritizing a close study of landscape as part of PROPOSAL

Courtesy of Shuang Wu

This pavilion type can generally be found until the treeline vanishes into meadow and tundra. Past this point, the pavilions would be located sporadically and only where an interesting rock formation or other landscape merited a close view.

At any point of vista, the Panoramic Shelter is located and tuned to provide attention on that view (Figure 10.35). This pavilion type had the highest elevation of the three types and maintained a single priority – create a platform for an incredible outlook or the framing of a scene. The form of the pavilion, in this situation, visually identifies the direction of the event to be considered. There is a single focus for each of these forms and it is fully externalized, unlike the Pause and Browse Shelters. The lattice allows for climbing when the form is vertical. As the pavilion form transitions from the vertical to the horizontal, the continuous lattice provides the structure to support surface cladding. The two uses of the single structure allow a human body to both climb and stand.

The final presentation of the architectural proposal maintained its coherence with the priorities set up in the hypothesis phase (Figure 10.36). It used the application of concept as an organizing principle as well as a way to identify judgement criteria for testing each decision made in the process. The use of shopping as an analogy became beneficial in this case as it allowed unique ways of considering architectural relationships through domain mapping. In the end, however, the analogy is not present except through choices made in the architectural response. There is no representation or symbolism of consumption, or any value judgement or critique of commercialism in the proposal. The analogy was used only to strengthen and enrich the architecture, not as cultural commentary.

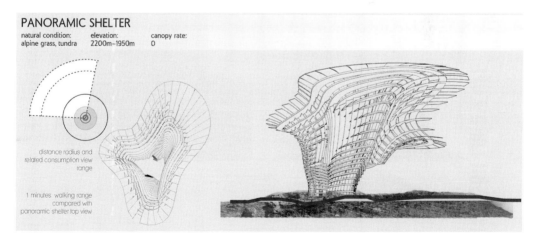

PANORAMIC SHELTER

| natural condition: | elevation: | canopy rate: |
| alpine grass, tundra | 2200m–1950m | 0 |

distance radius and related consumption view range

1 minutes walking range compared with panoramic shelter top view

Figure 10.35: Architectural resolution for the Panoramic Shelter prioritizing vista as part of PROPOSAL

Courtesy of Shuang Wu

Figure 10.36: Brochure representations of the three pavilion typologies in context

Courtesy of Shuang Wu

Political activism and architecture (Example 3)

The third example addresses how a political analogy can be used as a concept to generate an architectural design proposal. The project, Occupy Skyscraper, was developed by Ying Xiao and Shengchen Yang.[44] The designers started the project with a limit – the architectural proposal had to address the idea of the skyscraper based on changes in technology, typology, and globalization. It was also tasked to be 'an investigation on the public and private space and the role of the individual and the collective in the creation of a dynamic and adaptive vertical community'.[45] To this limit, the designers introduced their own bias – they were interested in addressing architecture as activism to support a democratic political structure. Researching the current status of democratic political action in October 2011, when the project commenced, highlighted the Occupy movement.[46] Occupy was then receiving international press coverage, and the movement, which had started in New York City on 17 September 2011, had quickly spread around the world (Figure 10.37). Within three weeks of the New York event, the movement had touched every continent except Antarctica, with protests in over ninety-five cities. For the designers, the movement had a strong potential to be engaged as part of an architectural proposal, as it was provocative, timely, and connected to their sense of ethics. The Occupy political agenda and the structure of the movement would act as an analogy for mapping into the proposal, moving from politics to architecture.

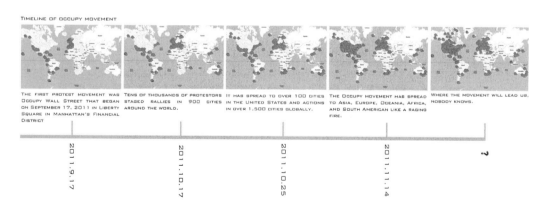

Figure 10.37: Growth of the Occupy movement worldwide in a three-month period during fall of 2011 as early research

Courtesy of Ying Xiao and Shengchen Yang

[HYPOTHESIS] After the initial exploratory and evaluative thinking phases that selected Occupy as a site for an architectural intervention, a design concept had to be developed. The designers understood the basic operations and beliefs of the movement. They wrote in a project brief that

> in a world driven by markets, the richest 1% of people write the rules of an unfair global economy. The other 99% – the vast majority of the people who live, love and die on our planet – are beholden to this sliver of a minority. As Goethe said, 'None are more hopelessly enslaved than those who falsely believe they are free'. The 99% are these enslaved, their rights distorted and treasure swindled. The carrot dangles, and the cart moves forward pulled by the 99%.[47]

Passionate rhetoric, however, does not necessarily make a strong architectural project.

The project limits and bias along with the selected subject created a simple concept to focus the proposal. As the stress was on verticality and the designers were using the New York City-based Occupy Wall Street as the situation to address, the concept was positioned to move the protests into three dimensions (Figure 10.38). There would still need to be analogy mapping to guide decisions,

VERTICAL OCCUPY

THE PROPOSAL IS SUPPORTING THE POLITICAL MOVEMENT ARCHITECTURALLY AND CONSTRUCTS A TOWER FOR DEMOCRACY. IT CHANGES THE ORIGINAL HORIZONTAL PROTEST TO A VERTICAL PROTEST AND FINALLY TO 3-D OCCUPATOIN

Figure 10.38: Concept for the Occupy Skyscraper proposal as HYPOTHESIS

Courtesy of Ying Xiao and Shengchen Yang

but the major judgement criterion was set by the concept. The next question became how architecture could support a grass-roots political movement and reinforce that movement's priorities.

[MAPPING/PROPOSE MOMENTS] Occupy Wall Street became both an analogy and a situation for the project. As an analogy, it was used to map the relationships and priorities of the movement into an architectural response that used this information as its decision-making structure. As a situation, Occupy Wall Street was used as context, site, programme, and client. While it is not necessary for a situation and analogy to be identical, in this case it strengthened the proposal to align both aspects of the architectural design.

Expanding into research about Occupy Wall Street, the designers explored the organization, its goals, strategies, beliefs, and methods. Evaluation of the research identified several relationships as possible points of mapping the analogy. The Occupy movement is a collective process that strives to be leaderless.[48] As such, decision-making is by consensus and through participatory democracy. There is no rigid structure, or even a clear shared mission statement – an arrangement for which the movement has been criticized. The general description of the global movement is the reinvention of twenty-first-century politics and financial structures. What was highlighted for the designers was the process of change from the grass roots, with small elements making a radical change in the greater whole, along with a suppression of hierarchy.

As a situation, the designers analysed Occupy Wall Street and the related Occupy events for content to engage the analogical mapping. Through exploratory thinking, a programme of the protest's needs was developed. While not a traditional client for an architect, the designers considered the participants of the Wall Street protest as their patron and user group. Spaces that would be required were identified. These included orientation space for speeches and large gatherings, workshop space for the fabrication of placards and flags, rallying space for smaller groups to assemble and organize, recreation space for casual interactions away from the protest, large meeting space away from the front lines, conference space for the General Assembly to discuss strategy, and sleep/rest space as a residential component. All of these spaces were catalogued for their qualities and needs. The general factors considered were based on the bias of elevation as a factor of safety, the proximity to the protest event, and the density of users.

Mapping from the relationships and priorities of the Occupy movement, the architectural form was suggested to be additive, participatory, and non-hierarchical.

As a democratic structure, the material choices should be readily available, non-premium, and adaptable from everyday sources. The structure should grow based on need and the increasing density of protesters. It should not be structured by top-down planning or a rigid system that does not allow incremental growth. Moving through another exploratory phase based on assembly and materiality, the designers explored all the possible ways these priorities could be met. The evaluation of that information ultimately selected a system based on rope, canvas, tents, and carabiners (Figure 10.39).

Existing buildings would be used as the primary structure since they were available in the context of Occupy Wall Street. This allowed the proposal to be internally non-structured and non-hierarchical. Attached to the existing structure would be ropes and carabiners, used to produce a web system on which programmatic spaces would be developed as needed (Figure 10.40). The web could be arranged without echelons or a rigid organization. It could also expand based on need. Connected to the web system would be a panel system using tents, canvas, and connectors. The panel system was used to create contained space for different types of occupation.

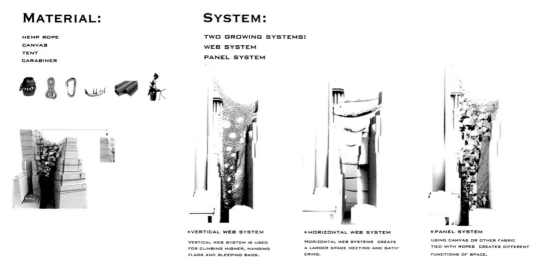

MATERIAL:

HEMP ROPE
CANVAS
TENT
CARABINER

SYSTEM:

TWO GROWING SYSTEMS:
WEB SYSTEM
PANEL SYSTEM

•VERTICAL WEB SYSTEM

VERTICAL WEB SYSTEM IS USED FOR CLIMBING HIGHER, HANGING FLAGS AND SLEEPING BAGS.

•HORIZONTAL WEB SYSTEM

HORIZONTAL WEB SYSTEMS CREATE A LARGER SPACE MEETING AND GATHERING.

•PANEL SYSTEM

USING CANVAS OR OTHER FABRIC TIED WITH ROPES CREATES DIFFERENT FUNCTIONS OF SPACE.

Figure 10.39: Assembly and materiality selection from analogical mapping as part of MAPPING/ PROPOSE MOMENTS

Courtesy of Ying Xiao and Shengchen Yang

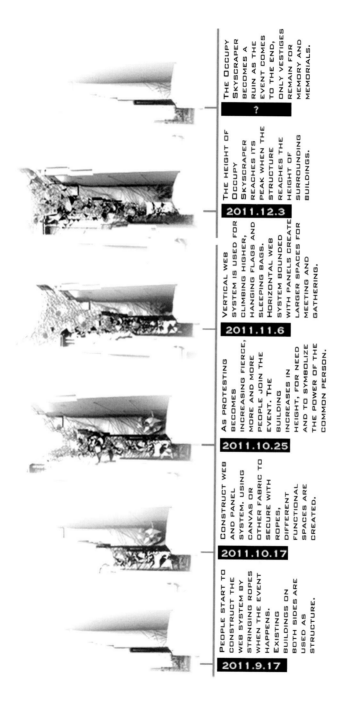

Figure 10.40: Mappings of temporalness and shifting needs from situation analysis as part of MAPPING/PROPOSE MOMENTS

Courtesy of Ying Xiao and Shengchen Yang

Other priorities of the movement, such as non-violence, were mapped to programmatic relationships as a response to context. Non-violence was translated to the architectural by considering height and location of use types. The street would be the location of protest as well as police, corporate representatives, and civic authorities. Any threat to the protesters would be considered to occur on the street level. The designers chose to address safety not through shielding and impenetrable materials, if deadly violence were used, but through the removal of threat as a factor of elevation. The tensile structure was pulled up vertically, away from the street, as the primary site of conflict, touching it lightly. This information would be used to start to arrange programmatic spaces within the 'skyscraper'.

[ARRANGE ELEMENTS] Once the major mapping was completed and material systems identified, the project needed refinement to address particular occupations and site conditions. The situational content was brought into the design as elements that could adjust the structural arrangement. Several variations of the assembly were explored (Figure 10.41), resolving into a finalized structural system generated as a general model and then analysed for programme opportunities (Figure 10.42). Since the web and panel system were selected for maximum flexibility, the programme responded to spatial quality only. Traditional architectural qualities of circulation, light, privacy, and isolation were not used for the programmatic arrangement. While not undermining the importance of these forces, the designers intended a narrow focus for the proposal. They used qualities that would support the concept and provide coherence to the overall design. The qualities used were those identified earlier in the process: the requirements of factors of safety, the proximity to the protest event, and the density of users.

While not fixed, the designers suggested a possible arrangement of programmatic spaces based on their architectural system (Figure 10.43). Orientation space would be located on the street, or just above it, with the skyscraper providing a stage area performing as the major focal point for the protest. This would be one of the largest defined spaces and the closest to the action. Workshop space would also be near the ground, so protesters would not need to carry equipment or supplies too far while climbing the structure. Rallying space was considered flexible in terms of location, scale, and purpose. These spaces would be opportunistic, carved out based on the whim and need of the users. Recreation and large meeting spaces were to be pushed away from the street to provide some degree of safety. The recreational space might need some infrastructural resources that would affect its

Figure 10.41: An early exploratory manifestation of the system as suggested by analogical mappings

Courtesy of Ying Xiao and Shengchen Yang

location – such as electricity leached from adjacent buildings. The most protected spaces would be the sleeping spaces and the conference space. The location of the sleeping spaces was suggested as in proximity to rallying or meeting spaces, but still with a high degree of safety. There should be multiple redundant clusters of these spaces spread through the skyscraper complex. The conference space would be set the highest and would constantly shift locations as the structure grew. The abandoned conference space would be appropriated as a meeting space. While easily accessible internally, the conference space should be obscure to view or monitoring from the outside.

[PROPOSAL] The final proposal responded to the needs of the Occupy movement 'through broadcast and shelter'.[49] The proposal stressed adaptability and temporary shelter while becoming an alternative image of the power structure it opposed – the skyscraper as symbol of corporate hegemony (Figure 10.44). The design is not site specific, but it is context specific. More than just a mapping from the political to the architectural, the designers intended the proposal to map back from the architectural into the political. The temporary edifice would become a symbol of human outcry, participatory democracy, and solidarity. While not

Figure 10.42: A refined manifestation of the system through evaluation and selection as part of
ARRANGE ELEMENTS

Courtesy of Ying Xiao and Shengchen Yang

present in the project's method, the effect of the final work would have an aspect
of the symbolic – as a positive side-effect of use rather than a design intention.

WORKSHOP SPACE ② RECREATION SPACE ⑤

ORIENTATION SPACE ① LARGE MEETING SPACE ③ SLEEP/REST SPACE ⑥

Figure 10.43: Suggested composition and arrangement of programme spaces based on architectural system as part of ARRANGE ELEMENTS

Courtesy of Ying Xiao and Shengchen Yang

Coherent thinking

Most projects pursuing architectural competitions use concept as a design framework in order to develop a proposal. One of the strengths of concept-based methods is the ability quickly to communicate a core set of priorities to which the proposal responds. In a competition, this is important as there is little time to build an understanding of a subtle and nuanced experiential project. The strength is also the danger, however. Concept operates by producing an overlying set of priorities that are used to select and arrange elements within the body of the proposal. The selection of the concept and the mapping of content are both based on the skill, sensitivity, and experience of the architectural designer. In addition, while concept-based methods can use either internal or external source material, they also use techniques from both typological patterns and forces as part of the process. In this context, pattern and force information is directed by concept's judgement criteria, creating coherence to an overall position or idea, rather than emergence.

Figure 10.44: Final poster image of the Occupy Skyscraper in context as PROPOSAL

Courtesy of Ying Xiao and Shengchen Yang

Notes

1 Boullée, Étienne-Louis, 'Architecture: An Essay on Art.' In *Papiers de E.-L. Boullée in the Bibliothèque Nationale, Paris.* Translated by de Vallée, Sheila, edited by Rosenau, Helen. London: A. Tiranti, 1953: 82–116, at 83.

2 Baumgarten, Alexander Gottlieb, *Meditationes Philosophicae de Nonnullis ad Poema Pertinentibus.* Translated by Aschenbrenner, Karl and William B. Holther. Berkeley and Los Angeles: University of California Press, 1954: 43–47.

3 Ibid.: 36.

4 Ibid.: 42.

5 Horace was a Roman poet and critic who wrote at the time of the Emperor Augustus. He is considered one of the finest of the Roman poets and was highly influencial in later Western poetry and literature.

6 Original text is: '§70. Since order in a succession of representations is called method, method is poetic, §69. And, with Horace, when he attributes a lucid order to poets, let us call that poetic method lucid'. Baumgarten, Alexander Gottlieb, *Meditationes Philosophicae de Nonnullis ad Poema Pertinentibus.* Translated by Aschenbrenner, Karl and William B. Holther. Berkeley and Los Angeles: University of California Press, 1954: 63.

7 Original text is: '§5. Connected sensate representations are to be apprehended from sensate discourse, §2, §4.' Ibid.: 39.

8 There are correlations to the content of a domain of knowledge as discussed in Chapter 7, where a domain is constructed from objects, object-attribute, and relations between objects. Representations map to attributes, interrelationships to relations between objects and words as objects. Baumgarten's writing refers to the part as: '§10. The several parts of a poem are: (1) sensate representations, (2) their interrelationships, (3) words as their signs, §9, §6.' Ibid.: 40.

9 Extensive clarity as discourse is described as: '§8. A sensate discourse will be the more perfect the more its parts favor the awakening of sensate representations, §4, §7.' Ibid.: 39.

10 Boffrand wrote, 'An Edifice, through its design, is expressive as if on a theatrical Stage, where the scene be Pastoral or Tragical, a Temple or a Palace, and whether it is a public Edifice destined for a certain manner of use, or a private House. These different edifices, through the arrangement of their parts, their structure and the manner in which they are decorated, must announce their purpose to the observer, and if they do not, true expression is falsified, and they

are not as they should be.' See Boffrand, Gabriel-Germain, *Book of Architecture Containing the General Principles of the Art and the Plans, Elevations and Sections of Some of the Edifices Built in France and in Foreign Countries.* Translated by Britt, David, edited by van Eck, Caroline. Burlington, VT: Ashgate, 2003: 8.

11 Russell, Abby Osborne, *An English Paraphrase of Horace's Art of Poetry.* New York: William R. Jenkins, 1896: 5.

12 Boffrand, Gabriel-Germain, *Book of Architecture Containing the General Principles of the Art and the Plans, Elevations and Sections of Some of the Edifices Built in France and in Foreign Countries.* Translated by Britt, David, edited by van Eck, Caroline. Burlington, VT: Ashgate, 2003: 8.

13 Ibid.

14 Ibid.: 6.

15 Ibid.

16 Kruft, Hanno-Walter, *A History of Architectural Theory: From Vitruvius to the Present.* London and New York: Zwemmer/Princeton Architectural Press, 1994: 149.

17 Blondel wrote in 'Lessons on Architecture' (Vol. 1), 'It is said when speaking of a building that its Architecture is symbolic when the style that characterises its decoration appears to be taken from the reasons that led to it being constructed.' See Blondel, Jacques-François, 'Lessons on Architecture (Vol. 1).' In *The Emergence of Modern Architecture: A Documentary History from 1000 to 1810,* edited by Lefaivre, Liane and Alexander Tzonis. New York: Routledge, 2004 [1771]: 388–395, at 391.

18 Kruft, Hanno-Walter, *A History of Architectural Theory: From Vitruvius to the Present.* London and New York: Zwemmer/Princeton Architectural Press, 1994: 163.

19 Boullée, Étienne-Louis, 'Architecture: An Essay on Art.' In *Papiers de E.-L. Boullée in the Bibliothèque Nationale, Paris.* Translated by de Vallée, Sheila, edited by Rosenau, Helen. London: A. Tiranti, 1953: 82–116, at 88.

20 Le Corbusier and Pierre Jeanneret, 'Five Points towards a New Architecture.' In *Programs and Manifestos in Twentieth Century Architecture.* Translated by Bullock, Michael, edited by Conrads, Ulrich. Cambridge, MA: The MIT Press, 1971 [1926]: 99–101.

21 Curtis, William J. R., *Le Corbusier: Words and Forms.* New York: Rizzoli, 1986: 178.

22 Ibid.: 179.

23 Postmodernism can be seen as a crisis of faith with the Enlightenment ideas of certainity, determinism, and absolute truth. As Pam Morris wrote, 'Underpinning Enlightenment thought is an optimistic belief that human beings can adequately reproduce by means of verbal and visual representations, both the objective world that is exterior to them and their own subjective responses to that exteriority. Such representations, verbal and visual, are assumed to be mutually recognisable by fellow human beings and form the basis of knowledge about the physical and social worlds.' See Morris, Pam, *Realism*. New Critical Idiom. London and New York: Routledge, 2003: 9. This idea was challenged by Postmodern thought which then opened a search for access to meaning. Source books representing architectural theory after 1968 are expansive in their inclusion of alternative domains of knowledge and disciplinary priorities. See Hays, K. Michael, *Architecture Theory since 1968*. Cambridge, MA: The MIT Press, 1998; Nesbitt, Kate, *Theorizing a New Agenda for Architecture: An Anthology of Architectural Theory, 1965–1995*. New York: Princeton Architectural Press, 1996; Harrison, Charles and Paul Wood, *Art in Theory 1990–1990: An Anthology of Changing Ideas*. Oxford: Blackwell, 1992; and Hays, K. Michael, *Oppositions Reader: Selected Readings from a Journal for Ideas and Criticism in Architecture, 1973–1984*. New York: Princeton Architectural Press, 1998.

24 Poe, Edgar Allan, 'The Philosophy of Composition.' *Graham's Magazine* 28, no. 4 (April 1846): 163–167.

25 Poe wrote, 'I prefer commencing with the consideration of an *effect*. Keeping originality *always* in view. For he is false to himself who ventures to dispense with so obvious and so easily attainable a source of interest [...] Having chosen a novel, first, and secondly a vivid effect, I consider whether it can be best wrought by incident or tone.' Vividness is that part that strikes the mind and memory with particular force, separating foreground detail from background clutter. See ibid.: paragraph 4.

26 Baumgarten wrote, '§71. The general rule of the lucid method is this: poetic representations are to follow each other in such a way that the theme is progressively represented in an extensively clearer way. Since the theme is to be set forth in a sensate manner, §9, its extensive clarity is maintained, §17. Now if the earlier representations represent more clearly than those that follow, the latter do not accord with what is to be poetically represented. But they ought to accord, §68. Therefore, the later representations ought to set forth the theme

more clearly than the earlier.' See Baumgarten, Alexander Gottlieb, *Meditationes Philosophicae de Nonnullis ad Poema Pertinentibus.* Translated by Aschenbrenner, Karl and William B. Holther. Berkeley and Los Angeles: University of California Press, 1954: 63.

27 Poe, Edgar Allan, 'The Philosophy of Composition.' *Graham's Magazine* 28, no. 4 (April 1846): 163–167: paragraph 10.

28 Ibid.: paragraphs 13–14.

29 Ibid.: paragraph 15.

30 Boullée, Étienne-Louis, 'Architecture: An Essay on Art.' In *Papiers de E.-L. Boullée in the Bibliothèque Nationale, Paris.* Translated by de Vallée, Sheila, edited by Rosenau, Helen. London: A. Tiranti, 1953: 82–116, at 89.

31 Poe, Edgar Allan, 'The Philosophy of Composition.' *Graham's Magazine* 28, no. 4 (April 1846): 163–167: paragraph 24.

32 See Chapter 1 for a discussion of internal and external content, and Chapter 7 for domain-to-domain transfer techniques.

33 Prince-Ramus, Joshua, *Joshua Prince-Ramus on Seattle's Library.* Long Beach, CA: TED, 2006. http://www.ted.com/talks/joshua_prince_ramus_on_seattle_s_library.html.

34 Ibid.

35 Ibid.

36 Gang, Jeannie, *Reveal: Studio Gang Architects.* Edited by Simon, Dan. New York: Princeton Architectural Press, 2011: 145.

37 Ibid.: 146.

38 Studio Gang Architects stressed that if the topography analogy did not bring positive benefits, it would have been dropped and another analogy sought for a conceptual beginning. In conversations between the office and the author, it was stressed that there 'was no direct intent to mimic the form of the cliff' and 'one of the benefits of topography [as an idea] is the special views it offers, so the team then began to investigate how the tower could provide specific views of city landmarks. This led to the idea of achieving a specific elevational topography by using unique floor slabs, which resulted in the design team studying the multiple benefits made possible by varying the balconies – one of which was the wind studies and subsequent elimination of the mass damper, etc.' They made an important point about the iterative nature of design processes and relevance when stating that 'chronological order doesn't equal a hierarchy of importance – the topography concept would probably have been dropped, for

example, had we not discovered compelling reasons (like the wind disruption) to keep pursuing it.' Personal correspondence between Studio Gang Architects and the author, 21 November 2012.

39 Snøhetta, 'The Architect's Intentions.' In *Oslo Opera House* [*Operaen*], edited by Beck, Jon Otter. Oslo: Opera Publishing, 2008: 20.

40 Ibid.

41 Ibid.

42 Ibid.: 21.

43 Opengap.net, 'Innatur_2 Competition.' http://www.opengap.net/index. php?p=ficha_concurso_cerrado&id=189.

44 The project won an honourable mention in the Evolo 2012 Skyscraper Competiton (www.evolo.us) and has been published in several magazines worldwide. Occupy Skyscraper was done in a senior design studio led by the author. See Xiao, Ying, Shengchen Yang, and Philip Plowright, 'Occupy Skyscraper.' *Boundaries: International Architectural Magazine* 4 (April–June 2012): 80–81.

45 *eVolo*, '2012 Skyscraper Competition.' http://www.evolo.us/category/2012/.

46 Occupytogether, 'Homepage.' http://www.occupytogether.org/.

47 Personal communication with the author.

48 Occupy Wall Street. http://occupywallst.org/.

49 Personal communication with the author.

Chapter Eleven

Conclusion

There is a perception of increased complexity in our current cultural period. Many different terms have been thrown out in the last couple of decades to denote a paradigm shift, a self-defined description of Western society's changing intellectual construction. These include terms about emergency, complexity, networks, systems, non-linearity, hypertexting, liquidity, and postindustrial society.[1] What all these terms address is a significant technological and structural change that has occurred in information flow, economic connectivity, the ability to process 'big data', and the way humans rationalize their context. Writing almost twenty years ago, the architectural and cultural theorist Sandford Kwinter prophetically noted that our 'culture is moving decisively away from classical mechanism and reductionism. More specifically, the physics model as the system and method of explanation that has dominated our modernity for nearly five centuries is giving way to a biological model.'[2] Others, such as Manuel Castells, point out the dominance of media and their inherent disconnection with ethical and political responsibility.[3] As the Enlightenment heralded a shift in the approach to knowledge, moving from mysticism to the analogies of mechanics and the grid, now our culture is moving to the analogies of biology and the network. Many discussions are framed by these analogies as a way to invest a sense of realness in what is hopelessly virtual. The collective cultural agreement behind the analogies is that contemporary life is complex – exponentially more complex, it is held, than even a couple of decades ago, and even though that period was more complex than a couple of decades earlier. We are also beginning to realize our environment is interminably an extension of our bodies and our bodies are extensions of the environment. The clockwork model of the universe no longer suffices as a model of reality.

As architecture is a discipline that touches many aspects of what is said to be driving the cultural paradigm shift – technology, communications, economics, cognition, and politics – it cannot help but be affected. Architecture is fundamentally a manifestation of social life. A crisis or shift in a society's self-definition will affect architecture as an aspect of framing, starting bias, and transferred content. At the core of architectural design is the relationship between information and knowledge – explicitly related to the engagement of the human body with spatial and formal articulation, but implicitly about how a society represents itself and what values it holds. The increase in complexity also has information and knowledge at its centre – where does it come from, how much is there, how does it move, and, ultimately, what does it mean?

Complexity does not, however, mean randomness. It means that the complex event is difficult to map, describe, understand, and act upon using the exact knowledge of cause and effect. Complexity also does not necessarily mean complicated.[4] Complex systems have underlying structure even though it may be concealed from immediate human comprehension. The revealing of patterns in chaos and non-periodic movement was a critical point in the development of the knowledge of complexity. Chaos as a field of study can be traced back to the 1880s and the work of Henri Poincaré on the three-body problem of celestial objects. Poincaré's work led to contemporary chaos theory and the related fields of complexity and catastrophe theory. Recent work by Rima Al Ajlouni, an architectural researcher at Texas Tech University, has shown the ability to develop complex, non-periodic patterning through the use of a framework and a seed pattern.[5] Rather than a series of local rules such as matching, overlapping, or subdividing based on adjacency, Al Ajlouni found that the idea of a framework was critical to the development of complex outcomes. While not prescriptive, the framework guided overall development; the seed pattern was then the starting state and the tool for scaling. The technique was originally used by ancient Muslim designers for architectural tile patterns, yet it seems to hold one of the keys to understanding contemporary research in the formation of quasicrystalline formations. While the tile patterns seem complex, that complexity is generated by simple rules. The rules structure primary formal choices, while leaving large points of flexibility as points of engagement for human choices, artistic desire, and personal interest. Reduced to this description, there can often be deceptively simple patterns behind complexity.

It is even more critical to understand underlying purposes and thinking structures when considering that complex situations found in architectural design
contexts contain many competing priorities. Framing and starting biases for design
have already become more varied, pushed by economic, political, philosophical,
and cultural theory, combined with communication technology and massive
databases. Analytical tools continue to be refined, while generative structures of
design remain obscure. Disciplines are subdividing into more specialized units
and, though multidisciplinary work is stressed, it is difficult to develop a shared
understanding of value when a discipline's syntax is not well understood, or even
appreciated, by other disciplines. There needs to be clarity to issues of relevance, as
well as content that directly affects that relevance. Architectural design frameworks
provide this structure. The frameworks have remained stable over many hundreds
of years. This is because they developed from disciplinary priorities through syntax
engaging ultra-stable boundaries. Because the frameworks developed naturally,
they are highly relevant to outcomes that *are* architecture, and hence they are
difficult to replace. However, the frameworks are also extremely flexible and
non-restrictive – that is, there is no really good reason to want to replace them.

There are many valid paths to a successful architectural design proposal using
methods generated from the three major frameworks of pattern, force, and
concept. The purpose of those frameworks, and the various related methods,
should be considered to augment the human designer, rather than to create
automated decisions. The role of method, like a recipe, is to provide a structure
which limits, and hence guides, approach and content. This allows decisions to be
made, enforces coherence of the proposal's elements, filters for significant content
and selects tools by which to engage disciplinary syntax. Frameworks are a scaffold
for addressing content rather than the content itself. Changing a framing position,
scale of focus, or starting bias has no effect on the framework itself although it
could change the application of the method generated from that framework.

Methods developed from the pattern-based framework identify existing formal
arrangements between architectural elements and then reapply those arrangements
to a similar situation. These methods operate from the elements to the whole
as a bottom-up approach. Methods developed from the force-based framework
examine the qualities and properties of elements to set up synergies between
opportunities and assets while suppressing or exploiting the negatives of threats
and constraints. This approach is also bottom-up, or inductive; the elements project
the whole. Both pattern-based and force-based methods would be considered as

emergent processes, where the final proposal is not predetermined but emerges from the organization of the elements. In contrast, methods developed from the concept-based framework use an overall structure to organize the relationships between elements, ensuring coherence by selecting those elements that will support the desire of the whole. Concept-based methods use a top–down or deductive approach. In a design situation, the framework approaches are combined with, and influenced by, framing, bias, and starting state. These are not internal to any method. They are applied by the architectural designer as a context to help select a framework and method as well as focusing judgement criteria. A final architectural proposal is assembled by the choices made within the applied method and guided by judgement criteria. The location of the judgement, rather than the judgement itself, is fixed by the frameworks.

In this book, frameworks have been presented at their largest scale, operating as an overarching structure behind a single method. The examples of applied method have been presented in simplified versions for the sake of clarity. Many of the explorations, dead-ends, secondary, and tertiary ideas that the designers developed have been glossed over because, while formative, these aspects were ultimately abandoned as part of the process. The purpose of the applied architectural examples was to illustrate a single approach – be it pattern, force, or concept. What can make architectural design complex, though, is that methods from all three frameworks are often used in a single design process. A hybrid method uses processes from multiple frameworks arranged in a hierarchical structure – there is a dominant framework in which secondary and tertiary frameworks are nested. The secondary frameworks operate at a different scale from the overarching framework, and, if necessary, occur multiple times within the primary method. For example, the final example, Occupy Skyscraper, used a primary method based on a concept framework. The overarching method set the starting state and the judgement criteria for the project. However, many of the decisions that are required to develop a quality of architectural space were only tangentially associated with that concept. The major placement of the programmatic spaces could be driven by creating coherence with the concept, but smaller-scale design choices needed a different type of information. In order to design spaces for occupation that went beyond the large-scale gestures, the needs of the human body would have to be considered, using forces and qualities to examine environmental and social content. This would allow access to information about light, privacy, connectivity, and view as secondary information in the shaping of spaces. The concept-based method still drives the design proposal. If the primary framework were force-based, the environmental and social pressures would have been used not only to refine the spaces, but to locate them. In addition, since the Occupy Skyscraper project was using known events – the protests – it would have been possible to use patterns to map social to formal interactions in the various activities. Patterns are already implicitly involved in the placement of the various programmatic spaces; whenever social-to-formal information is applied based on known interactions, patterns are accessed. However, as a method, the location and composition of the conference room, resting areas, and rallying points, as examples, could have been extracted from case-study analysis. Again, the pattern-based method is producing information to be used within an overarching concept-based approach.

One or more methods from any framework can be nested in any other – concept to focus forces, forces to augment patterns, or patterns to develop concept. Frameworks, like all other tools, work in a situation where they have relevance. Methods based on concept address cultural mythology and identity, those based on forces access spatial qualities, and pattern-based methods map human events to their formal context.

The concern of this book was to reveal the underlying structure and conceptual tools for architectural designers that allow for exploratory, creative, and innovative design proposals. Those proposals need also to be defensible and relevant. Design methods are not used, nor can they be used, to develop correct starting states, to make choices in the process itself, to automate creative or analytical thinking, or to decide on framing positions – these require, and reveal, the abilities of a human designer. Everything else is just an idle tool.

Notes

1 A good summary in architectural terms for this shift in perception can be found in Taylor, Mark C., *The Moment of Complexity: Emerging Network Culture*. Chicago: University of Chicago Press, 2001; and Bachman, Leonard R., *Two Spheres: Physical and Strategic Design in Architecture*. Abingdon and New York: Routledge, 2012. While they have different priorities, they address the same underlying factors. To address the same issues in political and social terms, see: Bauman, Zygmunt, *Liquid Modernity*. Cambridge: Polity Press, 2000.

2 Kwinter, Sandford, 'Soft Systems.' In *Culture Lab 1*, edited by Boigon, Brian. New York: Princeton Architectural Press, 1996: Vol. 1: 207–228, at 212.

3 Castells, Manuel, *The Rise of the Network Society*. 2nd edn. Oxford: Wiley–Blackwell, 2000.

4 Complicated and complex are related terms but do not mean the same thing. Complicated events or actions have the ability to be precisely mapped and orchestrated. There are hundreds of moving parts but the relations between each of those parts is known and there is a linear effect – if 'a' happens, then 'b' happens. Hierarchically, complicated things can be managed with top-down organization. Complex events or actions also have hundreds of moving parts, but those parts are at different scales, have different priorities, and may or may not be visibly connected. The hierarchical structure is more diffused with no clear line of authority. The introduction of change into a complex system may have completely unexpected results – if 'a' happens, then 'k' is blue and 'x' starts to sing. The effects can be exponential, non-linear, and non-discrete.

5 Al Ajlouni, Rima A., 'The Global Long-Range Order of Quasi-Periodic Patterns in Islamic Architecture.' *Acta Crystallographica Section A* 68, no. 2 (2012): 235–243.

Bibliography

Al Ajlouni, Rima A. 'The Global Long-Range Order of Quasi-Periodic Patterns in Islamic Architecture.' *Acta Crystallographica Section A* 68, no. 2 (2012): 235–243.

Alberti, Leon Battista. *On the Art of Building in Ten Books*. Cambridge, MA: The MIT Press, 1988.

Alexander, Christopher. *Notes on the Synthesis of Form*. Cambridge, MA: Harvard University Press, 1964.

Alexander, Christopher. *The Timeless Way of Building*. New York: Oxford University Press, 1979.

Alexander, Christopher, Sara Ishikawa, and Murray Silverstein. *A Pattern Language: Towns, Buildings, Construction*. New York: Oxford University Press, 1977.

Alison, Archibald. *Essays on the Nature and Principles of Taste*. 2nd American edn. Hartford, CT: G. Goodwin & Sons, 1821.

Allen, Stan. 'The Future that is Now.' In *Architecture School: Three Centuries of Educating Architects in North America*, edited by Ockman, Joan. Cambridge, MA: The MIT Press, 2012.

Altshuller, Genrich, Lev Shulyak, and Steven Rodman. *The Innovation Algorithm: TRIZ, Systematic Innovation, and Technical Creativity*. Worcester, MA: Technical Innovation Center, 1999.

Archer, Bruce L. 'Design as a Discipline.' *Design Studies* 1, no. 1 (1979): 17–20.

Argan, Giulio Carlo. 'On the Typology of Architecture.' In *Theorizing a New Agenda for Architecture: An Anthology of Architectural Theory 1965–1995*, edited by Nesbitt, Kate. New York: Princeton Architectural Press, 1996 [1963]: 242–246.

Aristotle. 'Metaphysics.' In *The Complete Works of Aristotle: The Revised Oxford*

Translation, translated by Ross, W. D., edited by Barnes, Jonathan. Bollingen Series edn. Princeton, NJ: Princeton University Press, 1984: Vol. 2: 1552–1728.

Aristotle. 'Physics.' In *The Complete Works of Aristotle: The Revised Oxford Translation*, translated by Hardie, R. P. and R. K. Gaye, edited by Barnes, Jonathan. Bollingen Series edn. Princeton, NJ: Princeton University Press, 1984: Vol. 1: 315–446.

Aristotle and Jonathan Barnes. *The Complete Works of Aristotle: The Revised Oxford Translation*. Bollingen Series edn. Princeton, NJ: Princeton University Press, 1984.

Aristotle and John Henry MacMahon. *The Metaphysics of Aristotle*. Bohn's Classical Library. London: G. Bell and Sons, 1896.

Aristotle, W. D. Ross, and J. A. Smith. *The Works of Aristotle*. Oxford: Clarendon Press, 1908.

Ashley, Maurice. *The Age of Absolutism, 1648–1775*. Springfield, MA: G. & C. Merriam Co., 1974.

Aureli, Pier Vittorio. *The Possibility of an Absolute Architecture*. Cambridge, MA: The MIT Press, 2011.

Bachman, Leonard R. *Two Spheres: Physical and Strategic Design in Architecture*. Abingdon and New York: Routledge, 2012.

Baird, George. 'Studies on Urban Morphology in North America.' In *Morphologie Urbaine et Parcellaire*, edited by Merlin, Pierre. Saint-Denis: Presses Universitaires de Vincennes, 1988.

Ballantyne, Andrew. *Deleuze and Guattari for Architects*. London and New York: Routledge, 2007.

Banfield, Edward. 'Ends and Means in Planning.' *International Social Science Journal* 11, no. 3 (1959): 361–368.

Basadur, Min, George Graen, and Mitsuru Wakabayashi. 'Identifying Individual Differences in Creative Problem Solving Style.' *Journal of Creative Behavior* 24, no. 2 (1990): 111–131.

Basadur, Min and Milena Head. 'Team Performance and Satisfaction: A Link to Cognitive Style within a Process Framework.' *Journal of Creative Behavior* 35, no. 4 (2001): 227–248.

Bauman, Zygmunt. *Liquid Modernity*. Cambridge: Polity Press, 2000.

Baumgarten, Alexander Gottlieb. *Aesthetica*. Hildesheim: G. Olms, 1961.

Baumgarten, Alexander Gottlieb. *Meditationes Philosophicae de Nonnullis ad Poema Pertinentibus*. Translated by Aschenbrenner, Karl and William B. Holther. Berkeley and Los Angeles: University of California Press, 1954.

Bayazit, Nigan. 'Investigating Design: A Review of Forty Years of Design Research.' *Design Issues* 20, no. 1 (2004): 16–29.

Beardsley, Monroe C. *Aesthetics from Classical Greece to the Present: A Short History.* New York: Macmillan, 1966.

Behne, Adolf. *The Modern Functional Building.* Santa Monica, CA: Getty Research Institute for the History of Art and the Humanities, 1996.

Benjamin, Andrew. 'Eisenman and the Housing of Tradition.' In *Rethinking Architecture: A Reader in Cultural Theory*, edited by Leach, Neil. New York: Routledge, 1997: 286–301.

Bhatt, Ritu. 'Christopher Alexander's *Pattern Language*: An Alternative Exploration of Space-Making Practices.' *Journal of Architecture* 15 no. 6 (2010): 711–729.

Blackwell, A. F. 'The Reification of Metaphor as a Design Tool.' *ACM Transactions on Computer–Human Interaction* 13, no. 4 (2006): 490–530.

Blondel, Jacques-François. 'Lessons on Architecture (Vol. 1).' In *The Emergence of Modern Architecture: A Documentary History from 1000 to 1810*, edited by Lefaivre, Liane and Alexander Tzonis. New York: Routledge, 2004 [1771]: 388–395.

Boehm, Barry. 'A Spiral Model of Software Development and Enhancement.' *ACM SIGSOFT Software Engineering Notes* 11, no. 4 (1986): 14–24.

Boffrand, Gabriel-Germain. 'Book of Architecture.' In *The Emergence of Modern Architecture: A Documentary History from 1000 to 1810*, edited by Lefaivre, Liane and Alexander Tzonis. New York: Routledge, 2004 [1745]: 316–317.

Boffrand, Gabriel-Germain. *Book of Architecture Containing the General Principles of the Art and the Plans, Elevations and Sections of Some of the Edifices Built in France and in Foreign Countries.* Translated by Britt, David, edited by van Eck, Caroline. Burlington, VT: Ashgate, 2003.

Bonta, Juan Pablo. *Architecture and its Interpretation.* New York: Rizzoli, 1979.

Bosanquet, Bernard. *A History of Aesthetic.* 2nd edn. London and New York: Allen & Unwin, 1966.

Boullée, Étienne-Louis. 'Architecture: An Essay on Art.' In *Papiers de E.-L. Boullée in the Bibliothèque Nationale, Paris.* Translated by de Vallée, Sheila, edited by Rosenau, Helen. London: A. Tiranti, 1953: Vol. MS. 9153: 82–116.

Buchanan, Richard. 'Wicked Problems in Design Thinking.' *Design Issues* 8, no. 2 (1992): 5–21.

Capon, David Smith. *Le Corbusier's Legacy Principles of Twentieth-Century Architectural Theory Arranged by Category.* Chichester: Wiley, 1999.

Capon, David Smith. *The Vitruvian Fallacy: A History of the Categories in Architecture and Philosophy*. Chichester: Wiley, 1999.

Cassirer, Ernst. *The Philosophy of the Enlightenment*. Boston, MA: Beacon Press, 1960.

Castells, Manuel. *The Rise of the Network Society*. 2nd edn. Oxford: Wiley-Blackwell, 2000.

Ching, Francis D. K. *Architecture: Form, Space, and Order*. Hoboken, NJ: John Wiley & Sons, 2007.

Chong, Dennis and James N. Druckman. 'Framing Theory.' *Annual Review of Political Science* 10, no. 1 (2007): 103–126.

Colquhoun, Alan. 'Typology and Design Method.' *Perspecta* 12 (1969): 71–74.

Conway, Hazel and Rowan Roenisch. *Understanding Architecture: An Introduction to Architecture and Architectural Theory*. New York: Routledge, 2005.

Conzen, Michael R. G. *Alnwick, Northumberland: A Study in Town-Plan Analysis*. London: Institute of British Geographers, 1960.

Cook, Peter. *Archigram*. New York: Princeton Architectural Press, 1999.

Cret, Paul P. 'The École des Beaux-Arts and Architectural Education.' *Journal of the American Society of Architectural Historians* 1, no. 2 (1941): 3–15.

Croft, William and D. Alan Cruse. *Cognitive Linguistics*. Cambridge: Cambridge University Press, 2004.

Crompton, Dennis, Barry Curtis, William Menking, and the Archigram Group. *Concerning Archigram*. 3rd edn. London: Archigram Archives, 1999.

Cronon, William. 'Inconstant Unity: The Passion of Frank Lloyd Wright.' In *Frank Lloyd Wright: Architect*, edited by Riley, Terance and Peter Reed. New York: Museum of Modern Art, 1994: 8–31.

Crook, J. Mordaunt. *The Dilemma of Style: Architectural Ideas from the Picturesque to the Post-Modern*. Chicago: University of Chicago Press, 1987.

Cross, Nigel. *Design Thinking: Understanding How Designers Think and Work*. New York: Berg, 2011.

Cross, Nigel. 'Designerly Ways of Knowing: Design Discipline versus Design Science.' *Design Issues* 17, no. 3 (2001): 49–55.

Cummings, Jonathon N. and Sara Kiesler. 'Collaborative Research across Disciplinary and Organizational Boundaries.' *Social Studies of Science* 35, no. 5 (October 2005): 703–722.

Curtis, Nathaniel Cortland. *The Secrets of Architectural Composition*. New York: Dover Publications, 2011.

Curtis, William J. R. *Le Corbusier: Words and Forms*. New York: Rizzoli, 1986.

Daniell, Thomas. 'Fitting in: Small Sites in Urban Japan.' In Daniell, Thomas, *After the Crash: Architecture in Post-Bubble Japan*. New York: Princeton Architectural Press, 2008: 163–169.

Davidoff, Paul. 'Advocacy and Pluralism in Planning.' *Journal of the American Institute of Planners* 31, no. 4 (1965): 331–338.

De Zurko, Edward Robert. *Origins of Functionalist Theory*. New York: Columbia University Press, 1957.

Demkin, Joseph A., ed. *The Architect's Handbook of Professional Practice*. 14th edn. New Jersey: John Wiley & Sons, 2008.

Den Norske Opera & Ballett. *Oslo Opera House [Operaen]*. Edited by Beck, Jon Otter. Oslo: Opera Publishing, 2008.

Descartes, René. *Discourse on Method, Optics, Geometry, and Meteorology*. Rev. edn. Indianapolis, IN: Hackett, 2001.

Descartes, René, Valentine Rodger Miller, and Reese P. Miller. *Principles of Philosophy*. Dordrecht, Boston, MA, and Hingham, MA: Reidel, 1983.

D'Hooghe, Alexander, Raf De Preter, Luk Peeters, and Natalie Seys. *ORG Architects and Urban Designers, Office for Permanent Modernity: Selected Work*. Boston, MA: Office for Permanent Modernity, 2009.

Dickie, George. *The Century of Taste: The Philosophical Odyssey of Taste in the Eighteenth Century*. New York: Oxford University Press, 1996.

Dickie, George and R. J. Sclafani. *Aesthetics: A Critical Anthology*. New York: St. Martin's Press, 1977.

Docherty, Thomas. *Postmodernism: A Reader*. New York: Columbia University Press, 1993.

Dorst, Kees and Judith Dijkhuis. 'Comparing Paradigms for Describing Design Activity.' *Design Studies* 16, no. 2 (1995): 261–274.

Draper, Joan. 'The Ecole des Beaux-Arts and the Architectural Profession in the United States: The Case of John Galen Howard.' In *The Architect: Chapters in the History of the Profession*, edited by Kostof, Sprio. New York: Oxford University Press, 1986: 209–237.

Dupré, Louis K. *The Enlightenment and the Intellectual Foundations of Modern Culture*. New Haven, CT: Yale University Press, 2004.

Durand, Jean-Nicolas-Louis. *Précis of the Lectures on Architecture; with Graphic Portion of the Lectures on Architecture*. Translated by Britt, David. Los Angeles, CA: Getty Research Institute, 2000.

Eames, Charles. 'What is Design? An Interview with Charles Eames.' In *Eames Design: The Work of the Office of Charles and Ray Eames*, edited by Neuhart, John, Charles Eames, Ray Eames, and Marilyn Neuhart. New York: H. N. Abrams, 1989: 14–15.

Eisenman, Peter. 'Aspects of Modernity: Maison Dom-Ino and the Self-Referential Sign.' In *Oppositions Reader: Selected Readings from a Journal for Ideas and Criticism in Architecture, 1973–1984*, edited by Hays, K. Michael. New York: Princeton Architectural Press, 1998: 189–198.

Eisenman, Peter. *Diagram Diaries*. New York: Universe Publishing, 1999.

Else, Gerald Frank. *Aristotle's Poetics: The Argument*. Cambridge, MA: Harvard University Press, 1957.

Ericsson, K. Anders. 'The Influence of Experience and Deliberate Practice on the Development of Superior Expert Performance.' In *The Cambridge Handbook of Expertise and Expert Performance*, edited by Ericsson, K. Anders, Neil Charness, Robert R. Hoffman, and Paul J. Feltovich. Cambridge: Cambridge University Press, 2006: 685–706.

Etlin, Richard A. *Symbolic Space: French Enlightenment Architecture and its Legacy*. Chicago: University of Chicago Press, 1996.

Falkenhainer, B., K. D. Forbus, and D. Gentner. 'The Structure-Mapping Engine: Algorithm and Examples.' *Artificial Intelligence* 41, no. 1 (1989): 1–63.

Ferguson, Ronald W., Kenneth D. Forbus, and Dedre Gentner. 'Incremental Structure-Mapping.' *Proceedings of the Cognitive Science Society* 16 (August 1994): 313.

Finke, Ronald A., Thomas B. Ward, and Steven M. Smith. *Creative Cognition: Theory, Research, and Applications*. Cambridge, MA: The MIT Press, 1992.

Forty, Adrian. *Words and Buildings: A Vocabulary of Modern Architecture*. London: Thames & Hudson, 2000.

Foucault, Michel. 'The Order of Discourse (Inaugural Lecture at the Collège de France, Given 2 December 1970).' In *Untying the Text*, edited by Young, Robert. Boston, MA: Routledge & Kegan Paul, 1981 [1971]: 52–64.

Friedman, Ken. 'Theory Construction in Design Research: Criteria: Approaches, and Methods.' *Design Studies* 24, no. 6 (2003): 507–522.

Friedman, Mildred and Frank O. Gehry. *Gehry Talks: Architecture + Process*. New York: Universe Publishing, 2002.

Friedmann, John. *Retracking America: A Theory of Transactive Planning*. Garden City, NY: Anchor Press, 1973.

Gang, Jeannie. *Reveal: Studio Gang Architects*. Edited by Simon, Dan. New York: Princeton Architectural Press, 2011.

Gelernter, Mark. *Sources of Architectural Form: A Critical History of Western Design Theory*. Manchester and New York: Manchester University Press, 1995.

Gentner, Dedre. 'Metaphor as Structure Mapping: The Relational Shift.' *Child Development* 59, no. 1 (1988): 47–59.

Gentner, Dedre. 'Structure-Mapping: A Theoretical Framework for Analogy.' *Cognitive Science* 7, no. 2 (1983): 155–170.

Gentner, Dedre, Keith James Holyoak, and Boicho N. Kokinov. *The Analogical Mind: Perspectives from Cognitive Science*. Cambridge, MA: The MIT Press, 2001.

Gentner, Dedre and Arthur B. Markman. 'Structure Mapping in Analogy and Similarity.' *American Psychologist* 52, no. 1 (1997): 45–56.

Gentner, Dedre and Robert M. Schumacher. 'Use of Structure Mapping Theory for Complex Systems.' Presented at the Panel on Mental Models and Complex Systems, IEEE International Conference on Systems, Man and Cybernetics (1986).

Gentner, D. and C. Toupin. 'Systematicity and Surface Similarity in the Development of Analogy.' *Cognitive Science* 10, no. 3 (1986): 277–300.

Gerard, Alexander, Voltaire, Jean Le Rond d'Alembert, and Charles de Secondat, Baron de Montesquieu. *An Essay on Taste*. New York: Garland, 1970 [1759].

Gibbs, Raymond W., Jr., ed. *The Cambridge Handbook of Metaphor and Thought*. New York: Cambridge University Press, 2008.

Gigerenzer, Gerd, Peter M. Todd, and ABC Research Group. *Simple Heuristics that Make Us Smart*. New York: Oxford University Press, 1999.

Goldschmidt, Gabriela. 'The Designer as a Team of One.' *Design Studies* 16, no. 2 (1995): 189–209.

Goldstein, Daniel G. and Gerd Gigerenzer. 'Models of Ecological Rationality: The Recognition Heuristic.' *Psychological Review* 109, no. 1 (2002): 75–90.

Gombrich, E. H. *Norm and Form*. London: Phaidon, 1966.

Grabow, Stephen and Allan Heskin. 'Foundations for a Radical Concept of Planning.' *Journal of the American Institute of Planners* 39, no. 2 (March 1973): 106–114.

Groak, Steven. *The Idea of Building: Thought and Action in the Design and Production of Buildings*. London: E. & F. N. Spon (Taylor & Francis), 1990.

Gutting, Gary. *The Cambridge Companion to Foucault*. 2nd edn. Cambridge: Cambridge University Press, 2005.

Hanlon, Don. *Compositions in Architecture*. Hoboken, NJ: John Wiley & Sons, 2009.

Harrison, Charles and Paul Wood. *Art in Theory 1990–1990: An Anthology of Changing Ideas*. Oxford: Blackwell, 1992.

Hartman, Henry G. *Aesthetics: A Critical Theory of Art*. Columbus, OH: R. G. Adams & Co, 1919.

Hays, K. Michael. *Architecture Theory since 1968*. Cambridge, MA: The MIT Press, 1998.

Hays, K. Michael. *Oppositions Reader: Selected Readings from a Journal for Ideas and Criticism in Architecture, 1973–1984*. New York: Princeton Architectural Press, 1998.

Hearn, M. F. *Ideas that Shaped Buildings*. Cambridge, MA: The MIT Press, 2003.

Hegel, Georg Wilhelm Friedrich. *The Philosophy of Fine Art*. New York: Hacker Art Books, 1975.

Hegel, Georg Wilhelm Friedrich and Bernard Bosanquet. *The Introduction to Hegel's Philosophy of Fine Art*. London: Kegan Paul, Trench, Trübner, 1905.

Hegel, Georg Wilhelm Friedrich and John Steinfort Kedney. *Hegel's Aesthetics: A Critical Exposition*. 3d edn. Chicago: Scott Foresman, 1897.

Hippocrates. 'Praeceptiones (Precepts) 1.' In *Hippocrates Collected Works*, edited by Jones, W. H. S. Cambridge, MA: Harvard University Press, 1957 [1923]: Vol. 1: 313–315.

Hogarth, William. *The Analysis of Beauty. Written with a View of Fixing the Fluctuating Ideas of Taste*. London: R. Scholey, 1810.

Holl, Steven. *Parallax*. New York: Princeton Architectural Press, 2000.

Holl, Steven and Lebbeus Woods. *Steven Holl: Architecture Spoken*. New York: Rizzoli, 2007.

Hummel, John E. and Keith J. Holyoak. 'Distributed Representations of Structure: A Theory of Analogical Access and Mapping.' *Psychological Review* 104, no. 3 (1997): 427–466.

Hurtienne, Jörn and Lucienne Blessing. 'Metaphors as Tools for Intuitive Interaction with Technology.' *Metaphorik.De* 12 (2007): 21–52.

Hvattum, Mari and Christian Hermansen. *Tracing Modernity: Manifestations of the Modern in Architecture and the City*. London and New York: Routledge, 2004.

Isenberg, Barbara. *Conversations with Frank Gehry*. New York: Alfred A. Knopf, 2009.

Iser, Wolfgang. *How to Do Theory*. Malden, MA: Blackwell, 2006.

Jencks, Charles. *The Language of Post-Modern Architecture*. New York: Rizzoli, 1977.

Johnson, Mark. *The Body in the Mind: The Bodily Basis of Meaning, Imagination, and Reason*. Chicago: University of Chicago Press, 1987.

Johnson, Mark. *The Meaning of the Body: Aesthetics of Human Understanding*. Chicago: University of Chicago Press, 2007.

Johnson, Paul-Alan. *The Theory of Architecture: Concepts, Themes and Practices*. New York: Van Nostrand Reinhold, 1994.

Jonas, Wolfgang. 'Design as Problem-Solving? Or: Here is the Solution – What Was the Problem?' *Design Studies* 14, no. 2 (1993): 157–170.

Jones, J. Christopher. *Design Methods: Seeds of Human Futures*. London: Wiley-Interscience, 1973.

Kant, Immanuel and J. H. Bernard. *Kant's Kritik of Judgment*. London and New York: Macmillan and Co., 1892.

Kelman, Mark. *The Heuristics Debate*. New York: Oxford University Press, 2011.

Kolocotroni, Vassiliki, Jane Goldman, and Olga Taxidou. *Modernism: An Anthology of Sources and Documents*. Edinburgh: Edinburgh University Press, 1998.

Koolhaas, Rem. 'Precarious Entity.' In *Anyone*, edited by Davidson, Cynthia C. New York: Rizzoli, 1991: 148–155.

Koolhaas, Rem, Bruce Mau, Jennifer Sigler, and Hans Werlemann. *S, M, L, XL*. New York: Monacelli Press, 1998.

Koolhaas, Rem and Office for Metropolitan Architecture. *Content*. Edited by McGetrick, Brendan, Simon Brown, and Jon Link. Köln: Taschen, 2004.

Koolhaas, Rem and Nobuyuki Yoshida. *Oma@work*. Tokyo: A+U Publishing, 2000.

Krier, Léon. *The Architecture of Community*. Edited by Thadani, Dhiru A. and Peter J. Hetzel. Washington, DC: Island Press, 2009.

Krippendorff, Klaus. *The Semantic Turn: A New Foundation for Design*. Boca Raton, FL: CRC/Taylor & Francis, 2006.

Kruft, Hanno-Walter. *A History of Architectural Theory: From Vitruvius to the Present*. London and New York: Zwemmer/Princeton Architectural Press, 1994.

Kubose, Tate T., Keith J. Holyoak, and John E. Hummel. 'The Role of Textual Coherence in Incremental Analogical Mapping.' *Journal of Memory and Language* 47, no. 3 (2002): 407–435.

Kwinter, Sandford. 'Soft Systems.' In *Culture Lab 1*, edited by Boigon, Brian. New York: Princeton Architectural Press, 1996: Vol. 1: 207–228.

Lakhani, Karim R., Lars Bo Jeppesen, Peter A. Lohse, and Jill A. Panetta. *The Value *of Openness in Scientific Problem Solving*. HBS Working Paper Number 07-050. Cambridge, MA: Harvard University, 2007.

Lakhani, Karim R. and Jill A. Panetta. 'The Principles of Distributed Innovation.' *Innovations: Technology, Governance, Globalization* 2, no. 3 (Summer 2007): 97–112.

Lakoff, George and Mark Johnson. *Metaphors We Live By*. Chicago: University of Chicago Press, 1980.

Lakoff, George and Mark Johnson. *Philosophy in the Flesh: The Embodied Mind and its Challenge to Western Thought*. New York: Basic Books, 1999.

Lakoff, George and Mark Turner. *More than Cool Reason: A Field Guide to Poetic Metaphor*. Chicago: University of Chicago Press, 1989.

Latour, Bruno. *We Have Never Been Modern* [*Nous n'Avons Jamais Été Modernes*]. Cambridge, MA: Harvard University Press, 1993.

Laugier, Marc-Antoine. *An Essay on Architecture* [*Essai sur l'Architecture*]. Translated by Herrmann, Wolfgang and Anni Herrmann. Los Angeles, CA: Hennessey & Ingalls, Inc., 1977 [1753].

LaVine, Lance. *Constructing Ideas: Understanding Architecture*. Dubuque, IA: Kendall/Hunt Publishing Company, 2008.

Lawson, Bryan. *How Designers Think: The Design Process Demystified*. Oxford: Architectural Press, 2006.

Le Camus de Mézières, Nicolas. *The Genius of Architecture, Or, the Analogy of that Art with our Sensations*. Santa Monica, CA, and Chicago: Getty Center for the History of Art and the Humanities, 1992.

Le Corbusier. *Towards a New Architecture*. New York: Dover Publications, 1986.

Le Corbusier and Pierre Jeanneret. 'Five Points towards a New Architecture.' In *Programs and Manifestos in Twentieth Century Architecture*. Translated by Bullock, Michael, edited by Conrads, Ulrich. Cambridge, MA: The MIT Press, 1971 [1926]: 99–101.

Leach, Neil. *Rethinking Architecture: A Reader in Cultural Theory*. New York: Routledge, 1997.

Ledoux, Claude-Nicolas. *L'Architecture Considerée sous la Rapport de l'Art, des Moeurs et de la Legislation*. Paris: H. L. Perronneau, 1804.

Lefaivre, Liane and Alexander Tzonis. *The Emergence of Modern Architecture: A Documentary History from 1000 to 1810*. London and New York: Routledge, Taylor & Francis Group, 2004.

Locke, John. *An Essay Concerning Human Understanding*. London and New York: J. M. Dent/Dutton, 1961.

Mallgrave, Harry Francis. *Modern Architectural Theory: A Historical Survey, 1673–1968*. Cambridge and New York: Cambridge University Press, 2005.

Melville, Herman. *Moby Dick, Or the Whale*. New York: Charles Scribner's Sons, 1902.

Mitrović, Branko. *Philosophy for Architects*. New York: Princeton Architectural Press, 2011.

Moneo, Rafael. 'On Typology.' *Oppositions* 13 (1978): 23–45.

Moore, Kathryn. *Overlooking the Visual: Demystifying the Art of Design*. Abingdon and New York: Routledge, 2010.

Morris, Pam. *Realism*. New Critical Idiom. London and New York: Routledge, 2003.

Moudon, Anne Vernez. *Built for Change: Neighborhood Architecture in San Francisco*. Cambridge, MA: The MIT Press, 1986.

Muratori, Saverio. *Studi per una Operante Storja Urbana di Venezia*. Rome: Istituto Poligraphico dello Stato, 1959.

Nesbitt, Kate. *Theorizing a New Agenda for Architecture: An Anthology of Architectural Theory, 1965–1995*. New York: Princeton Architectural Press, 1996.

Neuhart, John, Charles Eames, Ray Eames, and Marilyn Neuhart. *Eames Design: The Work of the Office of Charles and Ray Eames*. New York: H. N. Abrams, 1989.

Newman, Barnett. 'Remarks at the Fourth Annual Woodstock Art Conference.' In *Barnett Newman: Selected Writings and Interviews*, edited by Newman, Barnett and John P. O'Neill. Berkeley: University of California Press, 1992: 242–247.

Nickerson, Raymond S. 'Enhancing Creativity.' In *Handbook of Creativity*, edited by Sternberg, Robert J. New York: Cambridge University Press, 1999: 392–430.

Osborn, Alex. *Applied Imagination: Principles and Procedures of Creative Problem Solving*. New York: Charles Scribner's Sons, 1953.

Padovan, Richard. *Towards Universality: Le Corbusier, Mies, and De Stijl*. London and New York: Routledge, 2002.

Palladio, Andrea. *The Four Books on Architecture*. Cambridge, MA: The MIT Press, 1997.

Pinker, Steven. *The Blank Slate: The Modern Denial of Human Nature*. New York: Penguin, 2003.

Pinker, Steven. *The Stuff of Thought: Language as a Window into Human Nature*. New York: Viking Adult, 2007.

Plowright, Philip. 'Agency and Personification: Core Analogical Operators in the Architectural Design Process.' In *Proceedings of the 2013 ARCC Architectural Research Conference* (27–30 March 2013): 156–164.

Poe, Edgar Allan. 'The Philosophy of Composition.' *Graham's Magazine* 28, no. 4 (April 1846): 163–167.

Popper, Karl. *The Logic of Scientific Discovery*. Abingdon: Routledge Classics, 2002.

Prina, Francesca. *Architecture: Elements, Materials, Form*. Princeton, NJ: Princeton University Press, 2008.

Protzen, Jean-Pierre and David J. Harris. *The Universe of Design: Horst Rittel's Theories of Design and Planning*. New York: Routledge, 2010.

Puccio, Gerard J., Mary C. Murdock, and Marie Mance. 'Current Developments in Creative Problem Solving for Organizations: A Focus on Thinking Skills and Styles.' *Korean Journal of Thinking and Problem Solving* 15, no. 2 (2005): 43–76.

Quatremère de Quincy, M. Antoine-Chrysostome. *The True, the Fictive, and the Real: The Historical Dictionary of Architecture of Quatremère de Quincy*. Translated by Younés, Samir. London: Andreas Papadakis, 1999.

Rittel, Horst and Melvin Webber. 'Dilemmas in a General Theory of Planning.' In *Developments in Design Methodology*, edited by Cross, Nigel. Chichester: J. Wiley & Sons, 1984: 135–144.

Rittel, Horst and Melvin Webber. 'Dilemmas in a General Theory of Planning.' *Policy Sciences* 4 (1973): 155–169.

Rorty, Richard. *Philosophy and Social Hope*. New York: Penguin, 1999.

Rorty, Richard. *Philosophy and the Mirror of Nature*. Princeton, NJ: Princeton University Press, 1979.

Rossi, Aldo. *The Architecture of the City*. Translated by Ghirardo, Diane and Joan Ockman. Cambridge, MA: The MIT Press, 1984.

Rowe, Peter. *Design Thinking*. Cambridge, MA: The MIT Press, 1987.

Ruskin, John. *The Seven Lamps of Architecture*. New York: J. Wiley & Sons, 1884.

Russell, Abby Osborne. *An English Paraphrase of Horace's Art of Poetry*. New York: William R. Jenkins, 1896.

Sadler, Simon. *Archigram: Architecture without Architecture*. Cambridge, MA: The MIT Press, 2005.

Schön, Donald A. *The Reflective Practitioner: How Professionals Think in Action*. New York: Basic Books, 1983.

Schumacher, Patrik. *The Autopoiesis of Architecture*. Chichester: John Wiley & Sons, 2011.

Serlio, Sebastiano. *The Five Books of Architecture: An Unabridged Reprint of the English Edition of 1611*. New York: Dover Publications, 1982.

Serlio, Sebastiano, Vaughan Hart, and Peter Hicks. *Sebastiano Serlio on Architecture*. New Haven, CT: Yale University Press, 1996.

Serlio, Sebastiano and Myra Nan Rosenfeld. *Serlio on Domestic Architecture*. New York: Courier/Dover Publications, 1997.

Shelley, Mary Wollstonecraft. 'Introduction.' In *Frankenstein: Or, the Modern Prometheus*. London: George Routledge and Sons, 1891 [1831]: v–xii.

Shiner, Larry. *The Invention of Art: A Cultural History*. Chicago: University of Chicago Press, 2003.

Simon, Herbert A. *The Sciences of the Artificial*. Karl Taylor Compton Lectures. Cambridge, MA: The MIT Press, 1969.

Snodgrass, Adrian and Richard Coyne. *Interpretation in Architecture: Design as a Way of Thinking*. New York: Taylor & Francis, 2006.

St. Amant, Robert, Clayton T. Morrison, Yu-Han Chang, Paul R. Cohen, and Carole Beal. 'An Image Schema Language.' *Proceedings of the 7th International Conference on Cognitive Modelling* (April 2006): 292–297.

Stempfle, Joachim and Petra Badke-Schaub. 'Thinking in Design Teams: An Analysis of Team Communication.' *Design Studies* 23, no. 5 (2002): 473–496.

Sullivan, Louis. *Kindergarten Chats and Other Writings (Documents of Modern Art)*. New York: Dover Publications, 2012 [1918].

Taylor, Mark C. *The Moment of Complexity: Emerging Network Culture*. Chicago: University of Chicago Press, 2001.

Thompson, D'Arcy Wentworth. *On Growth and Form*. Cambridge: Cambridge University Press, 1992 [1917].

Thornley, Denis G. 'Design Method in Architectural Education.' In *Conference on Design Methods*, edited by Jones, J. Christopher and Denis G. Thornley. Oxford: Pergamon Press, 1963: 37–51.

Todd, Peter M. and Gerd Gigerenzer. 'Bounding Rationality to the World.' *Journal of Economic Psychology* 24, no. 2 (2003): 143–165.

Tschumi, Bernard. *Architecture and Disjunction*. Cambridge, MA: The MIT Press, 1994.

Unwin, Simon. *Analysing Architecture*. 3rd edn. New York: Routledge, 2009.

Venturi, Robert, Denise Scott Brown, and Steven Izenour. *Learning from Las Vegas: The Forgotten Symbolism of Architectural Form*. Rev. edn. Cambridge, MA: The MIT Press, 1996.

Vidler, Anthony. 'The Third Typology.' *Oppositions* 7 (Winter 1976): 1–4.

Vignola and Branko Mitrović. *Canon of the Five Orders of Architecture*. New York: Acanthus Press, 1999.

Viollet-le-Duc, Eugène-Emmanuel. *How to Build a House: An Architectural Novelette*. Translated by Bucknall, Benjamin. 2nd edn. London: Sampson, Low, Marston, Searle, and Rivington, 1876.

Viollet-le-Duc, Eugène-Emmanuel. *Lectures on Architecture*. New York: Dover Publications, 1987.

Viollet-le-Duc, Eugène-Emmanuel. *The Architectural Theory of Viollet-Le-Duc: Readings and Commentary*. Edited by Hearn, M. Fillmore. Cambridge, MA: The MIT Press, 1990.

Viollet-le-Duc, Eugène-Emmanuel. *The Foundations of Architecture: Selections from the Dictionnaire Raisonné*. New York: G. Braziller, 1990.

Viollet-le-Duc, Eugène-Emmanuel. *The Story of a House*. Translated by Towle, George M. Boston, MA: James R. Osgood and Company, 1874.

Vitruvius Pollio, Marcus. *Architecture of Marcus Vitruvius Pollio in Ten Books*. Translated by Gwilt, Joseph. London: Priestley and Weale, 1826.

Vitruvius Pollio, Marcus and Frank Stephen Granger. *Vitruvius, on Architecture*. The Loeb Classical Library. Cambridge, MA: Harvard University Press, 1962.

Vitruvius Pollio, Marcus, M. H. Morgan, and Herbert Langford Warren. *Vitruvius, the Ten Books on Architecture*. Cambridge, MA: Harvard University Press, 1914.

von Meiss, Pierre. *Elements of Architecture: From Form to Place*. New York: E. & F. N. Spon/Routledge, 1998.

Wallington, A. M., J. A. Barnden, S. R. Glasbey, and M. G. Lee. 'Metaphorical Reasoning with an Economical Set of Mappings.' *DELTA Documentacao de Estudos em Linguistica Teorica e Aplicada* 22, Special Issue (2006): 147–171.

Ware, William R. and Vignola. *The American Vignola, Part I: The Five Orders*. 5th edn. Scanton, PA: International Textbook Co., 1928.

Weinberg, Steven. *Facing up: Science and its Cultural Adversaries*. Cambridge, MA: Harvard University Press, 2003.

Winston, Patrick H. 'Learning and Reasoning by Analogy.' *Communications of the ACM* 23 12 (1980): 689–703.

Winters, Edward. *Aesthetics and Architecture*. London: Continuum, 2007.

Wright, Frank Lloyd. *An Autobiography*. New York: Duell, Sloan and Pearce, 1943.

Wright, Frank Lloyd. *The Future of Architecture*. New York: Horizon Press, 1953.

Wright, Frank Lloyd. *The Natural House*. New York: Horizon Press, 1954.

Wright, Frank Lloyd, Andrew Devane, and Frederick Albert Gutheim. *In the Cause of Architecture, Frank Lloyd Wright: Essays*. New York: Architectural Record, 1975.

Xiao, Ying, Shengchen Yang, and Philip Plowright. 'Occupy Skyscraper.' *Boundaries: International Architectural Magazine* 4 (April–June, 2012): 80–81.

Young, Robert. *Untying the Text: A Post-Structuralist Reader*. Boston, MA: Routledge & Kegan Paul, 1981.

Index

aesthetics 55, 245

affinity diagram 87–8; *see also* clustering

Al Ajlouni, Rima 311

Alberti, Leon Battista 15, 45, 59, 184n32, 186–88, 241n3

Alésia Museum 275

Alexander, Christopher 23, 30n3, 32n21, 35, 40, 42–3, 51n32, 136, 142; and first principles 98

algorithm *see* tools, disciplinary

analogy 44–5, 46, 107–13, *111*, 129n3, 249, 257, 262–4, 270–3, 277, 287–8; transfer through structure-mapping 121–29

analytical thinking *see* evaluative thinking

Andraos, Amale *see* WORKac

Aqua Tower 262–8

architecture as response to situation 26–8, 43, 66, 102, 190, 278, 312; and research 90

architectural syntax *see* syntax, architectural

architectural design: definition 5–6; as a system 6, 13, 18, 26–7, 40; as disciplinary knowledge 16

art: architecture as art 249–250; judgement of 34, 59–60; of building 38; relationship to architectural design 2, 8n2, 112–13, 245–6, 311; social role 34; *see also* use of non-architectural content; poetry

artistic unity *see* coherence

Asimow, Morris 75

assets, design 40–3, 63, 90, 105, 185, 187, 194–205, 222, 268; light as an asset 192; constraints as assets 228–9, 231–7; infrastructure as asset *see* Nature-City

Atelier Tekuto *see* Reflection of Mineral House

attribute mapping *see* mapping, attribute

avant garde practice: relation to discourse 15

axis 140, *141*, *143*, 145

axonometric *see* tools, disciplinary

Ballantyne, Andrew 61–2

Banfield, Edward 24, 75, 92n3

Baumgarten, Alexander Gottlieb 245–6

beliefs *see* bias, architectural; value system

Bernard Tschumi Architects 275; *see also* Alésia Museum

bias, architectural 8, 17–20, 47–8, 62, 216, 222; and Frank L. Wright 203; and OMA 204, 263; and Studio Gang 263; and Viollet-le-Duc 194, 198; and WORKac 226, 228–9; in convergent techniques 88; *see also* priorities, disciplinary; bounded thinking; *see also* starting state

big idea as design source 44; *see also* concepts; frameworks, concept-based

Blondel, Jacques-François 248

Boehm's Spiral Model 75, *76*

Boffrand, Gabriel-Germain 45, 245–8